SUICIDE NOTES

SUICIDE NOTES

Predictive Clues and Patterns

Antoon A. Leenaars, Ph.D., C. Psych.

Windsor
Ontario, Canada

HUMAN SCIENCES PRESS, INC.
72 FIFTH AVENUE
NEW YORK, N.Y. 10011-8004

72 Fifth Avenue, New York, New York 10011

Printed in the United States of America
987654321

Library of Congress Cataloging-in-Publication Data

Leenaars, Antoon A.
Suicide notes.

Bibliography: p.
Includes indexes.
1. Suicide. I. Title.
HV6545.L367 1988 362.2 87-21362
ISBN 0-89885-399-0

CONTENTS

PREFACE

From the first day that I found a copy of Shneidman and Farberow's book, *Clues to Suicide,* suicide notes have been a focus of mine in studying suicidal phenomena. Suicide is a human malaise and suicide notes are the penultimate act giving a voice to this malaise. If I may quote my friend and "teacher": Shneidman, in *Voices of Death,* wrote that such personal "documents contain special revelations of the human mind and that there is much one can learn from them." Suicide notes allow us to learn about a person, to advance the nomothetic and idiographic approaches in science, and to aid in the aims of science in general—understanding, prediction, and control.

This is a book in both the theoretical and empirical traditions. My goal is to present, as straightforwardly as possible, the formulations of 10 suicidologists: Alfred Adler, Ludwig Binswanger, Sigmund Freud, Carl G. Jung, Karl A. Menninger, George Kelly, Henry A. Murray, Edwin S. Shneidman, Harry Stack Sullivan, and Gregory Zilboorg. These men have given us a rich history of suicidological thought. It is not the intent here to present their complete theories of personality but only their formulations regarding suicide. The book is also a presentation of new data: the common and differentiating variables in suicide notes and, by implication, suicide; the differences and similarities of suicide notes from 1945–1954 and 1983–1984; and some observations on age and sex.

My driving need behind this book is the belief that understanding of suicide notes and, by implication, suicide can be used to assist us in preventing the event. When understanding is inadequate and based not on *any* sound empiricism, remediation (i.e., prevention, intervention, and postvention) is likely to be ineffective. It is hoped that the definition of suicide derived from suicide notes will assist a needful individual in some way.

In the appendices, there is a collection of suicide notes. These are within the public domain and were kindly provided through the office of the Los Angeles Coroner. However, the suicide notes themselves are disguised to avoid any invasion of privacy. The notes remind us that we are talking about people—people who experienced unbearable pain and saw suicide as the *only* solution. We are in debt to these individuals for letting us know what it was like for them at the last moments of their life.

Edwin Shneidman is a special person to me. He has been the guiding light to this book and my study of suicide and people in general. Anyone who knows his work will know his influence on me.

A.L.
June, 1987

FOREWORD

Not at all surprisingly, I am extremely happy to be asked to write a foreword to an extraordinarily fine book in which my own work is examined and discussed. For me, this act has something of the quality of a silent self-directed prayer: To call a blessing on oneself.

Part of my qualifications in this present instance is that I have had a long and keen interest in suicide notes. Since 1949—when I came upon hundreds of suicide notes in the vaults of the Los Angeles County Coroner's Office and almost continuously since then—I have been fascinated with suicide notes as a special kind of thematic material—a response, as it were, to the Blank card of the Thematic Apperception Test written by a person in a suicidal context, and amenable to the rules of thematic interpretation in general.

Over the past almost 40 years I have held more than one view about the power and usefulness of suicide notes as "golden windows" into the world of suicide. Like an amateur Hegelian philosopher I have undergone my own dialectical process, first (in 1952) believing the *thesis*—that suicide notes were *the* absolutely best way to study the affective and cognitive components of the suicidal act; then (in 1973), proposing the *antithesis*— that suicide notes, written, as I asserted, in a state of great constriction and closed-mindedness, could not, by virtue of the circumstances in which they were composed, be the wide-ranging and revelatory documents I first thought them; and finally (in 1980), the *synthesis*—in which I appreciated that both the thesis and the antithesis had been overstatements, and that many suicide notes, when put in the context of life history of that individual who wrote the note, could throw enormous light on the life, just as the life could help illuminate many aspects of the note. I now believe that, in the overall study of suicide, suicide notes are very important documents and play a special role both in the study of suicidal phenomena generally and in the analysis of specific cases of suicide.

Dr. Antoon Leenaars has done the kind of study with suicide notes that I highly endorse. He has embedded his intensive study of suicide notes within the larger context of suicide theory. His previous published studies of this genre include his analyses of notes-and-theory of Binswanger, George Kelly, and Freud. And now he has turned to other published work on suicide, including my own.

Here, in Dr. Leenaars's book is the first extensive operational study which attempts to combine notes with suicidal theory. Hypotheses generated from theory are, through the examination of suicide notes, put to empirical test. Leenaars's attempts to use suicide *notes* as the vehicle for establishing an empirical suicidology are the most extensive that I know. He is doing the marvelous thing of scientizing our field by use of its most dramatic personal documents. I support and applaud his efforts and give him every encouragement in this exciting and fruitful endeavor. I recommend this book to every practicing or aspiring suicidologist for both its brilliant methodology and its insightful clinical implications.

Edwin Shneidman, Ph.D.
UCLA
1988

ACKNOWLEDGMENTS

First and foremost, I need to make explicit my debt to E. Shneidman. Not only are his formulations central to this book, he read the entire manuscript several times. He made numerous suggestions for improvement, all of which added to its scholarly aspect. I wish, with the deepest gratitude, to thank him for his sense of "generativity."

I am pleased to acknowledge the assistance of W. Balance, who worked for years with me on the research and assisted the book with his fine Southern pen. The Judges—P. Arnaut, J. Berek, D. Chernets, S. Clyne-Jackson, T. Fellbaum, C. Loughner, C. McMullin, D. Mooney, D. Rudzinski, and S. Wenckstern—who obviously worked long hours, made the data possible. The patient secretarial assistance of L. Brown, N. Dawid, R. Edwards, and L. LaPorte are greatly appreciated. The support of my family, former teachers, friends and colleagues has been encouraging. My wife, Susanne, made various suggestions that improved the book. My children, Lindsey and Heather, allowed me to work on the book (despite the occasional, "No dada, Me!")

I am extremely appreciative of the editorial guidance of Norma Fox, editor-in-chief and her excellent staff at Human

Sciences Press, Inc. A word of thanks to May Dikeman for a thoughtful editing of the manuscript.

Appreciation is acknowledged to the following for permission to reproduce materials that appear in this volume:

Excerpts from "The Case of Ellen West" in *Existence: A New Dimension in Psychiatry and Psychology* by L. Binswanger. (W. Mendel & J. Lyons, Trans; R. May, E. Angel & H. Ellenberger, Eds.) Copyright, 1958 Basic Books, Inc. Reprinted by permission of Basic Books, Inc.

Excerpts from "Mourning and Melancholia" from Volume XIV, "A Case of Homosexuality in a Woman" from Volume XVIII and "The Ego and the Id" from Volume XIX of *The Complete Psychological Works of Sigmund Freud* by S. Freud. (J. Strachey, Ed. and Trans.) Copyright, 1974, Sigmund Freud Copyrights Ltd, The Institute of Psycho-Analysis and The Hogarth Press. Reprinted by permission.

Excerpts from *Collected Papers, Vol. 2, by Sigmund Freud,* Authorized Translation under the supervision of Joan Riviere. Published by Basic Books, Inc. by arrangement with The Hogarth Press Ltd. and The Institute of Psycho-Analysis, London. Reprinted by permission.

Excerpts from *Collected Papers, Vol. 4, by Sigmund Freud,* Authorized Translation under the supervision of Joan Riviere. Published by Basic Books, Inc. by arrangement with The Hogarth Press Ltd. and The Institute of Psycho-Analysis, London. Reprinted by permission.

Excerpts from "The Ego and the Id" from Volume XIX of *The Complete Psychological Works of Sigmund Freud* by S. Freud. Reprinted with permission from W.W. Norton & Co., Inc.

Excerpts from "Psychological Types" from Volume VI, "The Relations Between the Ego and the Unconscious" from Volume VII, and "Symbol and the Interpretation of Dreams" from Volume XVIII of *The Collected Works of C. G. Jung* by C. G. Jung (R. Hull, Trans.). Copyright, 1974, 1977, by Princeton University Press/Routledge & Kegan Paul. Reprinted by permission of Princeton University Press.

Excerpts from *Man Against Himself* by K. Menninger. Copyright, 1983, 1966 by Karl A. Menninger. Reprinted by permission of Harcourt, Brace, Jovanovich, Inc.

Excerpts from *Voices of Death* by Edwin Shneidman. Copyright, 1980, 1982, by Edwin Shneidman. Published by Harper and Row, 1980 and Bantam Books, 1982. Reprinted by permission of Edwin Shneidman.

Excerpts from *Definition of Suicide* by Edwin Shneidman. Copyright, 1985, Edwin Shneidman. Reprinted by permission of John Wiley & Sons, Inc.

Excerpts from *Clues to Suicide* by E. Shneidman and N. Farberow (Eds.) Copyright, 1957, by McGraw-Hill Book, Co. Reprinted by permission of McGraw-Hill Book Co.

Excerpts from *The Collected Works of Harry Stack Sullivan* by H.S. Sullivan. Copyright 1940, 1956, 1962, 1964 by W.W. Norton & Co., Inc. Reprinted by permission of W.W. Norton & Co., Inc.

Excerpts from "Differential diagnostic types of suicide," *Archives of Neurology and Psychiatry,* 1936, *35,* 270–291, by G. Zilboorg. Copyright, 1986, by American Medical Association. Reprinted by permission of American Medical Association.

Excerpts from "Considerations on suicide, with particular reference to that of the young," *American Journal of Orthopsychiatry,* 1937, *7,* 15–31, by G. Zilboorg. Copyright, 1937, by American Orthopsychiatry Society. Reprinted by permission of American Orthopsychiatry Society.

Part I

SUICIDE NOTES AS PERSONAL DOCUMENTS

Understanding suicidal phenomena—like understanding all complicated human acts—is a complex endeavor, involving information and insights drawn from many sources. One obvious source is the suicide note. This volume introduces the reader to a definition of suicide in terms of suicide notes. Part I consists of three chapters: A discussion of suicide notes and personal documents; a review of the literature on suicide notes; and an outline for a theoretical analysis of suicide notes. All this is preliminary to Part II which presents a study of 10 suicidologists. Part III presents some implications and applications.

Chapter 1

SUICIDE, SUICIDE NOTES, AND OTHER PERSONAL DOCUMENTS

No one really knows why human beings commit suicide. One of the most frequent questions asked about suicide is, "Why do people kill themselves?" or, more specifically, "Why did that individual commit suicide?" People are perplexed, bewildered, confused, and even overwhelmed when they are confronted with suicide. Indeed, the very person who takes his own life may be, at the moment of decision, the least aware of the essence of the reasons for doing so. Understanding suicide—like understanding any complicated human act—is a complex endeavor, involving knowledge and insights drawn from many points of view.

Definition of Suicide

Briefly defined, suicide is the human act of self-inflicted, self-intentioned cessation (Shneidman, 1973). It is not the definition we shall end with, but it will suffice for a start. Suicide is not a disease (although there are many who think so); it is not an immorality (although it has often been treated so); it is not a biological anomaly (although biological factors may play a role in some suicides); and it is not a neurological dysfunction (although even minimal brain dysfunction may play an additive role in some suicides).

It is unlikely that any one theory will ever define or explain phenomena as varied and as complicated as acts of human self-destruction. Our own initial definition is fraught with complexities and difficulties. Even the word "is"—"Suicide is"—has its philosophical complexities (Heidegger, 1962).

The history of our key word provides only initial assistance. "Suicide," in fact, is a relatively recent word. According to *The Oxford English Dictionary,* the word was used in 1651 by Walter Charleton when he said, "To vindicate ones self from . . . inevitable Calamity, by Sui-cide is not . . . a Crime." However, the exact date of its first use is open to some question. Some claim that it was first used by Sir Thomas Browne in his book, *Religio Medici,* published in 1642. Edward Philips, in his 1662 edition of his dictionary, *A New World of Words,* claimed to have invented the word. The word "suicide" does not appear in Robert Burton's *Anatomy of Melancholy* (1652 edition), nor in Samuel Johnson's *Dictionary* (1755). Before the introduction of the word, other terms, of course, were used to describe "the act"—among them self-destruction, self-killing, self-murder, and self-slaughter. Burton's phrases for suicide include "to make way with themselves" and "they offer violence to themselves." The classical (and current) German term is in keeping with this tradition—*Selbstmord,* or self-murder.

In the present scene, individuals who have attempted to define the term (e.g., Beauchamp, 1978, Frey, 1980, Graber, 1981, Windt, 1980) have given scholarly definitions, but suffer from intellectual overkill (Shneidman, 1985). An excellent discussion of the problem of definition was offered by Jack Douglas (1967). Douglas outlines the fundamental dimensions of meanings that are required in the formal definition of suicide which include aspects of initiation, willing, motivation, and knowledge.

Suicide may today be defined depending on the purpose of the definition—medical, legal, administrative, etc. In the United States and Canada (and most of the countries reporting to the World Health Organization), suicide is defined (by a medical examiner or coroner) as one of the four possible modes of death.

An acronym for the four modes of death is NASH: natural, accidental, suicidal, and homicidal. This fourfold classification of all deaths also has its problem. Its major deficiency is that it treats the human being in a Cartesian fashion, namely as a biological machine, rather than appropriately treating him as a motivated psychosocial organism; that is, it obscures the individual's *intentions* in relation to his own cessation and, further, completely neglects the contemporary concepts of psychodynamic psychology regarding intention, including unconscious motivation.

The topic of definition of suicide was the focus of a recent book by Shneidman (1985). Shneidman's book, *Definition of Suicide,* can be seen as a necessary step to more effective understanding and treatment of suicide. It argued that we desperately need a clarification of the definitions of suicide—definitions that can be applied to needful persons. The present volume can be seen as an attempt at definition in terms of suicide notes.

History of Suicide

The modern era of the study of suicide began around the turn of the twentieth century, with two main threads of investigation, the sociological and psychological, associated primarily with the names of Emile Durkheim (1858–1917) and Sigmund Freud (1856–1939), respectively. Much earlier, during classical Greek times, suicide was viewed in various ways. Pythagoras of Samos, who introduced the theory of number to understand man and the universe ("Number is all things and all things are number"), proposed that suicide would upset the spiritual mathematics of all things. All was measurable by number and to exitby suicide might result in an imbalance, unlike other deaths that were in harmony with all things. Plato's position (428–348 B.C.), best expressed in the *Pheodo* in his quotation from Socrates, is as follows:

> Cebes, I believe. . . . that the gods are our keepers, and we men are one of their possessions. Don't you think so?
>
> Yes I do, said Cebes.
>
> Then take your own case. If one of your possessions

> were to destroy itself without intimation from you that you wanted it to die, wouldn't you be angry with it and punish it, if you had any means of doing so?
>
> Certainly.
>
> So if you look at it in this way I suppose it is not unreasonable to say that we must not put an end to ourselves. . . .

There are, however, provisions for exceptions. The above quotation continues:

> . . . until God sends some compulsion like the one which we are facing now.

The compulsion, of course, was the condemnation by the Athenian court of Socrates for "corrupting the minds of the young and of believing in deities of his own invention instead of the gods recognized by the state" *(Apology)*. Socrates drank poison, hemlock.

Aristotle (384–222 B.C.) espoused the view that suicide was against the state and, therefore, wrong. Man was answerable for all to the state and thus liable for wrongdoing and was to be punished for such acts, including suicide. In the *Nicomachean Ethics,* Aristotle further noted that:

> . . . to die to escape from poverty or love or anything painful is not the mark of a brave man, but rather of a coward; for it is softness to fly from what is troublesome, and such a man endures death not because it is noble but to fly from evil.

In classical Rome, in the centuries just before the Christian era, life was held rather cheap and suicide was viewed either neutrally or, by some, positively. The Roman Stoic, Seneca (4 B.C.–65 A.D.) said: "Living is not as long as he can . . . He will always think of life in terms of quality not quantity . . . Dying early or late is of no relevance, dying well or ill is . . . even if it is true that while there is life there is hope, life is not to be bought at any cost." Zeno, the founder of Stoic philosophy, after putting his toe out of joint in a fall at age ninety-eight, hanged himself. The history of Rome is filled with such incidences, where life was given up for seemingly trivial reasons. The history of Rome's civilization itself was, indeed, inimical; the life-style in Rome truncated that civilization's very existence.

The Old Testament does not directly forbid suicide, but in Jewish law suicide is wrong. There was a value for life. In the Old Testament one finds only six cases of suicide: Abimelech, Samson, Saul, Saul's armor-bearer, Ahithapel, and Zimni. The New Testament, like the Old, did not directly forbid suicide. During the early Christian years, in fact, there was excessive martyrdom and tendency toward suicide, resulting in considerable concern on the part of the Church Fathers. Suicide by these early martyrs was seen as redemption and thus the Fathers began increasingly to associate sin and suicide. In the fourth century, suicide was categorically rejected by St. Augustine (354–430). Suicide was considered a sin because it precluded the possibility of repentance and because it violated the Sixth Commandment, "Thou shalt not kill." Suicide was a greater sin than any sin one might wish to avoid. This view was elaborated by St. Thomas Aquinas (1225–1274) who emphasized that suicide was, not only unnatural and antisocial, but also a mortal sin in that it usurped God's power over man's life and death (echoing the views of Aristotle). By 693, the Church, at the Council of Toledo, proclaimed that individuals who attempted suicide were to be excommunicated. The notion of suicide as sin took firm hold and for hundreds of years played an important part in western man's view of self-destruction. Only during the Renaissance and the Reformation did a different view emerge, although, as Farberow (1972) has documented, the Church remained powerful and against suicide among the lower classes into this century.

The writers and philosophers from the 1500s began to present a variety of different views on suicide. William Shakespeare (1564–1616), for example, has provided us with an excellent array of such views. Shakespeare wrote a number of tragedies, with 14 suicides occurring in his plays.

The French philosopher, Jean-Jacques Rousseau (1712–1778), emphasized the natural state of man. He transferred sin from man to society, making man generally good (and innocent) and asserting that it is society that makes him bad. The disputation as to the locus of blame—whether in man or in society—is a major theme that dominates the history of suicidal thought. David Hume (1711–1776) was one of the first major Western philosophers to discuss suicide apart from the concept of sin. In his essay, "On Suicide," he refutes the view of suicide as a crime by arguing that suicide is not a transgression of our duties to God, to our fellow citizens, or to ourselves. He asserts that ". . . prudence and courage should engage us to rid ourselves at once of existence when it becomes a burden. . . . If it be no crime in me to divert the Nile or Danube from its course, were I able to effect such purposes, where then is the crime in turning a few ounces of blood from their natural channel?"

Whereas Hume tried to decriminalize suicide and make it our right, others, including Immanuel Kant (1724–1804), wrote that human life was sacred and should be preserved, in an anti-Stoic sense, at any cost. Johann Wolfgang von Goethe (1749–1832) in his novel, *The Sorrows of Young Werther,* presents the opposite view. Life does not need to be preserved. Werther killed himself in the face of unbearable emotional pain. It is a story of Werther's intoxication—"complete possession," "flood of emotions," in which "everything around about ceased to exist," "the purest joy of life," "Heaven"—with Lotte, who is betrothed to and marries another. The book itself is written as if it were the personal documents—letters, diary—of Werther. *The* final document, a suicide note, reads:*

> Everything is so calm around me and my soul is so calm. I thank thee, Lord, who gives these last moments. This warmth, this strength!
>
> I step to the window, my dearest, and see, and still see through the stormy, fleeting clouds some stars in the eternal heavens. No, you will not fall! The Eternal Father carries you near his heart, and me. I see the stars of the shaft of the Dipper, the loveliest of all the constellations. When I left you at night and passed your gate, it was in front of me.

---

*Translated from the German by Susanne Wenckstern.

With what intoxication have I so often looked at it, raised up my hands to it as a symbol, and made it a sacred token of my bliss! And even now—oh Lotte, what is there that does not remind of you? Are you not about me always? And have I not, like a child, greedily seized every trifle which you, dear saint, had touched!

Beloved silhouette! I return it to you, Lotte, and ask that you take good care of it. I have bestowed a thousand, thousand kisses on it, waved a thousand greetings to it whenever I went out and returned home.

I left a note for your father entreating him to protect my body. In the churchyard there are two linden trees, in a far corner, next to the field, there I wish to rest. He can and will do this for his friend. Do ask him to. I will not ask pious Christians to allow their bodies to lie next to that of a poor, unhappy man. Oh I wished you would bury me by the wayside, or in a lonely valley, that priest and Levite might cross themselves as they pass the stone which marked the spot, and the Samaritan may shed a tear.

There, Lotte! I do not shudder to take the cold, dreadful cup from which I am to drink the ecstasy of death! You have given it to me, and I do not fear. All, all the desires and hopes of my life are fulfilled. So cold, so stiff, to knock at the iron gate of death.

That I might have been granted the happiness to die for you, Lotte, to sacrifice myself for you! I would die gladly, I would die cheerfully, if I could restore the peace and happiness of your life. But alas! it was granted to but a few noble souls to shed their blood for those they loved, and by their deaths to kindle for them a new life enhanced a hundredfold.

I want to be buried in these clothes, Lotte. You have touched and sanctified them. I have also asked your father to carry out this request. My soul hovers over the coffin. Let them not search through my pockets. This rose-coloured ribbon which you wore on your bosom the first time I met you surrounded by your children—oh! Kiss them a thousand times and tell them the fate of their unhappy friend. The darlings! how they swarm around me. Oh! how I attached

> myself to you, how I could not keep away from you from the first moment!—Let this ribbon be buried with me. You gave it to me on my birthday! How eagerly I accepted all this!—Alas! I did not think the way would lead to this!—Be calm! I beg you, be calm!
>
> They [the pistols] are loaded—The clock strikes twelve! So be it then!—Lotte! Lotte! Farewell! Farewell!

Werther had strong impact in Europe; Goethe himself became known only as "the author of *Werther*." Even the clothes Werther wore became fashionable. A contagious suicide effect seemed to occur; a concern that preoccupies many suicidologists to this day. However, it should be noted that Goethe himself battled against his own emotional difficulties, for example, working on *Faust* for 60 years until he had it completed.

During more recent times, other main threads of suicidal study evolved. Existentialism, for example, has brought suicide into sharp focus, best exemplified in Albert Camus's *The Myth of Sisyphus* (1955). In the opening lines, he wrote:

> There is but one truly serious philosophical problem, and that is suicide. Judging whether life is or is not worth living amounts to answering the fundamental question of philosophy. All the rest and whether or not the world has three dimensions, whether the mind has nine or twelve categories—comes afterwards.

The two giants in the field of suicidal theorizing at the turn of the twentieth century were Durkheim and Freud. Durkheim in *Suicide* (1897) focused on society's inimical effects on the individual, while Freud, eschewing the notions of either sin or crime, gave suicide back to man, but put the locus of action in man's unconscious. Since around 1900, a host of psychological theories besides Freud's have focused on the individual; for example, those of Alfred Adler, Ludwig Binswanger, Carl G. Jung, Karl Menninger, George Kelly, Henry A. Murray, Edwin Shneidman, Harry Stack Sullivan, and Gregory Zilboorg. One purpose of this book is to outline and provide a current context for suicide by way of these 10 modern suicidologists. Indeed, our view of the history of suicide shows not only a constant development in defining suicide, but also that suicide is open to various constructions.

Suicide Facts and Myths

The lore about suicide contains a large number of interesting and esoteric items. People are not only perplexed and bewildered, but they believe a number of misconceptions of suicide. Here are some common fables and facts of suicide, formulated by Shneidman around 1952 and incorporated in a number of publications (e.g., Shneidman & Mandelkorn, 1970):

1. Fable: People who talk about suicide don't commit suicide.
   Fact: Of any 10 persons who kill themselves, 8 have given definite warnings of their suicidal intentions.
2. Fable: Suicide happens without warning.
   Fact: Studies reveal that the suicidal person gives many clues and warnings regarding his suicidal intentions.
3. Fable: Suicidal people are fully intent on dying.
   Fact: Most suicidal people are undecided about living or dying, and they "gamble with death," leaving it to others to save them. Almost no one commits suicide without letting others know how he is feeling.
4. Fable: Once a person is suicidal, he is suicidal forever.
   Fact: Individuals who wish to kill themselves are suicidal only for a limited period of time.
5. Fable: Improvement following a suicidal crisis means that the suicidal risk is over.
   Fact: Most suicides occur within about three months following the beginning of "improvement," when the individual has the energy to put his morbid thoughts and feelings into effect.
6. Fable: Suicide strikes much more often among the rich—or, conversely, it occurs most exclusively among the poor.

Fact: Suicide is neither the rich man's disease nor the poor man's curse. Suicide is very "democratic" and is represented proportionately among all levels of society.

7. Fable: Suicide is inherited or "runs in the family."
   Fact: Suicide does not run in families. It is an individual pattern.

8. Fable: All suicidal individuals are mentally ill, and suicide always is the act of a psychotic person.
   Fact: Studies of hundreds of genuine suicide notes indicate that although the suicidal person is extremely unhappy, he is not necessarily mentally ill.

There is also the misconception that we talk about "myths" as if we really knew what people actually believe or know. Recently, studies by McIntosh, Hubbard, and Santos (1983) and Leenaars, Balance, Pellarin, Aversano, Magli, and Wenckstern (1988) addressed this topic. Their findings supported the belief that people's information levels regarding suicide on some facts and fables are poor (but generally well above what was anticipated from the previous anecdotal literature). Ginsburg (1971) had previously documented that people often see suicide as something "just happening" to a person. Others, according to Kalish, Reynolds, and Farberow (1974), believe that people who kill themselves are crazy or mentally ill. Still others, as will be evident to any reader of current popular formulations regarding suicide, see suicide as simply due to an external event; i.e., a rejection, an illness, or other misfortune. On the other hand, Kalish et al. (1971) and Leenaars et al. (1988) have also pointed out that many people are aware of some facts regarding suicide, such as that it is not the outcome of mental illness.

Apart from knowledge, people's attitudes towards suicide or suicide attempts are either negative or ill-informed. Kalish et al. (1971) have emphasized that the milieu cannot be omitted. Cultural attitudes, norms, and values (as any historical review shows) influence behavior. Domino, Moore, Westlake, and Gibson (1982) have demonstrated that today there is considerable complexity in the attitudes regarding suicide. Yet Ansel and Gibson (1971) have demonstrated that such attitudes are often negative and held not only by people in general but by the care givers themselves. Such a situation appears to be especially true regarding the suicide attempter. Ginsburg (1971) has noted that there frequently continues to be an aura of disgrace around suicide, which tarnishes even the survivors. Kalish et al. (1974) further note that a large number of people display little or no sympathy for individuals who attempt or threaten to commit suicide, although Ramsay and Bagley (1985) have indicated that in the 1980s there is a more accepting attitude to suicide than reported previously.

Attempted Suicide

Although it is obvious that one has to "attempt" suicide in order to commit it, it is equally clear that the event of "attempting suicide" does not always have death (cessation) as its objective. It is an acknowledged fact that often the goal of "attempted suicide" (such as cutting oneself or ingesting harmful substances) is to change one's life (or to change the behavior of the "significant others" around one) rather than to end it. On some very rare occasions death is actually intended and only luckily avoided. We will meet some of these "fortuitous survivors" as well as some "attempters" in this book; they are case illustrations that various suicidologists have documented and utilized to exemplify their formulations regarding suicide. We will also meet some who committed suicide. However, at this point, we wish to stress, as have others (e.g., Stengel, 1964), that it is useful to think of the "attempter," now often referred to as the parasuicide, and the "completer," as two sets of overlapping populations: (1) a group of those who attempt suicide, a few of whom go on to commit it, and (2) a group of those who commit suicide, many of who previously attempted it. A great deal has to do with *perturbation* and *lethality* of the event. Perturbation refers to how upset (disturbed, agitated, sane-insane) the individual is—rated as low-medium-high (or alternatively on a 1 to 9 scale)—and may be measured by various means (e.g., self-reports, biological markers, psychological tests, observations). Lethality is roughly synonymous with the "deathfulness" of the act and is an important dimension in understanding any potentially suicidal individual. Lethality can be rated as low-moderate-high (or alternatively on a 1 to 9 scale). An example for measuring lethality is the following, derived from Shneidman (1967): "During the last 24 hours, I felt the chances of my actually killing myself (committing suicide and ending my life) were: absent, very low, low-medium, fifty-fifty, high medium, very high, extra high (came very close to actually killing myself)." Smith, Conroy, and Ehler (1984) have presented a sound psychometric scale of lethality. A critical distinction in suicide is that lethality—not perturbation—kills. All sorts of people are highly perturbed but are not suicidal. The ratio between suicide attempts and commits is about 8 to 1—one committed suicide for every eight attempts.

The "attempter," a parasuicide (along with self-assaultive and self-mutilative behavior) and "completer," share some commonalities; however, they are, by and large, operationally quite different. There is a third group, the "contemplators," whose numbers are so vast that it is difficult to begin to highlight their commonalities, who are again quite different. The differences (and commonalities) between suicide and parasuicide have been recently presented by Shneidman (1985). He presents the following schema: (1) whereas the common *stimulus* in suicide is unendurable psychological pain, in parasuicide it is intense, potentially endurable, psychological pain; (2) whereas the common *purpose* in suicide is to seek a solution to an overbearing problem, in parasuicide it is to reduce tension and to evoke a response; (3) whereas the common *goal* in suicide is cessation of consciousness, in parasuicide it is reordering of the life space; (4) whereas the common *emotion* in suicide is hopelessness-helplessness, in parasuicide it is loss and rejection, disconnectedness and disenfranchisement; (5) whereas the common *internal attitude* in suicide is ambivalence, in parasuicide it is trivalence among living (life), suffering, and dying (death); (6) whereas the common *cognitive state* in suicide is constriction, in parasuicide, it is obsessional, with some planfulness; (7) whereas the common *interpersonal act* in suicide is communication of intention, in parasuicide it is communication of unhappiness, a call to rescue, evocation; and (8) whereas the common *action* in suicide is egression, in parasuicide it is communication, importuning. There are also some similarities, although the content of such characteristics may be quite different. Shneidman (1985), for example, provided the following two: (1) the common *stressor* in both is frustrated needs; and (2) the common *consistency* in both is with lifelong adjustment patterns.

Suicide attempts have many meanings and, whatever the level of lethality, ought to be taken seriously. A person who attempts suicide may not necessarily mean that he wants to die but that the situation was so intense that he had to communicate the pain. Words like "manipulation" or "blackmail" or "attention" add only a pejorative emotional tone, revealing our own attitudes and fears.

Partial Death and Substitutes for Suicide

Freud (1901), Shneidman (1963), Murray (1963), Leenaars and Balance (1984b), and others have speculated that beyond intentional suicides, there is a vast array of subintentional inimical behaviors. The very life-style of such individuals seems to truncate and demean their life so that they are as good as dead. In 1901, Freud stated:

> It is well known that in the severe cases of psychoneurosis instances of self injury are occasionally found as symptoms and that in such cases suicide can never be ruled out as a possible outcome of the physical conflict . . . many apparently accidental injuries that happen to such patients are really instances of self-injury. (p. 178–179)

Freud further notes that such self-destruction is not rare. Often alcoholism, drug addiction, mismanagement of physical disease, auto accidents, and masochistic behavior can be seen in this light. Farberow (1980) has edited a book on (borrowing from the title of the book) "the many faces of suicide." Therein, he asks a number of relevant questions. For example, he asks (somewhat paraphrased):

> Why did a person stop taking insulin when he knew he had to take it regularly to stay well, or even to stay alive?

> Why did a person, knowing what drugs can do to you, get hooked?
>
> Why did a person drive so fast on the curving mountain roads when he had known for the last three months how bad his brakes were?

There may be no intent to kill himself, but he is "as good as dead." Karl Menninger, the chief theorist on the concept of partial death, in *Man Against Himself* (1938), writes of (1) *chronic* suicide—including asceticism, martyrdom, neurotic invalidism, alcohol addiction, antisocial behavior, and psychosis; (2) *focal* suicide—focusing on a limited part of the body—including self-mutilation, multiple surgery, purposive accidents, impotence, and frigidity; and (3) *organic* suicide—focusing on the psychological factors in organic disease, especially the self-punishing aggressive, and erotic components. Freud (1901) has speculated that there is, in fact, a suicidal thread in all of us. The answer to why some exhibit chronic, focal, or organic suicide may be related to some or all of those characteristics listed by Shneidman (1985) regarding parasuicide.

A related concept is of "subintentioned death" (Shneidman, 1963). This concept asserts that there are many deaths that are neither clearly suicidal nor clearly accidental or natural, but deaths in which the decedent played some covert or unconscious role in "permitting" his death to occur, sort of "accidentally" or by "inviting" homicide, or by unconsciously disregarding what could be a life-extending medical regimen, and thus dying sooner than "necessary." Freud (1901) speculated:

> Anyone who believes in the occurrence of half-intentional self-injury—if I may use a clumsy expression—will be prepared also to assume that in addition to consciously intentional suicide there is such a thing as half-intentional self-destruction (self-destruction with an unconscious intention), capable of making skillful use of a threat of life and of disguising it as a chance mishap (p. 180–181).

We shall meet a few people like this in our case examples, such as Zilboorg's Hessler.

SUICIDE NOTES

How do we look at suicide? What raw data can we legitimately use? After all, unlike most other areas of research regarding complicated human acts, we cannot ask the dead suicidal person. This forces us to look elsewhere. Shneidman and Farberow (1957), Maris (1981) and others have suggested the following alternatives: statistics, third-party interviews, the study of nonfatal suicide attempters and documents (including *personal documents*). All of these have their limitations. Statistics reflect by themselves only numbers and are, at best, only a fraction of the true figures. A third party can only provide a point of view which is not the suicide's. Nonfatal attempters are different from completers. Documents may provide, to use Maris's word (1981), only a snapshot of an event that requires a full-length movie. But sometimes they provide a vignette of sufficient length so that some essential essences of the entire movie can be reasonably inferred. Examples of such documents are case histories, psychological test results, death certificates, suicide notes, and a host of others as will be seen in the case of Natalie in a later chapter at the end of this book.

Of course, there is the problem of obtaining any of these data, statistics, interviews, reports by attempters, and personal documents. Maris (1981) has discussed at length some of these problems; he states, "One of the major problems in understanding self-destructive behaviors is that the data base for such potential explanations is conspicuously absent." Maris further points out that this is because "most researchers have been trapped by either the Scylla of official or 'vital' statistics or the Charybdis of individual case histories." However, such a formulation should not deter us in our study of suicide. Rather, it should make us rethink the problem (and the specific problems with each source of data) anew, look at it alternatively with the beginning understanding, as Maris (1981) has pointed out, that "the real world of suicide is never captured in [the act of] suicide." Something will always remain omitted, but something also will always be learned.

A related (if not embedded) problem is the one that is the ubiquitous issue of psychology itself: the mind-body problems;

or, the admissibility of introspective accounts as opposed to objective reports. This resonates to Windelband's (1904) division of two possible approaches to knowledge between the nomothetic and the idiographic. The tabular, statistical, arithmetic, demographic nomothetic approach deals with generalizations, whereas the idiographic approach involves the intense study of individuals—the clinical methods, history, biography. In this latter approach *personal* documents are frequently utilized—personal documents such as letters, logs, memoirs, diaries, autobiographies, suicide notes. Let us, before addressing the topic at hand, explore the views on the idiographic approach in more detail; the other—the nomothetic approach—is well engrained in psychology and science in general.

Allport (1962) has provided us with a classical statement on the advantages of an idiographic approach. All 10 suicidologists in this book have made use of the idiographic approach in their formulations. Allport (1962) notes that psychology is "committed to increasing man's understanding of man," man in general and man in the particular. What concerns psychology deeply is individual human personality. John Stuart Mill proposed that we make such a distinction in science, both being critical, although some psychologists object strongly to the study of individual cases.

Allport (1962) provides the following:

> Suppose we take John, a lad of 12 years, and suppose his family background is poor; his father was a criminal; his mother rejected him; his neighborhood is marginal. Suppose that 70 percent of the boys having a similar background become criminals. Does this mean that John himself has a 70 percent chance of delinquency?

Allport answers:

> Not at all. John is a unique being (p. 411).

Allport (1962) noted that the real concern about the idiographic and nomothetic is developing methods that are more rich, flexible, and precise, that "do justice to the fascinating individuality" of each individual.

Runyan (1982a & b, 1983) has more recently outlined a detailed defense for idiographic approaches. The criticisms of idiographic studies and Runyan's defenses are as follows:

1. It is difficult to generalize from them. Defense: Psychology is not only concerned with the general.
2. There is no such thing as a unique trait or element. Defense: A concept can be created to describe an individual; it can be later applied to others.
3. It is useful for generating hypotheses, not for testing them. Defense: There are not only general laws but also unique. Equally, there are not only general methods but also single case methods.
4. It is impossible to conduct an idiographic study of every individual. Defense: Indeed one cannot study all, but one can study individuals of particular interest.
5. It is not science. Defense: It is clearly untenable that science is not concerned with particulars (e.g., a comet, a star, a volcano, a whale, or a human).
6. There are no adequate methods. Defense. There are, indeed, adequate methods.

This present volume, in fact, is one such approach. Our book is explicitly about several methods to study one source of relevant data, suicide notes. Our methods, we hope, will allow us to study the suicidal person. But the book is also about the general: what suicide notes have in common and, by inference, what suicidal individuals may have in common.

Suicide Notes and Other Personal Documents

Allport (1942) has noted that personal documents have a significant place in psychological research. Shneidman (1980), in *Voices of Death,* a book about letters, diaries, notes, and other personal documents relating to death, has stated that such "documents contain special revelations of the human mind and that there is much one can learn from them." Although Allport (1942) cites some shortcomings in the use of personal documents in psychological science—unrepresentativeness of sample, self-deception, blindness to motives, errors of memory—he makes a clear case for the use of personal documents, citing the following: learning about the person, advancing both nomothetic and idiographic research, and aiding in the aims of science—understanding, prediction, and control. One is also reminded of Maslow's view (1966) that much of scientific psychology is "mechanistic and ahuman." Most psychologists only know the controlled experiment. But, according to Maslow (1966), if we want to know the *person,* we have to be more open-minded. The experiment has an important place, but so do other methods (and questions). Maslow (1966) has noted, for example, that we can use the subjective reports in psychology as well as "covert communications, paintings, dreams, stories, gestures, etc.—which we can interpret." Personal documents provide this invaluable source of data. As an interesting footnote to his trailblazing work, Allport wrote about diaries, memoirs, logs, letters, autobiographies, but it did not occur to his capacious mind to think of perhaps the most personal document of all: suicide notes.

This book about personal documents is not defensive about their use or pleading for their occasional admissibility. On the contrary, it emphasizes their special virtues and their special power in doing *the main business of psychology*—the intensive study of the human person.

Furthermore, the use of personal documents does not mean that the essential method of science, Mill's method of difference, has to be abandoned, as the comparison between genuine and simulated suicide notes clearly illustrate. We believe that personal documents provide a unique place in human science where maximum *relevance* can be mated with acceptable *precision.* There are not many marriages like that in psychology.

Suicide notes are the ultrapersonal documents. They are the unsolicited productions of the suicidal person, usually written minutes before the suicidal death. They are an invaluable starting point for comprehending the suicidal act and for understanding the special features of the people who actually commit suicide and what they share in common with the rest of us who have only been drawn to imagine it. Suicide notes are a way through the looking glass to suicide although, unlike Alice, we will not find "beautiful things" there, but unbearable pain.

Early research on suicide notes largely utilized an anecdotal approach that incorporated descriptive information of individual notes. Subsequent methods of study have primarily included classification analysis and content analysis, whereas very few studies have utilized a theoretical analysis—a deficiency which this book seeks to redress.

How representative are suicide notes? To what extent can one generalize from the note-writers to those who do not leave a note? Regarding the latter, it seems that approximately 12 to 15 percent of people who commit suicide leave notes. Erwin Stengel in *Suicide and Attempted Suicide* (1964) stated:

> Whether the writers of suicide notes differ in their attitudes from those who leave no notes behind it is impossible to say. Possibly, they differ from the majority only in being good correspondents. At any rate, the results of the analysis of suicide notes are in keeping with the observation . . . common to most suicidal acts. (p. 44–45)

We believe that research in suicide notes has been useful and can be made more so, even though suicide notes by themselves do not give a complete account of suicidal thinking. The notes must be put in the context of people's lives (Shneidman, 1980) and in the context of broad theoretical formulations about suicide and personality functioning in general.

We make formulations about things (sometimes singular, sometimes general) (Husserl, 1907/1973). A common point of view is that personal documents are open to different formulations. Runyan (1982a), for example, has noted that "it is claimed that Freud's case studies suffer from the critical flaw of being open to many interpretations." The studies of most people's lives are open to any number of theoretical templates. Gergen (1977) has argued that the events of people's lives allow the investigator freedom to support his or her formulations. We would agree that such misuse is possible, not only in the application of personal documents but, we would add, in *any* form of research. Statistics too can be manipulated by one's formulations. Runyan (1982a) suggests that to avoid this misuse, one must "critically evaluate alternative explanations and interpretations," which is what this book intends to do. We shall look not only at Freud's formulations but at 10 different explanations and interpretations, various constructions by 10 suicidologists. Indeed, being open to different points of view constitutes the very richness of personal documents rather than some experiment that is preplanned to address one's favorite theory. Balance (1975) and Bringmann (1975) have presented an interesting similar point of view in their historical investigations and have provided convincing examples of the richness of documents in their study of archives of nineteenth-century German psychology.

A related issue is that theory should not play any role in research. This view holds that research, of whatever type, should be atheoretical. However, we believe that theory, explicit and implicit, plays some role in research, whether solving a specific problem, testing an existing theory, developing new theories, or expanding existing theories. The problem is that frequently the theory is not stated. Regrettably, much of the research to date on suicide notes is atheoretical—the theory is not stated. We will attempt to look at this in our book by way of a logical empirical approach to a theory, derived from Carnap (1931/1959).

As a source of data, suicide notes are not uncontroversial regarding the utility of such documents. Some see suicide notes as the key to unlocking the mysteries of suicidal phenomena, or the looking glass to suicide. Others believe that suicide notes, unlike other personal documents, cannot ever be illuminating. Suicide notes are no looking glass at all; indeed, suicide notes are written by the very person, who because of his constriction, "knows" *least* why he is doing it. Our own point of view, at this time, is these notes may be bountiful, but they are rarely banal. Suicide notes can have a great deal of meaning if, as commented earlier, they are put within the context of the details of that person's life (Shneidman, 1980). Furthermore, if put in the context of different *formulations* of suicide and personality functioning in general, we believe that suicide notes can provide us important information, both for idiographic and nomothetic use.

SUICIDE DIARIES

Another fascinating kind of personal document left by suicides is the suicide diary. A suicidal diary is a suicide note with a history. It meets the following criteria: It is a lengthy, literate document kept over a fairly long period of time, often years; the diarist writes explicitly about suicide, including his suicidal thoughts, impulses, reflections, and resistances; and, the diarist commits suicide. The suicidal diary is but one subgroup of people who keep a book about their life, a book about what happened.

Currently, there is a resurgence of interest in the topic of diaries in general. Two recent first-rate books about diaries are Paul Rosenblatt's scholarly, *Bitter, Bitter Tears: Nineteenth Century Diarists and Twentieth Century Grief Theories* (1983) and Thomas Mallon's fascinating *A Book of One's Own: People and Their Diaries* (1984).

Paul Rosenblatt notes that diaries "allow one to see . . . clearly day-to-day changes, long-term trends, and the effects of specific events." A diary is a document about how life is lived. Most of us are curious about the diaries as we are about other personal documents. To cite a diarist, Evelyn Waugh, "the routine of their day properly recorded is always interesting." The personality of its keeper is richly found within a diary—a document not only of events but the very writer himself.

Why do people keep such a document? Thomas Mallon cites Virginia Woolf, who later drowned herself, reflecting on her diary, "I wonder why I do it. . . . Partly I, think, from my old sense of the race of time 'Time's winged chariot hurrying near.' Does it stay it?" Anais Nin notes that the diary is a personal document, an exploration, a growth, a meaningful personal relationship and much more. Both Mallon and Rosenblatt point out that there is a large variety of diaries that are written, for various reasons—all diarists wanting to write "it" down on pages like the writer of the suicide note. Both the diary and the note are rich personal documents left by their writers, something they wanted to communicate to themselves and, almost always, to unknown others.

Diaries sometimes show us the wretchedness and unbearable pain as it unfolds day to day for the keeper. Kafka, as he worked on *The Castle* and *The Trial,* contemplated and wrote about suicide in his diary. Others write about their own suicide attempts. Mallon, for example, cites Lee Harvey Oswald, who attempted suicide and later wrote, "I decide to end it. Soak wrist in cold water to numb the pain, then slash my left wrist . . . I watch my life whirl away." Some diaries are about extremely inimical life-styles, such as *Go Ask Alice;* a diary by a fifteen-year-old runaway girl, who finally died of a drug overdose. A few diarists write about their death. Only a relatively small number of suicide diaries are available. The list includes, among others, the diary of Benjamin Robert Haydon (1786–1846), English historical painter who committed suicide by both gunshot and razor.

Benjamin Haydon's diary according to Mallon "read(s) like a lifelong harangue." Haydon's life was dramatic; he was constantly "fighting off bill collectors and the indifference of his countryman." In his diary, he writes:

> Came home in excruciating anxiety, not being able to raise the money for rent for the Hall, and found a notice from a broker for a Quarter's rent from Newton, my old landlord for 22 years! For a moment my brain was confused! I had paid him half and therefore there was only 10 left. I went into the painting room in great misery of mind.

Some of Haydon's diary reads, indeed, like a suicide note. Haydon's own final entry:

> God forgive-me-Amen
> Finis
> of
> BR Haydon
> "Stretch me no longer on this tough
> World"—Lear
> End
> XXVI Volume.

Mallon provides other accounts of suicide diaries—of Sylvia Plath, Dora Carrington, and others. Daniel Aaron has recently (1985) edited a fascinating two-volume record of the Arthur Inman diaries. These are the personal documents—written between 1919 and Inman's suicide in 1963—of "a warped and deeply troubled man" whose aberrations call for suicidological probing. Mallon also, interestingly, cites the diary of Joe Orton, which ends up being a confession for his own killer, his lover Kenneth Halliwell—a homicide-suicide. The diary describes a calamitous relationship, one of loss and rejection, frustrated needs, pain, and much more. Orton writes on April 23, 1967, a few months before the homicide-suicide,

> Dreary day, Kenneth in an ugly mood. Morning, I said, "You look like a zombie." He replied, heavily, "So I should lead the life of a zombie."

On August 9, 1967, Halliwell repeatedly hit Orton's head with a hammer, killing him. He then left the following suicide note on Orton's diary:

> If you read his diary all will be explained.
> K.H.
> p.s. Especially the latter part.

Suicide Notes and Ethics

The very study of suicide can create ethical questions (Battin & Maris, 1983). Our research itself raises various ethical issues. No one has discussed such issues directly regarding suicide notes, but Paul Rosenblatt (1985) has recently discussed some ethical problems regarding the use of personal documents in general. The main issue is invasion of privacy. Rosenblatt has noted that when we read a personal document we are invading the person's private life, something that the person may never have intended. He notes that "even when a document like a suicide note is written with some particular person in mind, we are not those persons; we are intruding into a private world." However, as Rosenblatt himself further highlights, suicide notes are useful for research for us all. We will learn more about a person's death and, we hope that will save lives. A collection of actual suicide notes is printed in the appendices to this book, but care has been taken in changing identifying details, so that no person can be specifically identified.

Final Introductory Note

This book is more than about suicide notes. Rather, it touches on the tragedy of lives that were lived, illuminated by the viewpoints of 10 suicidologists and illustrated by case studies. The book is an attempt by means of a logical empirical investigation to understand "Why?", by way of 10 key formulations regarding suicide. It is an empirical investigation, redefining suicide in terms of suicide notes.

Chapter 2

PREVIOUS STUDIES OF SUICIDE NOTES

The purpose of this chapter is to provide a review of the literature on suicide notes. Suicide notes are a special kind of personal document. They are an unstructured and unsolicited communication by a person written just before the death in which that person conveys last thoughts, feelings, and wishes. The importance of such personal documents in the understanding of an individual, the building of theoretical models, and the undertaking of psychological research is not to be underestimated. Early descriptive presentations as well as the scientific study of suicide notes, beginning with Shneidman and Farberow's investigations (1957a), have revealed a series of clues to suicide that provide a valuable starting point in appreciating and understanding the suicidal individual's state of mind. Especially when notes are put in the context of the writers' lives (Shneidman, 1980) and in the context of broad theoretical formulations about suicide and personality in general (Leenaars & Balance, 1985), they have proven to be meaningful personal documents.

Although there are earlier descriptive presentations of suicide in the literature, Freud (1905), in his famous analysis of

Dora, began one of the first well-known clinical analyses of a note in which Dora wrote about killing herself. In his analysis, Freud reported that Dora's parents found "a letter in which she took leave of them because, as she said, she could no longer endure her life." Inasmuch as Dora did not kill herself (nor did Freud diagnose any serious lethality), Freud suggested rather that the note was reflective of Dora's psychodynamics and provided clues to understanding her and her relationships.

In this chapter, we will utilize the case of Dora as our clinical material to complement our survey of previous studies on suicide notes (cited individually in Appendix A). We shall report the original texts verbatim when possible, at the same time attempting to bring some unity to the specific data. It is our hope that Freud's case of Dora will serve as a device to make the review of the literature on suicide notes more meaningful and will allow us to frame our understanding of the case of Dora in a more empirical fashion.

A review of the previous research on suicide notes suggests that the topic can be subdivided under five broad subheadings, as follows:

1) The note reflects a communication about a *situation* for the survivors and/or others.
2) The note highlights the importance of a *relationship,* often one that involves a rejection, or needs (especially love) that are not being met.
3) The note exhibits the presence of an *emotional state,* usually a strong negative one (e.g., depression, hate, self-blame, grief, aggression, etc.) and a strong positive emotional state (e.g., love, affection, concern, gratitude, etc.) or, more accurately, an overall emotional state that can best be described as ambivalent, i.e., the simultaneous presence of both love and hate as well as other emotions.
4) The note exhibits language and reasoning suggestive of a *cognitive state* that is unusual and constricted.
5) Finally, suicide notes suggest the importance of *demographic variables,* notably age, in understanding suicide.

The following discussion of the literature will parallel this outline and will include illustrative examples of Freud's description of Dora.

SITUATION

Suicide notes are without question a communication—a communication about a situation (Hayakawa, 1957). Often the note is an effort of a person contemplating suicide to communicate with a significant other (e.g., a lover, a parent) about some very important situation. The note is more than just an everyday discussion, for it reflects that person's mental agony and psychic stress. Indeed, the person communicates in his note that the situation is unbearable and that he desperately wants a way out of it (Wagner, 1960, Jacobs, 1971; Shneidman, 1985). The suicidal person is highly perturbed (Bjerg, 1967) and is experiencing considerable dread (Spiegel & Neuringer, 1963) or pain (Shneidman, 1980). Most often the perturbation is related to a situation involving other people. There is, in fact, a high percentage of references to people in suicide notes with very specific details about them such as names, places, and addresses (Gottschalk & Gleser, 1960). Nouns, pronouns, references to third persons are much more frequently found in the genuine suicide notes than in simulated suicide notes.

Beyond a mere communication about a situation to another person, the notes reflect instructions to and restrictions upon the survivors (Shneidman & Farberow, 1957c; Spiegel & Neuringer, 1963; Jacobs, 1971). Although the message may be vague, the notes clearly reflect a wish to maintain a tie and to produce a persistent effect on others. There is, in fact, a demanding, commanding, pleading quality in suicide notes. Frequently, notes reflect a need of the writer that requires a response from another person for its satisfaction (Shneidman, 1980) but, unfortunately, the need can now never be met nor can the other person address it.

An illustration: Dora's "farewell letter" was left as a communication to her parents, although more directly to her father, about her perception of a situation. The note had been left in her desk where her parents could easily find it; for as Freud himself noted, Dora "had herself arranged for it to fall into their hands." The letter not only resulted in a state of great alarm in her parents but the letter and Dora's subsequent behavior resulted in significant changes in the behavior of the significant others around her, especially her father. Dora had previously attempted to use prayer, argument, and fainting spells, but these were unsuccessful in getting her basic wish gratified; namely, a close relation with her father. Freud, in his analysis of the case, speculated that perhaps Dora hoped to succeed in frightening her father by the note and thus make him more attached and attracted to her.

Relationship

The suicidal person has problems in establishing or maintaining interpersonal relationships. The sense of total rejection, in an individual who already depreciates himself, is often a root cause of self-destruction (Leenaars & Balance, 1981; 1984b; Shneidman, 1980). The relationship is often one that resulted in loss, rejection, or needs (especially love) not being met. The lack of success in establishing a satisfying relationship or the experience of a broken relationship (e.g., divorce, separation) are much more frequently cited in suicide notes than any other comparable item (such as illness, social disgrace, or alcoholism).

The loss, abandonment, or a rejection cited in a suicide note is not surprisingly related to a very important person (Leenaars & Balance, 1984b). The suicidal person is preoccupied with the person who had been lost or who had been rejecting and has developed a strong, direct or indirect, identification (or attachment) with the rejecting person. The person has unrealistic expectations of such a person (Bjerg, 1967) and exhibits heightened dependency needs in the suicide note (Darbonne, 1969a), to the point that the person's attachments and identification are regressive and unhealthy (Leenaars & Balance, 1984b).

An illustration: As noted previously, Dora's (unconscious) aim in her farewell note was to develop and increase her father's attachment to her and more indirectly to remove her mother from the relationship, since she had already fantasized that her father was now in love with Frau K., not her mother. Dora feared that she was losing her father to Frau K. It was this fantasized loss and rejection that acted as the precipitating event in the writing of the note.

Dora's aim by the note and her hysterical features was to detach her father from Frau K. and thus win her father, since she knew "how much he was attached to her." Freud suggested that this attachment began to be active in Dora's childhood during the period of normal affection and attachment to one's parents. Freud reconstructed that not only the note but all of Dora's hysterical reaction patterns were ways to maintain her regressive attachment. Freud further formulated that Dora was attempting by her behavior (including the note) to put herself in her mother's place. As Freud noted, Dora "felt and acted more like a jealous wife" than a concerned daughter.

Freud's analysis suggested that beyond the affection, there was a strong identification occurring with the significant others. He suggested that Dora was identifying herself both with the woman her father had once loved (mother) and with the woman he loved now (Frau K.). However, Dora was unaware of these dynamics. Her affection for her father was a much stronger one than she knew or would have cared to admit; namely, that she was in love with him erotically.

Emotional State

There are many emotional states found in suicide notes. For example, it is not difficult to find evidence of hostility in suicide notes. The hostility is often directed toward a person with whom the suicidal individual had been deeply attached but who had been lost or was rejecting (Leenaars & Balance, 1984b). Suicide notes of individuals who are separated or divorced exhibit an even greater amount of such outwardly directed aggression (Tuckman, Kliener, & Lavell, 1959; Tuckman & Ziegler, 1968).

In suicide notes, individuals often communicate feelings (as well as ideas) of vengefulness and aggression towards themselves; the person often sees the suicide as an act of self-punishment

(Leenaars & Balance, 1984b). Expressions of depression, guilt, and self-criticism are frequently cited (Chynoweth, 1977; Leenaars & Balance, 1984b). The suicidal person devalues himself and sees himself as worthless (Bjerg, 1967). A sense of shame, "loss of face," disgrace, or a sense of dereliction of duty can all be noted in some notes (Shneidman, 1980). However, analysis of suicide notes suggest that, despite these characteristics of aggression turned inward, the person appears to be angry toward someone else. Hate directed towards others and self-blame are both evident (Shneidman & Farberow 1957c). The person, in fact, appears to turn back upon himself murderous wishes or impulses which had been directed towards someone else, although, at times, these hostile themes are not directly stated but can be readily inferred (Leenaars & Balance, 1984b). Suicide may often be a veiled aggression which includes hurting the self and the wish to hurt and manipulate others (Darbonne, 1969; Leenaars & Balance, 1984b). Shneidman (1980) has called this process "murder in the 180th degree."

Suicide notes do not reflect aggression and hostility alone (Shneidman, 1980; Tuckman, Kliener, & Lavell, 1959). There are many other emotions evident such as despondency, shame, guilt, fear, despair, frustration, loss of autonomy, and especially, feelings of hopelessness and helplessness (Shneidman, 1985). There is also a positive emotional state evident in some notes. One study of suicide notes (Tuckman, Kleiner, & Lavell, 1959) reports that positive affect such as gratitude, affection, and concern for the welfare of others occurs more frequently in suicide notes than a negative emotional state or a neutral emotional state.

Analysis of genuine notes (as compared to simulated notes) suggests that the word "love" often occurs in the writings of the genuine suicide (Oglivie, Stone, & Shneidman, 1969). Love, especially frustrated love, seems to play as great a role in the suicide as aggression. However, it is the simultaneous presence of *both* love and hate (as well as other emotions) that occurs more frequently in suicide than either a negative or a positive emotion. There is considerable conflict in emotions and motives (Osgood & Walker, 1959). In fact, the person in the suicide note appears to be strikingly ambivalent (i.e., affectionate *and* hostile), for example, toward the same lost or rejecting person (Osgood &

Walker, 1959; Shneidman, 1980; Leenaars & Balance, 1984b). It is this ambivalence and the emotions of aggression, hopelessness, and helplessness that appear to be most critical in the emotional state of the suicide.

An illustration: Dora, according to Freud, exhibited positive feelings (affection, love) and negative feelings (hostility, aggression); she exhibited the simultaneous presence of both of these emotional states. Her feelings, according to Freud, can best be described as ambivalent. The analysis suggested that Dora was experiencing affection and love towards her father; in fact, she was identifying herself with the woman he had loved and was now in love with. At the same time, she was feeling pronounced hostility towards Frau K., a reaction that her father could not understand. Subsequent analysis suggested that the hostility was directed to her mother and a later analysis of a dream indicated that the negative feelings were directed to her father. Dora dreamed that she had received notice of her father's death in a letter. Freud reconstructed that this death was related to Dora's death in her farewell letter. On this basis, Freud postulated that her aggression directed inward in her letter was initially directed against her father.

Cognitive State

If there is a particular and unique cognitive state present immediately before one's suicide, this should be evident in the language and reasoning of the suicide note. Analysis of suicide notes (Osgood & Walker, 1959; Shneidman, 1980; Shneidman & Farberow 1957b) suggest that the notes indeed exhibit unusual modes of reasoning. They often contain suppressed premises (or beliefs) which lead to deadly conclusions (Shneidman & Farberow, 1957b). Some of the reasoning patterns in suicide notes observed by Tripodes (1976) are the following: It appears to the individual that his mode of reasoning is quite reasonable and objective. The individual in a suicide note describes what is perceived to be a very objective situation and appears unaware of his own distortions. The individual reports seeing events (e.g., a loss, a rejection), often full of irrelevancies, exactly as they are, making no discrimination between the relevant and irrelevant and accepting no alternatives. The note is written as though personal beliefs and perceptions are direct, absolute, and supreme. Likewise, feelings are perceived as equally relevant to assess either personal states or objective situations. Suicidal individuals trust their own premises and conclusions and expect others, often in a hostile and aggressive fashion, to understand and accept them. They ignore their own projections, fabrications, subjective state, cognitive disorganization and do not differentiate between inner states and outer situations.

In addition to these observations by Tripodes, analysis of suicide notes suggests that constriction and tunnel vision occur quite frequently in the note writer, evident by narrowing of focus, concreteness, a relative lack of cognitive awareness, and a greater amount of alienation (Shneidman 1980; 1981; 1985). The rigidity of thinking (cognitive constriction) seems to be a major component of the cognitive state in suicide (Henken, 1976; Neuringer, 1976; Shneidman, 1980). Writers of genuine notes (as compared to simulated-note writers) exhibit a narrower range of cognitive processes; greater difficulty in utilizing and relying on internal cognitive processes; greater polarizations or rather fixed perceptions; and a lesser ability to solve problems (Gottschalk & Gleser, 1960; Oglivie, Stone, & Shneidman, 1969). These traits are evident by the use of absolute words such as "only," (as in "*the* only way") "always," "never." The importance of people, places, things, and the concept "you" are denigrated and negated (Edelman & Renshaw, 1982). The notes are very present-oriented (Edelman & Renshaw, 1982). There is a decrease in references to the future, suggesting a lack of ability to construe oneself in the future. Furthermore, perceptions of oneself are also denigrated.

Analysis of suicide notes also indicates that premises or beliefs (in the "syllogism" of the note) lead to lethal conclusions (Shneidman & Farberow, 1957b). One finding is that the person cannot successfully imagine his own death, epitomized by thinking simultaneously and contradictorily of being absent and of giving orders as if one were going to be present to enforce them. The major finding in the importance of suppressed premises, however, is that the person who writes the note exhibits a confusion relating to the concept of the self, a problem having to do primarily with personal identification. The individual makes a fallacious identification between the self as experienced by oneself and the self as experienced by others. The individual, in fact, treats himself as if one were reacting to another person which Freud (1917a, 1917b) has termed a "Narcissistic" identification with another person.

Suicide notes suggest that the person has consciously planned to kill himself. If one reads the note just for the manifest content, one would, indeed, conclude that the individual was consciously aware of his thoughts, feelings, and behavior. However, quite frequently, others perceive in the suicide note that the act appears to be motivated by unconscious dynamics or intentions (Leenaars & Balance, 1984b). Volant (1986) has recently suggested, for example, that if one fills in "the empty spaces in the text," one can empathically interpret suicide notes as a rich source of moral values and religious symbols. Utilizing a semiotic analysis, he noted that the suicide in the note often expresses faith in the existence of life after life and the hope for salvation.

An illustration: Dora's reasoning (although largely unconscious) was unusual, although it was not reflective of gross distortions that may be seen in schizophrenia. Her note and other reaction patterns reflected a state that was not consistent with accepted modes of logical reasoning. Rather, Freud speculated that Dora's love relationship to her father likely resulted in "a revival of germs" of feelings and reasoning patterns "in infancy." Dora's reasoning, for example, resulted in amnesia and her belief in an imaginary relation between Frau K. and her father. She even constructed a "fairy tale" about a reported suicide attempt by her father which, according to Dora's belief, was actually a screen for his sexual relation to Frau K. Although Dora's reasoning was apparently not objective, Dora was unaware of this; in fact, she strongly believed her conclusions. There was also her belief that the farewell note would result in her father loving only her.

Age and Other Demographic Variables

Most formulations about suicide appear to omit or neglect the age of the suicidal person, despite the fact that research on suicide notes, since a study in 1957 by Shneidman and Farberow, has demonstrated—a finding repeatedly confirmed—that a developmental perspective across the life span is important in understanding suicide. Although research suggests that similarities exist regardless of age, important differences have been shown to exist depending on the age of the suicidal person. Using Menninger's ideas (1938), Farberow and Shneidman (1957) have shown that there is a decrease with age in the wish to be killed (referring to such themes as submission, masochism, self-blame, and self-accusation) and the wish to kill (referring to such themes as aggression, accusation, blame, eliminating, driving away, disposing of, annihilating, and revenge), and an increase with age in the wish to die (referring to such themes as hopelessness, fear, fatigue, despair, and references to illness and pain). Older suicides express less inwardly directed aggression and tend to be less explicit about their forthcoming suicide (Lester & Hummel, 1980). Younger suicides appear to be more harsh, critical, and severe towards themselves (Leenaars & Balance, 1984c) and tend to be very fatalistic about a situation in which they experienced rejection, loneliness, or other stress (Peck, 1983). They exhibit a greater sense of guilt and often perceive that they deserve no better fate than death. They are also more likely than older suicides to treat themselves as if they were reacting to someone else (Leenaars & Balance, 1984c). Tuckman, Kleiner, and Lavell (1959) have also noted that younger suicides show less affect (both positive and negative) in their suicide notes, a finding supported by Lester and Reeve (1982). These latter researchers noted that not only do younger people express less affect, they express more action and are more explicit about their suicide.

Analyses of the suicide notes also suggest that the reasons stated in the notes are quite different, depending on age (Darbonne, 1969b). The problem which seems to preoccupy the young adult (20–39) is concern over relationships. The 40 to 49 age group often communicate a state of being vanquished; they seem unequal to the demands of life and often express statements of departure or egression. The 50–59 age group often do not cite a reason; rather, they frequently use the note to give instructions and to leave information. The 60-and-over group often cite illness, pain, and physical disabilities and write more often about loneliness and isolation.

The above studies and others in which age is briefly noted (Capstick, 1960; Cohen & Fiedler, 1974; Shneidman & Farberow, 1960), support the position that the dynamics and reaction patterns vary with the age of the suicidal person. However, Leenaars and Balance (1984c) have noted that, when one attempts to describe the content of suicide notes, despite the fact that the dynamics of suicide appear to differ with age in some respects, the dynamics are also similar in other critical respects. These are the elements in suicide that are ubiquitous across the life span. Be that as it may, the research supports the position that age may be a significant variable when examining suicide notes and, by implication, when constructing a model to interpret suicide.

Other demographic variables such as social status, marital status, and sex appear to result in some differences in suicide notes, but these appear to be less important than age. The reason for the suicide and the affective state appear to differ somewhat depending on social status (Shneidman & Farberow, 1969). People from the upper classes often give no reason, although they do write more often about "being tired of life" or physical illnesses; the middle class often write about rejection and express much affect in their notes; and the lower class express the least affect, the greatest number of instructions, and often communicate about the pressure of their existence.

Marital status is obviously relevant in that separated and divorced people more often cite the separation as the cause of the suicide (Tuckman, Kliener, & Lavell, 1959; Tuckman & Zeigler, 1968). They express intense hostility and are critical of the rejecting spouse while they also express strong love and affection, mainly towards their children.

Analysis of sex differences (Cohen & Fiedler, 1974; Lester & Reeve, 1982) suggests greater similarities than differences, although females may express greater despondency, grief, and disappointment, while at the same time expressing greater concern for others. Females as compared to males may also be less direct in their communication.

As a result of the research with suicide notes of young and older people, we have come to learn that one must approach suicide within a developmental perspective. Nonetheless, many significant similarities across the life span do clearly exist.

Chapter 3

PROTOCOL ANALYSIS OF SUICIDE NOTES

Early research on suicide notes largely utilized an anecdotal approach that incorporated descriptive information. Subsequent methods of study have primarily included classification analysis and content analysis. Only a very few studies have utilized a theoretical-conceptual analysis despite the belief, since the first formal study of suicide notes, that such contributions offer a rich potential (Shneidman & Farberow, 1957). One criticism of most studies of suicide notes is that they are relatively atheoretical. The purpose of this chapter is to outline a logical, empirical approach to the investigation of suicide notes which offers an opportunity for a theoretical analysis of suicide notes. The second purpose of this chapter is to introduce the reader to the investigations of 10 suicidologists' theoretical formulations regarding suicide.

Leenaars (1979) and Leenaars and Balance (1984a) have suggested that suicide notes can be treated as the "personal documents" of an archival source and subjected to the scrutiny of control hypotheses, essentially combining the case-study approach (Allport, 1942, 1962; Runyan, 1982a, 1982b, 1983) and the ex post facto method (Kerlinger, 1964; Anderson, 1971). In this form of research, the antecedent or independent variables have already occurred and the researcher must begin with analysis of the consequent or dependent variable. The major problems with this type of research are the lack of control over extraneous variables, and the large number of potentially important antecedent variables and thus the danger of misinterpreting relationships. Kerlinger (1964) has suggested that these problems can be largely overcome by explicitly formulating not just a single research hypothesis but several "control" hypotheses as well, which specify the antecedent variables. Essentially, this procedure would call for the recasting of suicide notes into different theoretical contexts (hypotheses, theories, models, etc.) for which the lines of evidence of each of these positions can then be pursued in the data (Balance, 1975; Bringmann, 1975; Leenaars, 1985; Leenaars & Balance, 1984a). Psychodynamic, behavioral, cognitive, existential, and other perspectives can then be empirically investigated utilizing these procedures. Thus predictive validity can be introduced to the study of suicide notes where cross-sectional and current field studies are impossible. Yet, this cannot be a completely controlled experiment (Anderson, 1971) in that other factors that cannot be isolated may well contribute to the suicides. The current procedures, it is hoped, will give us greater control in isolating some common features of suicide and thus aid us in providing a better definition of suicide in terms of suicide notes.

Protocol Analysis

An intrinsic problem in developing a method that allows one to undertake a theoretical analysis of suicide notes is obtaining different testable hypotheses from abstract formulations. One answer to this problem is provided by Carnap's logical and empirical procedures (1931/1959). Carnap suggested that:

> A person tests (verifies) a system-sentence by deducing from it sentences of his own protocol language and comparing these sentences with those of the actual protocol (p. 166).

Carnap proposed that theoretical formulations be translatable into a "physical language"; i.e., specific *protocol sentences.* The protocol sentences must be publicly observable; i.e., one must be able to determine (test) the truth or falsity ("falsifiability") of these sentences. Psychological (metaphysical) language must be linked to physical language. The protocol sentences are, in fact, the meaning of the theory as they are logically and empirically matched (verified) with the data ("actual protocol"). Those sentences that are not verified are construed to be pseudostatements and are then discarded (Carnap 1932/1959). Carnap does not suggest that psychology should concern itself only with "physically describable situations"; rather, he stated:

> The thesis . . . is that psychology may deal with whatever it pleases, it may formulate its sentences as it pleases—these sentences will, in every case, be translatable into physical language. (p. 166)

An alternative perspective, presented by Leenaars and Balance (1984a), is that formulations related to various psychological concepts (e.g., latent or unconscious meanings) may not be observable utilizing Carnap's positivist procedures although they may be evident by way of other techniques.

Next, following Carnap, nomothetic ideas are established "by the so-called method of induction from the available singular sentences" (Carnap 1931/1959). The importance of logical, empirical research is the inductive generalization from verified protocol sentences, not from the whole theory, either a priori or a posteriori. One develops one's conclusions only from individual sentences, not whole theories. It is this focused positivist method that will be used in this book.

In his positivist method, Carnap does not clearly address the problem of what is "physical," i.e., what is publicly observable. One traditional approach to this question in psychology has been the use of inter-judge reliability (Kerlinger, 1964). This approach has been utilized in previous studies of suicide notes and appears to be a reasonable one in the theoretical analysis of such archival data. Leenaars and Balance (1984a) have further noted that judges should be independent of the researchers in order to add another important control to the investigation of suicide notes.

In these procedures independent judges need to make judgments about whether or not particulars of a note are included in a given classification (protocol sentence). This approach raises the issue of inter-judge reliability. In the current type of research, one must establish inter-judge agreement before one can state anything—a problem not always identified in some early research. In the studies to be reported in the next part of this book, two or three independent judges were used for each theorist. In all, seven different judges were utilized. Even so, there are still problems in the verification of the protocol sentences—greater reliability is desired. Should one use only data that all judges agree upon, or should a larger sample of judges be used and, subsequently, use the average of all judgments? The major problem with the latter possibility is getting judges to do the task.

Our experience with the judges has also raised a number of other concerns: 1) We have found that we can only use professional psychology raters. Attempts to utilize others, for example, undergraduate students, who had been screened for the task, generally produced unsatisfactory results because they have more difficulties with abstract, theoretical concepts and terms that are not directly observable. 2) We have found that our judges more easily verify concepts that are descriptive than concepts that are explanatory. Yet explanations are critical to theory construction and theory building. Theorists such as Kelly tend to be more explanatory than descriptive, resulting possibly in lower verification because of this problem rather than the properties of his theory. 3) We have also experienced the problem that Exner (1978) called the difficulty of the overincorporator-underincorporator. Early in our studies we found one judge to be a conspicuous underincorporator. This judge, when compared to a larger sample of judges, greatly underestimated the possible classifications, observing only a few possibilities. Underincorporators, on any relatively unstructured task (e.g., Rorschach), do not incorporate their environment fully, often being poor scanners, and thus make behavioral blunders. They are very quick. Overincorporators, on a similar task, tend to be excessive in scanning, being overly perfectionistic, and do not discriminate between what is important or not. They are very slow. In our case, the underincorporating judge performed the task in a few hours which took the other judges between 15 to 20 hours. We believe this factor in the use of judges to be an important variable in our procedures and likely results. 4) Motivational factors—for example, self-enhancement—may affect individuals' judgments of suicide notes (Sherman, Presson & Chassin, 1984). Finally, although problems are likely in the use of judges, we generally believe such use preferable to relying on oneself. It allows our interpretations to be more "testable, communicable and have a high measure of predictive power" (Allport, 1962).

Another problem in this type of research is the deduction of the protocol sentences. The sentences should be drawn up by investigators who are independent of the theorist, although the sentences must be representative of the theorist's formulations. Even though some sentences may be clearer and their implications more direct than others, depending on the theoretical constructs that are being utilized to describe or explain suicide, the sentences must also be publicly observable. Other problems include the following: The protocol sentences may not discriminate between genuine notes and the control simulated notes better than professional impressions of these same data; the sentences may refer to concepts such as "latent," "unconscious," etc. that are not overtly observed; and the sentences may not be mutually exclusive statements, but include several alternatives without specifying which alternative is observed.

In this method for the theoretical analysis of suicide notes, one must not alter the intent of the theorist's formulations in the protocol sentences. This problem of representativeness can be circumvented by formulating only "verbatim" sentences, subjecting the protocol sentences to external evaluation, formulating the sentences independently, and establishing subsequent interagreement among several researchers regarding the final set, and preferably (when possible) requesting the theorist himself to evaluate the representativeness.

There is, of course, the possible objection by some positivists, who would say that all this is not what Carnap intended. This is not logical empiricism. Protocol sentences refer to statements such as, "Water freezes at 0°C." But then we could get the cooperation of the chemist, who would be quick to point out that in the *natural* environment, one rarely verifies that statement. Impurities in the water result in an inexact one-to-one correspondence between the protocol sentence and the actual protocol. It is only in a laboratory environment that such events occur precisely. Thus we do not see this caveat from a critical positivist as an argument against our method. Suicide indeed occurs in a natural environment.

Hypothesis

If a suicide note can be seen as a projective written response to the blank card of the Thematic Apperception Test (TAT) in which the subject tells a story in a suicidal context, then our formulations regarding suicide can be seen as our attempt to understand that story. The subject is usually centered on telling only one story. Our formulations too can be centered.

Piaget (1970) has demonstrated in his famous experiment on volume, where the experimenter pours fluid from a short, fat beaker into a tall, thin one, that the young child will either say there is more fluid in the first or second one. The child is centered on only one dimension to the exclusion of others. Later in human development, the child can take into account both dimensions simultaneously, and use multiple perspectives on the same event. To be decentered, in general, is to be able to take an abstract view of things, rather than be influenced totally by the characteristics of concrete particulars, to be "stimulus bound." Analogously, the same appears true in suicide and can occur in our formulations regarding suicide. We could be like the young pre-conservative child—or in Piaget's terms, any individual who is centered. Since the study of suicide notes is still in its formative years, it may be best to take multiple perspectives, trying not to be concrete but also not overinclusive. In this sense, we follow Kelly's (1955) dictate of constructive alternativism:

> We take the stand that there are always some alternative constructions available to choose among in dealing with the world. No one needs to paint himself into a corner; no one needs to be completely hemmed in by circumstances; no one needs to be the victim of his biography. (p. 15)

We therefore choose, a priori, 10 alternative formulations regarding suicide to investigate suicide notes. These 10 theorists are viewed to have been influential in our understanding of suicide. Specifically, as earlier cited, investigations of Adler, Binswanger, Freud, Jung, Menninger, Kelly, Murray, Shneidman, Sullivan, and Zilboorg will be undertaken. We hope that the 10 perspectives will allow us to be sufficiently decentered. Despite events being open to alternative constructions, Kelly (1955) has warned us that

> some of them are undoubtedly better than others. They are better from our human point of view because they support more precise and more accurate predictions about more events. (p. 15)

Carnap's positivistic methods should allow us to see which formulations, constructs, or protocol sentences are more empirically precise and accurate. However, we wish to emphasize that the current investigations are not critical experiments designed to isolate which theory is correct.

Before turning to the methods themselves, a few historical comments about the actual studies are necessary. The investigations of the protocol sentences of Binswanger and Kelly are a rewrite of an earlier investigation (Leenaars, 1979). Freud's and Shneidman's protocol sentences are a condensation of larger sets of sentences, reported in Leenaars and Balance (1984b) and Leenaars, Balance, Wenckstern, and Rudzinski (1985), respectively. The original lists of protocol sentences for these theorists were reviewed for repetition as well as importance and were narrowed to 10 (from 25 for Freud and 50 for Shneidman). Shneidman's (1985) recent presentation of 10 commonalities in suicide was also used specifically in the reduction of his formulations to

10 classifications. The investigations of Adler, Jung, Menninger, Murray, Sullivan, and Zilboorg were generated for this volume. Ten statements will be investigated for each of the 10 theorists. These protocol sentences, all 100 of them, are then the equivalent to *the* hypothesis for the studies to be reported in this book.

METHOD

The protocol sentences were subjected to logical, empirical procedures as follows. Individuals, who have graduate degrees in psychology and are currently in clinical practice, served as judges. The judges were independently asked to verify whether the classes of content described by the individual protocol sentences did, in fact, occur in each of 66—33 each, paired—genuine and simulated suicide notes (Shneidman & Farberow, 1957). Shneidman and Farberow had obtained (with the cooperation of the Los Angeles County, Coroner's Office) the 33 genuine notes from a sample of 721 notes, written between 1945–1954, and had subsequently obtained the 33 simulated notes from nonsuicidal individuals who were matched by sex, age, and occupation. All 66 notes were written by individuals who were male, Caucasian, Protestant, U.S. native-born, and between the ages of 25 and 59. Both the notes and protocol sentences were presented in a randomized order and the judges were instructed:

> Enclosed, you will find a collection of suicide notes. Your task will be to verify whether the statements provided below correspond or compare to the contents of the suicide notes. The statements provided below are a classification of the possible content of suicide notes. You are to determine whether the contents in the suicide notes are a particular or specific instance of that classification or not. Your comparison should be *observable;* however, the classification may be more abstract than the specific instances. Thus, you will have to make judgments about whether particular contents of a note are included in a given classification or not. Your task is to either conclude, yes or no. Thank you.

Results

In the studies, substantial inter-judge reliability was demonstrated. The coefficient of concordance ranged from .57 to .88 (at the .05 to .01 level of confidence). Thus, generally, one can assume that one can make some probability statements from the data with a sufficient degree of reliability. The specific protocol sentences that were verified significantly more often within the genuine notes (as compared with the simulated notes) will be reported in the next 10 chapters, one each for each theorist. Chi-square tests for independent samples (Siegel, 1956) were performed to assess the significance of differences in verification instances for each of the protocol sentences.

General Findings

The current procedures—based on the results that will be reported next—are useful not only in research on suicide notes, but are also likely to be useful with other clinical material that is essentially archival in nature. The procedures subject the investigations of suicide notes to logical, empirical (ex post facto) research. Even positions that are clearly nonpositivistic, such as Freud's, are amenable to this empirical technique. The procedures may allow successful testing between theoretical positions, discriminate within theoretical positions, and facilitate the building of models.

It has been noted that if one attempts to describe the content of genuine and simulated suicide notes, it becomes evident that individuals under both conditions very frequently describe their behavior as highly similar in some critical respects and as significantly different in others. When a high frequency count occurs in both the real and simulated conditions, there is of course no statistical difference between them. Nonetheless, such high frequency data in the genuine notes is worth noting because it clearly provides us with pertinent descriptive information, although it is not based on significant differences and should be evaluated as such. In previous studies (Leenaars & Balance, 1984a, 1984b, 1985), a priori cutoff points were established. A more empirical approach appears to be possible now, by utilizing *a posteriori*, one standard deviation above the mean of all observations of all ten theorists. Thus the 100 protocol sentences were used as a sample to establish this critical observation. A mean of 13.8 (out of a possible range of 0 to 33) with a standard deviation of 8.5 was obtained, producing 22 as the critical cutoff point.

These findings will be utilized in the current studies to report the critical common variables in suicide notes. This will add some empirical value about what characteristics are most common in suicide notes in terms of our descriptions. These observations are important because statements that have high frequency in both genuine and simulated notes appear to describe those characteristics of suicidal individuals which were most understood and predicted by the nonsuicidal writers of the simulated notes and, by inference, one may suspect that these characteristics of suicide are relatively easily understood by people in general. In other words, the similarities probably point to the areas where people can accurately imagine what it is like to want to commit suicide. In contrast, the differences probably point to the areas that are most special to the people who actually commit suicide and are probably the ones which others find most difficult to understand. Both types of observations are important for both idiographic and nomothetic knowledge.

Despite various problems in the study of suicide notes (e.g., whether a suicidal person can provide an accurate and clear communication given the person's perturbation and mental constriction, whether the sample is representative, and whether one can generalize from the note writers to suicides who do not leave a note), it would appear that research in this area can be useful, although suicide notes may not by themselves give us a complete account of suicide. The notes must be put in the full context of a detailed account of people's lives (Shneidman, 1980) and in the context of broad theoretical formulations about suicide and personality functioning in general. It is hoped that the current procedures, outlined in this chapter, the epistemological issues that have been raised, and the findings that will be reported next, will allow researchers to investigate further suicide notes and other personal documents.

Part II

TEN SUICIDOLOGISTS

It is an unarguable advantage to come to the topic of suicide notes informed by diverse theoretical formulations regarding suicide. Such an approach can aid us in understanding suicide. After careful study we have chosen 10 suicidologists: Adler, Binswanger, Freud, Jung, Menninger, Kelly, Murray, Shneidman, Sullivan, and Zilboorg. For each of the 10 suicidologists, six subsections will be presented: a brief biography of that person; his theory of suicide based on his formulations regarding suicide; key protocol sentences (or classifications) derived from his work; discussion of the findings; and a bibliography of his work pertaining to suicide.

Chapter 4

ALFRED ADLER

PERSONAL HISTORY

Alfred Adler was born February 7, 1870 in a suburb of Vienna, Austria, the son of a middle-class merchant. His early years were marked by several key events; notably, the early development of a social interest in his community and the confrontation with death on several occasions (e.g., the death of his younger brother, Rudolf, at age three; narrowly escaping his own death twice in street accidents; and at age five, contracting pneumonia that was diagnosed as hopeless). Alfred entered Medical School in Vienna at eighteen, where his interest in socialism deepened, and he developed a lifelong interest in social medicine, being somewhat influenced by the works of Karl Marx. He graduated in 1895, practicing ophthalmology and general medicine and later shifting to neurology and psychiatry. In 1898 he published his first booklet, *Health Book for the Tailoring Trade,* which presents an orientation towards progressive social changes; e.g., medical care for the poor, improving all school systems, and advocating civil rights for all.

In 1902, Adler was invited by Freud to join an exclusive

discussion group that met on Wednesday evenings at Freud's home. This group marked the beginning of the Vienna Psychoanalytic Society. Adler eventually became the president and coeditor of its journal. One of these discussions in 1910 was on suicide, when Adler presented his early ideas on this topic. (The proceedings of this discussion have been edited by Paul Friedman (1967) in a book entitled *On Suicide.* The text itself presents many early classic views of suicide including the first enunciation, by Wilhelm Stekel, of the psychodynamic formulation that the yearning for the death of the self can only be the mirrored wish for the death of another.) By 1911, Adler's theoretical differences with Freud culminated in his resigning from the society. Adler, in 1907, had already written about his different formulation in *Study of Organ Inferiority and Its Psychical Compensation.* In 1912, he wrote *The Neurotic Constitution,* where he fully laid out his "Individual Psychology;" the same year he started the *Journal of Individual Psychology.* Subsequently he published numerous papers and monographs and lectured throughout Europe and the United States. He also continued his social interest, becoming active in education, including the training of teachers and establishing child-guidance centers in schools.

In 1935, he moved permanently with his family to the United States because of the rise of Hitler in Europe. Here, he continued his work including a paper in 1937 entitled "Suicide" (which is the only expression by Adler devoted solely to that topic). This paper has been reprinted in *Superiority and Social Interest.* He died on May 28, 1937 during a lecture tour in Scotland.

THEORY OF SUICIDE

In the 1910 symposium on suicide, Adler asked "[What clarifies] the psychological situation of the suicide, the dynamic force that drives him out of life? When we learn that the most densely populated parts of the world have the highest incidence of suicide, and that suicides cluster in certain months of the year, do we thereby learn a single adequate, explanatory motive?" Adler believed that environmental factors such as social privation or inadequate education do not answer that question. According to

Adler, suicide must be understood individually, even if social traumas had occurred, not only to develop general knowledge but also to develop implications for response.

Suicide is not an immediate unique response; it is arrived at under the same conditions that produce any disorder. Every child grows up in conditions where one is small, weak, and dependent, resulting in an overriding feeling of weakness and the need to bow to the caretakers. This historical actuality, according to Adler, results in various lifelong psychological patterns that predispose one's reaction to subsequent traumas during one's life. Childhood problems (excessive hurt feelings; poor adjustment to loss or defeat) all predispose one's reactions to new situations as they arise. Adler notes, for example, that most suicides have experienced a difficult childhood, suffering from "a particularly deep-seated feeling of inferiority." Lacking the ability to confront others directly, they attempted to influence others through complaining, sadness, and suffering. They collapse under pain whenever faced with difficulties and they utilize fantasies of sickness and death to hurt others and themselves. Thus, from early childhood, it appears that the unconscious has created a situation in which death is desired, partly in order to hurt or attack someone else who had slighted them. Initially, the parent is the target; but in later years it may be the teacher, the spouse, or society. To exemplify his view, Adler provides a case of a seventeen-year-old youth, the youngest in his family, who had been excessively spoiled by his mother. While staying with an elder sister, when his mother went on a journey alone, he committed suicide. He left the following suicide note:

> Don't tell mother what I have done. Her present address is ______. Tell her, when she comes back, that I no longer had any enjoyment in life. Tell her to put flowers on my grave every day.

The individual's aggression (and faulty logic) in this suicide appear to be obvious. Suicides, frequently, before their death, according to Adler, show various expressions of aggression turned inward, such as themes in their ideation and overt behavior of humility, submission, and devotion, subordination, flagellation, or masochism. Often, the would-be suicides dream of themselves as injured and being self-assaultive and engage in inimical behaviors. Adler cites a case of an eighteen-year-old girl, who was seen as good and capable by all and exhibited extreme religious conscientiousness. One day, after having sinful thoughts, she began to reproach herself and, after attempts by a religious advisor to relieve her of her self-accusations, placed herself in a street, endangering her life, shouting out her unworthiness.

Although the suicide from early years appears to be suffering from a particularly deep-seated feeling of inferiority-weakness, he attempts to escape from the recognition of such feelings. As in the case above, the would-be suicide frequently curses himself, reproaches himself and, ultimately, kills himself for the purpose of enhancing himself and depreciating the environment. Even after long training, he dismisses any interest in life; he promotes only the feeling of personal satisfaction, enhancing himself and achieving a heightened sense of superiority while disparaging the other person. The individual becomes lord and master over his own life and death, contributing nothing to the welfare of the general community and is more likely to disturb it, as by injuring another person. There is a lack of social interest, feeling or acceptance. The suicide itself arouses an elation of superiority ("I have done something not everybody could do. Formerly, nobody paid any attention to me, but now . . .")

Being superior, the individual is master, not inferior or weak, but his triumphs are only pseudovictories. Adler cites, for example, a case of a fifteen-year-old girl who, considering herself unfairly treated since childhood, created a favored situation at school which suddenly collapsed when a new teacher showed her "disfavor." This resulted in deep inferiority feelings and created a new need in the girl for warmth and pampering, which she attempted to obtain by "a loose way of life." Her promiscuity, however, (as is generally the case) did not provide the desired warmth, and led to a wish to kill herself which, fortunately, she was prevented by her mother from acting out.

Adler points out that individuals like the fifteen-year-old girl will defend their reasons, producing "intelligent" arguments to themselves and others, all toward the ("conscious and unconscious") goal of superiority. But, as Adler further points out, this is superiority "on the useless side". Since the individual wants to do away with himself, nothing can interest him, hindering him even further from social preparation in productive thinking, feeling, and acting.

All failures—neurotics, alcoholics, perverts, prostitutes, suicides, etc.—are failures because they lack social interest. Their goal of superiority and their successes are only for themselves; but such meaning has, according to Adler, no meaning. This lack is exemplified by the statement, "I do not think that life is worth living. For humanity, in general, I have nothing but the utmost contempt." It is this lack, rooted in childhood, that blocks adequate preparation for meeting all the problems of life. The suicide, who appears to have arrived at the end of his limited social interest, sees his suicide as an "intelligent" solution to any problem and to the general injustice of life. The individual considers himself too weak to overcome his personal difficulties and, therefore, (in revenge) rejects everything with one full swoop in order to escape the feeling of inferiority, and to act intelligently according to his goal of coping with the difficulties of life in disregard of the community—a beloved person, a teacher, society, or the world at large.

Adler concluded his remarks at the 1910 meeting with the statement, "Suicide and neurosis are both childish forms of reaction to a childish overestimation of motives, humiliations, and dissappointments. And so suicide represents—like neurosis and psychosis—an escape by antisocial means from the injustices of life."

PROTOCOL SENTENCES

The following 10 protocol sentences were derived from Adler's formulations regarding suicide:

In the suicide note:

1) Although the individual appears to be suffering from a particularly deep-seated feeling of inferiority, he ap-

pears to be attempting to escape from the recognition of this inferiority feeling.

2) There is a lack of or a foregoing of social interest, feeling, and/or acceptability.
3) The individual promotes the feeling of personal satisfaction, enhances the self, and/or achieves a heightened feeling of superiority without contributing to the welfare of the general community and is rather, likely to disturb it., e.g., injure another person, hurt another person.
4) The person's arguments appear to be "intelligent" to himself in respect to the ("conscious or unconscious") goal of personal superiority.
5) The person who appears to have arrived at the end of his limited social interest, sees his suicide as a solution for an urgent problem and/or the injustices of life.
6) The individual considers himself too weak to overcome his personal difficulties and therefore (in revenge) rejects everything with one full swoop in order to escape the feeling of inferiority, and/or to act intelligent according to his goal of coping with the difficulties of life (with disregard to the community—a beloved person, a teacher, society or the world at large).
7) The person enhances his esteem by disparaging the other person, becoming lord over life and death (his own life).
8) The communication suggests that childhood problems (excessive hurt feelings; poor adjustment to loss or defeat; use of complaining, sadness, and suffering; collapse under pain) are likely the predisposing factors in the individual's reaction to the current situation.
9) It appears that the unconscious has created a situation in which death is desired, partly in order to hurt/attack someone else, or as an act of revenge towards someone who has slighted him. One can conclude that the person by attacking himself is likely attacking another person.
10) The individual's aggression appears to have been turned inward. Themes of humility, submission, and

devotion, subordination, flagellation or masochism are evident.

Findings

Chi-square tests for two independent samples were performed to assess the significance of differences in verification instances for each of the protocol sentences derived from Adler's formulations as well as for the other nine suicidologists. No protocol sentence derived from Adler's ideas was verified significantly more often within the genuine notes as compared with the simulated notes.

As was noted previously, high frequency counts in the genuine notes are pertinent descriptions, despite the fact that these same observations may not discriminate between genuine and simulated notes (i.e., control data). Such statements are highly predictive of notes, not universal but *common* observations. A critical, empirically derived value, based on analysis of all 100 protocol sentences (10 for each theorist) was calculated to be approximately 22, one standard deviation above the mean. Incidentally, this value is equal to the verification of the protocol sentence in at least two-thirds of the notes.

The critical frequencies for Adler's statements were sentences 5, 6, 9, and 10. These sentences were related to the following classifications: A person who lacks social interest sees suicide as the solution to an urgent problem and/or injustice; the person, considering himself too weak or inferior to overcome difficulties, rejects everything except death; the person, by attacking himself, appears to be attacking someone else; and the person's aggression is turned inward.

Bibliography

Adler, A. (1951) *The practice and theory of individual psychology* (P. Radin, Trans.). New York: The Humanities Press, Inc.

Adler, A. (1956) *The individual psychology of Alfred Adler* (H. Ansbacher & R. Ansbacher, Eds.). New York: Harper & Row.

Adler, A. (1964) *Superiority and social interest* (H. Ansbacher & R. Ansbacher, Eds.). Evanston, Ill: Northwestern University Press.

Adler, A. (1967) Contribution to discussions of the Vienna Psychoanalytic Society—1910. In P. Friedman, Ed. *On suicide*. New York: International Universities Press, Inc. (Original published in 1910).

Chapter 5

LUDWIG BINSWANGER

Personal History

Ludwig Binswanger was born in Kreuzlingen, Thurgau, Switzerland on April 13, 1881 into a family of famous physicians and psychiatrists. This family background is generally seen as the key influence in Ludwig's early years. His own medical studies were in Lausanne, Heidelberg, and Zurich. He received his medical degree at the University of Zurich in 1907 in connection with studies under C. G. Jung, although his later work shares little with that of Jung's. He served as psychiatric intern under Eugene Bleuler in Zurich and as resident at the Psychiatric Clinic for Nervous Diseases at Jena University under his uncle, Otto Binswanger, and finally as an associate under his father, Robert, at the Sanatorium Bellevue at Kreuzlingen. After his father (and like his grandfather), Ludwig became Chief Medical Director of this sanatorium, until he stepped down in 1956.

Binswanger was a friend of Sigmund Freud and in fact attended some of the Wednesday evening seminars at Freud's home. Binswanger wrote about these relationships in 1958 in a book entitled, *Sigmund Freud: Reminiscences of a Friendship.* Despite this close contact, Ludwig's theoretical views were markedly different from Freud's. In 1936 Binswanger delivered an address on Freud's eightieth birthday, entitled "Freud's Concept of Man in the Light of Anthropology" on which Freud commented, "Truly one can put up with infinite amounts of praise. But, of course, I don't believe a word of what you say." Ludwig's real theoretical ground came from the existential point of view, namely from Heidegger and Husserl. His own *Daseinsanalyse* is an outgrowth of this view. In 1927, Martin Heidegger's *Sein und Zeit (Being and Time)* was published and provided Binswanger with a language for his approach to psychiatry. Heidegger had developed an ontology, based on the premise that to approach Being one must understand man as being-in-the-world. Binswanger utilized the concept of being-in-the-world as the basis for understanding the existence of his patients. One of his most famous examples—which is also one of the most famous examples of suicide in the twentieth-century literature—is that of Ellen West, published in Rollo May's edited book, *Existence* (1958). Being-in-the-world is also the title of a translated volume by J. Needelman of Ludwig's selected papers; this volume explicates the core of Binswanger's Daseinanalyse. Ludwig Binswanger died on May 2, 1966.

THEORY OF SUICIDE

Utilizing personal documents (i.e., poems, diaries) and testimonies of others, Binswanger has presented one of the most famous case histories in suicidology, namely of Ellen West. He provided a phenomenological analysis of Ellen's existence and death—her total existence, as being-in-the-world. In keeping with Binswanger's own outline, we will first present the history briefly since Binswanger has written the case in detail (see May's *Existence*), and then provide a synopsis of Binswanger's formulations regarding suicide that will allow us to frame Ellen's being-in-the-world and, perhaps, understand suicide more generally.

Ellen was the only daughter of a self-controlled, reserved man "for whom her love and veneration know no bounds." Her father came from a home where two brothers had killed themselves; one brother was very ascetic and inimical (e.g., practicing self-starvation) and two others had died at an early age. Ellen's mother was a soft, nervous woman whose background was also marked by early deaths, including her father's. Ellen had two brothers.

Ellen's birth was normal; at nine months she refused milk and had to be fed broth. Her early years were less striking until age seventeen when she began to write poetry like "Kiss Me Dead." By her twentieth year she saw herself as small and "wholly forsaken in a world which she cannot understand." At this time, *the* dread emerged—*the idea* of getting fat. Her mood became increasingly "depressive" and she developed anorexia. She bewailed her "loneliness of soul," breaking down at twenty-three after an unfortunate love affair. This affair was followed by another—a student who later became her lost ideal. This relation was broken off at the demand of her parents, resulting in severe depression. At twenty-six, she planned to marry her cousin (Karl) but vacillated for two years between her cousin and the student, until she finally married Karl.

Following her marriage, hoping to be rid of her "fixed idea," she was again quickly overwhelmed by dread that retained control of her existence. Ellen had a miscarriage and subsequently only hoped for a new, but never realized, pregnancy. By thirty-one, Ellen's being-in-the-world declined; she was described as old and haggard, being intensely preoccupied with the idea. She noted, "My thoughts are exclusively concerned with my body, my eating, my laxatives," attesting to both anorexia and bulimia. She thinned down to a skeleton, resulting in her entering her first "useless" psychoanalysis, at thirty-two and one-half. Feelings of dread became more frequent at this time, finding herself unable to get over "weeping, dread, and agitation." A second analysis at thirty-three was begun, but she despaired completely, marked by a separation from her husband, at the analyst's suggestion. On October 8, after expressing suicidal ideas, she made an attempt at suicide, followed by a series of attempts, until she was reunited with her husband. Her moods became more pronounced; the famous Kraepelin was consulted and the diagnosis of "melancholia" was made, but her analyst considered this incorrect. Another physician who was consulted recommended hospitalization. At this time, Ellen wrote:

> The comparison with imprisonment is not play on words. I am in prison caught in a net from which I cannot free myself. I am a prisoner within myself; I get more and more entangled, and every day is a new, useless struggle; the meshes tighten more and more. I am in Siberia; my heart is icebound, all around me is solitude and cold. My best days are a sadly comic attempt to deceive myself as to my true condition. It is insignificant to live on like this. Karl, if you love me, grant me death. (p. 258)

Ellen was hospitalized under the care of Binswanger at Bellevue Sanatorium in Switzerland from January 14 to March 30. In the clinic, with Karl's constant presence, her condition improved, but this was short-lived. In 7 days, she showed frequent fluctuations from one affective state to another. She found herself hopelessly despairing. On February 26, she reported four death dreams; one she described:

> I dreamt something wonderful. War had broken out, I was to go into the field. I say good-bye to everyone with the joyous expectation that I shall soon die. I am glad that before the end I can eat everything, have eaten a large piece of mocha cake. (p. 263)

By March 21, Ellen felt completely helpless, articulating more serious suicidal threats. Although the wish to die had been evident throughout her whole life, even as a child, when she wished to have a fatal accident, her behavior now became solely an attempt at suicide. The "ideal" of wanting to get thin was overvalent. Binswanger made the diagnosis of "a progressive schizophrenic psychosis (schizophrenia simplex)"; a diagnosis that was confirmed by E. Bleuler and another consulting psychiatrist. Ellen, however, requested to be discharged. She went home, being tormented not only by her idea but at her illness being brought even more on view.

Of Ellen's death, Binswanger wrote:

> On the third day of being home she is as if transformed. At breakfast she eats butter and sugar, at noon she eats so much but—for the first time in thirteen years she is satisfied by her food and gets really full. At afternoon coffee she eats chocolate creams and Easter eggs. She takes a walk with her husband, reads poems by Rilke, Storm, Goethe, and Tennyson, is amused by the first chapter of Mark Twain's "Christian Science," is in a positively festive mood, and all heaviness seems to have fallen away from her. She writes letters, the last one a letter to the fellow patient here to whom she had become so attached. In the evening she takes a lethal dose of poison and on the following morning she is dead. (p. 267)

For Binswanger, existence is a form of being-in-the-world. The essence of this view is the following: It is "in" the world that existence "lives." Forms are "being-in" a given world and refer to the self and the We-ness. World refers to the What (and the How and Who) within which existence exists. Temporality is the fundamental horizon (the ground) of this and all existence; one is being-ahead-of-oneself (future), having been (past), and being with (present). Temporality has meaning. It is from this phenomenological perspective that actual human existence such as Ellen West's can be analyzed.

Ellen West "makes an end" of its existence. What does this mean? To understand this end of being-in-the-world, according to Binswanger, one must suspend prejudgment and look at the suicide itself as it is given to us. Her suicide was when she ate food to nourish but, at the same time, to poison herself. It was a painful awakening to her existence. Yet her whole *life* was lived facing death; not just that one time. Her life was "encompassed" by death. Ellen West would like to die—and she killed herself. Binswanger asks, "How could these motives in Ellen and others who kill themselves become motives at all?" It is from this question that Binswanger provides his formulations regarding suicide.

Existence in the suicidal person becomes ripe for death. Death is the necessary fulfillment of the life-meaning of this existence, evidenced by its temporality. In the suicidal person, existence is ruled by the "supremacy of the past"; the individual is preoccupied, absorbed, and engrossed by his past. The suicidal person is cut off, detached from, or disinterested in his future and lives in a bare, empty present that is meaningless and purposeless. The past weighs the suicidal person down; one is "being-a-corpse-among-people." Dread is the what, the how, and who within which existence exists. The entire life suffers from this sickness. The individual experiences pronounced dread, and anticipates a future filled with fear and anxiety as was the past and is the present. The suicide is the necessary-voluntary outcome of this kind of being-in-the-world.

Existence ripens toward its death, separating from life. As seen in Ellen West, where, in the face of death, she eats without the anxiety of her "idea," the nearness of death shows itself as *brightness*. What does suicide mean? Death means absolute Nothingness—the negative and absolute annihilation of existence. Existence—the dread—stops with death. This is seen as a meaningful event against a background of an otherwise meaningless and purposeless life. The suicidal individual voluntarily chooses to kill himself; it is a consciously planned action. The carrying out of the suicidal act is the last practical act of this existence.

"Nothingness" is *positive* for the suicide. Existence here bases itself or rests upon Nothingness and absolute isolation of dread. The suicide is an act undertaken to isolate one's life, one's problems, and one's dread, *from* oneself. Yet the person dies as he has lived. The individual sees the suicide as meaningful but it is more accurately the contra-meaning—the meaning of being not oneself. Ellen desperately did not want to be herself, but different, not fat but thin. The suicidal person is tortured; one wants existence to be different, but it does not come; even death does not come. The suicide thus provides an act of liberation and freedom from one's life, one's problems, and one's dread. Death comes as a friend—a liberator from the fetters of life. The suicide authentically liberates and frees the individual. He resolves the situation by acting—an authentic present. He voluntarily chooses death, freeing one as "I am myself, I exist authentically." In this authenticity, existence has no being-ahead-of-oneself, only Nothingness.

To summarize: Ellen's life, according to Binswanger, was a painful existence; she was cut off from her future and was living in a bare, traumatic, empty present. Ellen's life was dreadful, painful, and devoid of meaning. She saw no alternatives to her existence but death. Suicide was, in fact, the only way that Ellen believed she could solve her problems; i.e., the idea of cessation gave Ellen a *meaning* to her present and a way of escaping from something far worse—the problems, the life, and the dread. For Ellen, her suicide was seen as an act of affirming herself and introducing authenticity into her existence. Yet, as Binswanger (1963) himself notes:

> "where existence can exist only by relinquishing life, there the existence is a tragic existence." (p. 298)

PROTOCOL SENTENCES

The following 10 protocol sentences were derived from Binswanger's formulations regarding suicide.

In the suicide note:

1) The person communicates that he is preoccupied, absorbed, and/or engrossed by his past.
2) The person communicates that he is cut off, detached, and/or disinherited from his future.
3) The person communicates that he is living in a bare empty present that is meaningless and/or purposeless.
4) The person communicates that he is experiencing pronounced dread; i.e., he seems to be anticipating and/or experiencing great fear or anxiety.
5) The person communicates that he sees his suicide as a meaningful event against the background of an otherwise meaningless, and/or purposeless life.
6) The person communicates that he is voluntarily choosing to kill himself.
7) The person communicates that his suicide is basically a consciously planned action.

8) The person communicates that his suicide is an act undertaken to isolate his life, his problems and/or his dread from himself.
9) The person communicates that his suicide is an act of liberation and freedom from his life, his problems and/or his dread.
10) The person communicates that he sees his death as giving him some personal meaning or purpose.

FINDINGS

No classifications that were deduced from Binswanger's theory were found to correspond significantly to the genuine notes, nor were any critical common frequencies observed in the genuine notes. However, specific aspects of his formulations were verified significantly more often within the simulated notes (as compared with the genuine notes), specifically the following: (8) the suicide being an act to isolate one's life, problems and/or dread ($x^2(1, N = 66) = 5.08$, $p < .01$); and (9) the suicide is seen as an act of freedom and liberation ($x^2(1, N=66) = 7.69$, $p < .01$).

BIBLIOGRAPHY

Binswanger, L. (1958). The case of Ellen West (W. Mendel & J. Lyons, Trans.). In R. May, E. Angel, & H. Ellenberger (Eds), *Existence.* New York: Basic Books. (Original published in 1944).

Binswanger, L. (1963) *Being-in-the-world* (J. Needleman, Trans.). New York: Harper & Row.

Chapter 6

SIGMUND FREUD

Personal History

Sigmund Freud was born on May 6, 1856 in Freiberg in Moravia (now Czechoslavakia). When Freud was four, his family moved to Vienna because of financial setbacks which continued to affect the family in his early years. From the beginning he was an excellent student, enjoying "special privileges." Influenced by Goethe and Darwin, he entered the faculty of Medicine at the University of Vienna in 1873, where he studied Helmholzian physiology in the laboratory of Dr. Ernest Brucke. A key idea that he learned here was that humans are dynamic physiological systems that are moved by the forces of attraction and repulsion, following the principle of the conservation of energy. This early work culminated in Freud's "project for a scientific psychology"; one to which he remained faithful in spirit in his more psychological descriptions of humans. In 1881 Freud received his medical degree, a few years after the death of his father; this death is generally acknowledged to have resulted in periods of deep depression for Freud. He subsequently entered private practice, beginning his own research on cocaine between 1884–1887.

In 1885 he established himself as a lecturer at the University of Vienna and in 1886 travelled to Paris to begin his famous studies under Jean Charcot, who influenced him in the areas of hypnosis, hysteria, and the sexual basis of maladjustment. Later he also worked with Joseph Breuer, this work culminating in a jointly authored book, *Studies in Hysteria.* In 1896 Freud introduced the term psychoanalysis to describe his methods for treating the hysteric and other patients. In 1900 he published his famous text, *The Interpretation of Dreams* and in 1901 *The Psychopathology of Everyday Life.* In 1902 he became a professor at the University of Vienna and the Vienna Psychoanalytic Society was founded with the Wednesday evening meetings at his home. The meetings were started by Freud and Wilhelm Stekel; members of the Society included Alfred Adler, Sandor Ferenczi, Carl Gustav Jung, Otto Rank, Karl Abraham, Ernest Jones, Paul Federn. As noted earlier, one such meeting in 1910 included a discussion on suicide, where Freud himself offered his formulations. Subsequently, a breakup of the society occurred; Jung, Adler, and others left to form their own schools of thought.

Freud's collected works include 24 volumes (*The Standard Edition of the Psychological Complete Works of S. Freud,* Ed. and Trans. by J. Strachey into English). Perpetually preoccupied over his lost disciples and other critics in his last book, *An Outline of Psychoanalysis* (1940) Freud stated, "The teachings of psychoanalysis are based on an incalculable number of observations and experiences, and only someone who has repeated those observations on himself and others is in position to arrive at a judgment of his own upon it."

Freud left Vienna in 1938, when Hitler took over Austria. These later years were onerous for him not only because of the war, but because, since 1923, he had suffered from cancer of the mouth and jaw. Nevertheless, in an aside in *Moses and Monotheism* (1939), he expresses gratitude to "hospitable England"; and in his last interview, he says, "But do not call me a pessimist." Freud died by his "own wish" on September 26, 1939, at the age of eighty-three.

THEORY OF SUICIDE

Freud's formulations of suicide have been outlined in his published works (1901, 1909, 1917, 1923, 1933, 1940). These texts suggest that the root of suicide—within a developmental context—is the experience of loss or rejection of a significant, highly cathected object (i.e., a person). The individual is singly preoccupied with this person who had been lost or who had rejected him. In addition to citing the loss, which is the manifest reason for the suicide, Freud (1920) has provided what he termed a "deeper interpretation" of what leads someone to kill himself after such a loss or rejection. He stated:

> Probably no one finds the mental energy required to kill himself unless, in the first place, in doing so he is at the same time killing an object with whom he has identified himself and, in the second place, is turning against himself a death wish which had been directed against someone else. (p. 162)

In addition to the lost object, the person had developed a strong direct or indirect identification with that same person. Attachment, based upon an important emotional tie with another person, is for Freud (1921) the meaning of identification; not only does the object exist outside, it becomes introjected into one's own personality (ego). With the loss, the energy (libido) in this attachment is withdrawn, but the person continues to exhibit an overly regressive attachment which Freud has termed a "narcissistic identification" with the object. In this state, the person treats himself as if he were reacting to another person; one treats *oneself*—one's ego—as the abandoned object and "it is subjected to all acts of aggression and expressions of vengefulness which had been aimed at the object."

The person's feelings and ideas of vengefulness and aggression towards another person are thus turned inward and directed towards oneself. However, he is, at a deeper level of interpretation, angry towards someone *else*. The suicide becomes a fulfillment of a wish; by killing *himself,* he has *gotten rid of the rejecting object.*

Ambivalence emerges with peculiar emphasis in such an individual. The individual usually feels quite ambivalent, i.e., both affectionate and hostile, towards the lost or rejecting person. The hostility gets expressed as an act of sadism not only directed towards oneself, but also towards another. The person's embitterment "strikes with a single blow at his own ego and at the loved and hated object." The person, when he kills himself (or exhibits other self-reproaches), turns back upon himself murderous impulses or wishes that had been directed towards someone else, the rejecting object. By killing himself, the person, thus, destroys someone else with whom he had identified. Freud (1917) wrote:

> We have long known, it is true, that no neurotic harbours thoughts of suicide which he has not turned back upon himself from murderous impulses against others, but we have never been able to explain what interplay of forces can carry such a purpose through to execution. The analysis of melancholia now shows that the ego can kill itself only if, owing to the return of the object cathexis, it can treat itself as an object—if it is able to direct against itself the hostility which relates to an object and which represents the ego's original reaction to objects in the external world. Thus in regression from narcissistic object-choice the object has, it is true, been gotten rid of, but it, nevertheless, proved more powerful than the ego itself. (p. 252)

The suicide is overwhelmed by these intense, aggressive reaction patterns.

There is, however, in suicide another motive besides fulfillment of a wish, and that is the fulfillment of punishment (self-punishment). A reproach from conscience (super-ego) occurs; before he kills himself, the person experiences, given the above "situation," a sense of guilt or, rather, criticism (self-criticism). The person develops prohibitions of extraordinary harshness and severity towards himself (ego). An excessively strong conscience rages against oneself. One must kill oneself, for one *deserves* no better. Freud (1923) put it:

> . . . we find that the exceedingly strong superego which has obtained a hold upon consciousness rages against the ego with merciless violence as if it has taken possession of the whole of the sadism available in the person concerned. Following our view of sadism, we should say that the destructive component had entrenched itself in the superego and turned against the ego. What is now holding sway in the superego is, as it were, a pure culture of the death instinct, and in fact it often enough succeeds in driving the ego into death. (p. 53)

The suicide consciously chooses the time, means, and opportunity to kill himself; however, the act is motivated by unconscious intentions. Such unconscious intentions are also, according to Freud, noted in accidental injuries and other forms of self-destruction ("instances of self-injury"). Freud (1901) stated that, "in addition, to consciously intentional suicide there is such a thing as half-intentional self-destruction (self-destruction with an unconscious intention), capable of making skillful use of a threat to life and of disguising it as a chance mishap" (p. 180–1). Self-destruction is not rare; the trend to self-destruction, according to Freud, is present to a degree in all of us. He further stated, "the unconscious of all human beings is full enough of such death-wishes, even against those they love" (1920).

In *An Outline of Psycho-Analysis,* Freud discussed how the instinct of self-preservation (Eros) in some individuals becomes reversed; how the aim of self-destruction (Thanatos) in all of us becomes nothing other than self-injury and self-destruction. People who kill themselves, in fact, he noted, aim at this alone—nothing other than self-injury and self-destruction. In such people, he explains, a far-reaching defusion of impulses has taken place, "as a result of which there has been a liberation of excessive qualities of the destructive instincts directed inwards" (p. 180). In an all-incompassing manner, given the excessive self-destructive wishes, the individual's personal organization of experiences is impaired, and/or he is no longer capable of any proper synthesis of his experiences.

Freud has explicated his formulations in a number of cases (not completed suicides), the most famous of which is Dora, which was presented in Chapter 2. In *New Introductory Lectures* (1933), Freud also provided another case who attempted suicide. To offer a brief synopsis:

A young man, involved in a liaison with a demimondaine, would repetitively provoke her with brutalities and subsequently reconcile with her. This not only deprived him of a wife and family but the liaison damaged his reputation. During his analysis, the man, after an abusive incident, asked the woman to write a note and submitted it to a graphologist, who interpreted the writing to be written by someone in deep despair and certain to commit suicide. The suicide did not occur but analysis succeeded in loosing the bonds with the demimondaine. The man then turned his attentions to a young girl with a view to making her his wife, but doubts about her worthiness arose. The man then took a note from the girl to the same graphologist, who confirmed his apprehensiveness. The man thereupon broke off with the girl.

To understand this man's behavior, Freud provides the following history: In his early youth, the man had fallen in love with a married woman who rejected him. He then made a suicide attempt, narrowly escaping death. The action deeply affected the woman and they became lovers. Twenty years later the man wanted to detach himself from the woman; at the same time, a "long-suppressed craving for vengeance on his mistress" arose. "As he had once tried to kill himself because she had spurned him, so he wished now to have the satisfaction of her seeking death because he left her." But, still loving her, he did not make the wish conscious, but took on the demimondaine as "a sort of whipping-boy" to satisfy his revenge. His brutalities inflicted on the demimondaine were actually a substitute for his wishes toward his lover of 20 years, evidenced by the fact that the man made the woman a confidante and adviser in his liaison, thus making her suffer.

The man's early suicide attempt show many central aspects of Freud's formulations, such as the role of loss and rejection, the regressive identification (attachment) with a highly cathected object and the turning of a death wish against oneself. The subsequent years after the man's attempt further suggests a key interpretation of Freud's theory of personality, namely that dynamics and reaction patterns have psychogenetic origin. The case also provides evidence for the formulation that there are both manifest and latent aspects to suicide.

PROTOCOL SENTENCES

The 10 following protocol sentences were derived from Freud's formulations regarding suicide.

In the suicide note:

1) The person communicates that he had consciously planned to kill himself; however, the act appears to be motivated by unconscious intentions.
2) The person communicates that he is preoccupied with a person he had lost or who had rejected him.
3) The person communicates that he is feeling quite ambivalent; i.e., affectionate and hostile towards a lost or rejecting person.
4) The person communicates that he is in some direct or indirect fashion identifying with a rejecting or lost person.
5) The person communicates that he is treating himself as if he were reacting to another person.
6) The person communicates feelings and/or ideas of vengefulness and aggression towards himself; however, he appears to be angry towards someone else.
7) The person communicates that he is turning back upon himself murderous impulses that had been directed against someone else.
8) The person communicates that his suicide is a fulfillment of punishment, i.e., self-punishment.
9) The person communicates that he is experiencing a sense of guilt or, rather, criticism.

10) The person communicates that his personal organization of experiences is impaired and/or that he is no longer capable of any coherent synthesis of his experiences.

FINDINGS

The protocol sentences that were verified significantly more often within the genuine notes (as compared with the simulated notes) were the following: (2) a loss or rejection with which one is preoccupied ($x^2(1, N=66) = 8.68, p < .01$); (3) the reported feeling of ambivalence ($x^2 (1, N=66) = 4.47, p < .05$); (4) identification, directly or indirectly, with a rejecting or a lost person ($x^2 (1, N=66) = 6.67, p < .01$); (6) the person communicating feelings and/or ideas of vengefulness and aggression towards himself; however, appearing to be angry towards someone else ($x^2(1, N = 66) = 6.13, p < .05$); (7) turning back upon oneself murderous impulses ($x^2(1, N=66) = 10.97, p < .01$); and (8) suicide seen as fulfillment of self-punishment ($x^2(1, N=66) = 6.67, p < .01$).

In the actual notes, the loss/rejection and the preoccupation with the loss was usually exemplified by the person stating that he could not "be," "do," or "go on" without a person whom he had recently lost (e.g., a rejecting parent, an unmet love, a separated or divorced partner). At times, the loss/rejection cited in a suicide note may be related to an object other than a person (e.g., social status, employment) although loss of a highly cathected person is clearly the most common experience. As one individual put it: "You left and did not say anything." The loss is beyond the person per se; as one person explained, he "lost the love" that he and his wife had shared for many years.

The suicidal person communicates a pronounced attachment—a deep emotional tie, an identification. In the actual notes, the person often reported a loss of a "loved" individual in a highly cathected relationship (e.g., lover, spouse, parent-child); the attachment-rejection theme was exemplified in the following: "I was really in love and I thought you were." The themes in the notes are also suggestive of ambivalence, both love and hate are often expressed to a specific person. Anger turned outward as well as anger turned inward are especially evident in the notes. The ambivalence and especially anger can best be clarified with a few examples.

In one note, the suicidal person communicated a history of marital conflict, ultimately resulting in a physical aggressive act by the person toward "the only one I ever loved." The individual then communicated a resulting loss/rejection (a separation), leading to a need for punishment—self-punishment. He declared, in a very self-critical manner, that he is "not worth it" and that he "never was much good," and deserved only the punishment of death for, as he added, "this is all I can do." At times, the aggression themes are not directly stated but clearly evident. For example, in one note the individual communicated a preoccupation with a sudden rejection by a spouse in what he perceived to be a happy marriage; toward the end of the suicide note to his wife he wished her "the best of everything" and concluded with "Thanks for everything." In another note, of an adolescent, this indirect (if not direct) aggression was expressed by "no one is to blame for this. I love you all" and concluded with "P.S., Happy Father's Day."

A frequency count of the sentences in the genuine notes indicated that no sentences occurred at the critical level of observation. The importance of the frequency count can now be highlighted by these results. Despite the ability to discriminate between genuine and simulated notes in terms of specific aspects of Freud's formulations regarding suicide, the frequencies of his formulations (protocol sentences) are relatively low compared to a number of observations regarding other theorists—frequencies of ⅔ were observed. Interestingly, some of Freud's statements in fact discriminated between genuine and simulated notes, but were observed very infrequently—an observation, as will be seen, that was made repeatedly in various factors that discriminated genuine from simulated notes. Some of these factors were observed so infrequently that one wonders if the low probabilities of such classifications in general contributed to the discriminations. Alternatively, it is possible, as Freud himself would note, that many of his formulations relate to unconscious or latent aspects of suicide which would not be readily open to the current manifest analysis of suicide notes.

Be that as it may, other theorists have formulated ideas that were observed very frequently—these being common elements of suicide. Interestingly, however, despite these high frequency counts in genuine notes, often many of these same statements have a high frequency count in the simulated notes as well, so that these protocol sentences did not usually discriminate between genuine and simulated suicide notes. Such statements appear to describe those characteristics of suicidal individuals that are easily understood by people in general—areas where people can accurately simulate what it is like to actually want to commit suicide.

The question arises, which data are most critical in defining suicide? We believe *all* are. The use of discriminations between genuine and simulated notes allows us to introduce the method of difference, isolating those factors that differentiate the suicide from others. The frequency data allow us to describe what is common. Here, the classifications at the established frequency (i.e., at least two-thirds of the notes) being the critical *empirical* commonalities in defining suicide from suicide notes. The most desirable data, of course, are those protocol sentences that are highly predictive *and* discriminative—five such observations were made.

It is imperative that the reader recognize that suicidal threats that reflect signs that are similar to the protocol sentences that neither discriminate nor predict the content in suicide notes do not necessarily mean that one should fail to respond (Leenaars & Balance, 1981). After all, except for one or two sentences, all protocol sentences were observed in one or more genuine suicide notes. Beyond the unique, however, those sentences that are highly predictive and/or discriminative—the sequence here is purposive for clinical implications—may well be ominous clues to a suicide in general.

Bibliography

Freud, S. (1974) Psychopathology of everyday Life. In J. Strachey (Ed. & Trans). *The standard edition of the complete psychological works of Sigmund Freud, Vol. VI*. London: Hogarth Press (Original published in 1901).

Freud, S. (1974) A case of obsessional neurosis. *Ibid, Vol. X.* (Original published in 1909).

Freud, S. (1974) Mourning and melancholia. *Ibid, Vol XIV*. (Original published in 1917).

Freud, S. (1974)) General Theory of neurosis. *Ibid, Vol XVI*. (Original published in 1917).

Freud, S. (1974) A case of homosexuality in a woman. *Ibid, Vol XVIII*. (Original published in 1920).

Freud, S. (1974) Group psychology and the analysis of the ego. *Ibid, Vol. XVIII* (Original published in 1921).

Freud, S. (1974) The ego and the id. *Ibid, Vol XIX*. (Original published in 1923).

Freud, S. (1974) New introductory lectures. *Ibid, Vol. XXII*. (Original published in 1933).

Freud, S. (1974) An outline of psycho-analysis. *Ibid, Vol. XXIII*. (Original published in 1940).

Chapter 7

CARL GUSTAV JUNG

Personal History

Carl Gustav Jung was born in Basel, Switzerland on July 26, 1875. A key influence during his early years was his religious and spiritual training, fueled by the fact that his father was a pastor. This influence continued throughout his life as related in his autobiography, *Memories, Dreams and Reflections* (1961). Jung was also, early on, interested in medicine, especially the study of "diseases of the personality" and psychic phenomena. He received his M.D. degree from the University of Basel in 1902. His thesis was the first statement on depth psychology entitled, "On the Psychology and Pathology of So-Called Occult Phenomena," wherein Jung put forward the view that each person moves toward a "totality of psyche."

From 1900 to 1907 he worked at Burgholzli Hospital, Zurich, under one of Freud's teachers, Bleuler. It was here that he developed the "word association method" to discover unconscious groups of ideas, which he termed "complexes." In 1905, he became a lecturer at the University of Zurich and a senior physician at the Psychiatric Clinic; later, he became professor at the University of Basel. His reputation became established in 1906 with his work on schizophrenia, *The Psychology of Dementia Praecox*. As a result of this work, Freud invited him to Vienna; their first meeting resulted in a close association. Freud, almost from the beginning, saw Jung as his heir. However, a rift occurred in 1909, culminating between 1912–1913 with Jung's publication of *The Psychology of the Unconscious* (renamed later as *Symbol of Transformation*), which highlighted the increasing theoretical disagreement between the two men. The break resulted in deep inner reflection for Jung from 1913–1917 and ultimately, a very productive explication of his own theory of analytic psychology (including his views on suicide), culminating in his book, *Psychological Types* (1921). Freud was clearly not the only influence on Jung; for example, when Einstein was a professor at Zurich, Jung knew him, and Einstein often discussed the theory of relativity with Jung. This likely influenced Jung as much as classical Newtonian physics, by way of Helmholz, influenced Freud.

In 1944, Jung suffered a severe heart attack which had a profound "mystical" effect on him. After his recovery, he began anthropological studies of the people of Africa and the Navajo Indians of America. He became interested in the religions of India and China, Greek mythology, and Christian mysticism (notably alchemy and Gnosticism). Two important books from this period were *Aion* (1951) and *Psychology and Alchemy* (1944). Jung died on June 6, 1961.

Theory of Suicide

According to Jung, ideally there is a normal harmony between man's conscious and unconscious. The fact is, however, that frequently the harmony is not there and "this is the reason for a vast number of psychogenic misfortunes," ranging from slips of the tongue to suicide. A normal psychological balance is a kind of self-regulation of the psychic system. Under certain circumstances and in certain cases, an imbalance may occur. A traumatic event (e.g., an unmet love, a failing marriage, disgust with one's work) results in certain individuals (for instance, in latent psychoses) in deep hurt, feelings of desperation, and destructive tendencies. One ultimate result may be suicide. In the suicide, therefore, there is, at least symbolically, a distance, a lack of balance, a lack of harmony between the conscious and the unconscious attitudes, impulses, etc, resulting in a conflict and the individual's destructive character.

The unconscious in such a disharmony brings about all kinds of "unwelcome disturbances" and "serious consequences." When unconscious impulses form a block in every way opposed to the conscious attitude, conflict and destructive behavior is evident (such as "a sudden zest for dangerous aerobatics," "hesitation in front of a motor-car," "mistaking corrosive sublimate for cough mixture," and so forth). However, according to Jung, such behavior is not a mere consequence to a traumatic event, for the person could previously be seen as exhibiting a "complex" in his personality, i.e., something discordant, unassimilated, and antagonistic (e.g., symptoms, ideas), perhaps as an obstacle, pointing to previous unresolved problems. Jung notes that it is only in individuals who have "weaker natures" that difficult circumstances lead to direct suicide. In others, destructive impulses are in some manner made conscious, allowing one to recognize and avoid situations that tempt one to self-destruction. What appears to occur in the suicide, however, is a conflict or clash between a demand for adaptation and the individual's constitutional inability to meet that challenge. For cultural reasons such individuals may also suppress infantile and primitive demands which leads to neurosis, the abuse of narcotics and, in extreme cases, suicide. Jung (1921) states:

> It is an outstanding peculiarity of unconscious impulses that, when deprived of energy by lack of conscious recognition, they take a destructive character. (p. 340)

A brief case of Jung's (1928), regarding the "mental case of a young sentimental youth," may best illustrate these formulations:

> (The youth) . . . had fallen in love with a girl and, as so often happens, had failed to ascertain whether his love was requited. His primitive participation mystique took it for

> granted that his agitations were plainly the agitations of the other, which on the lower levels of human psychology is naturally very often the case. Thus he built up a sentimental love-fantasy which precipitately collapsed when he discovered that the girl would have none of him. He was so desperate that he went straight to the river to drown himself. It was late at night, and the stars gleamed up at him from the dark water. It seemed to him that the stars were swimming two by two down the river, and a wonderful feeling came over him. He forgot his suicidal intentions and gazed fascinated at the strange, sweet drama. And gradually he became aware that every star was a face, and that all these pairs were lovers, who were carried along locked in a dreaming embrace. An entirely new understanding came to him: all had changed—his fate, his disappointment, even his love, receded and fell away. The memory of the girl grew distant, blurred; but instead, he felt with complete certainty that untold riches were promised him. (p. 61)

Regrettably, his link with the world had snapped, and believing that the treasure was in a local observatory, he found himself arrested for breaking into it.

According to Jung, the individual who kills himself had experienced unresolved problems before the act, problems where he has suffered defeat, at least for the time being, and where there is something he could not evade or overcome. Weak spots in every sense of the phrase are evident. A wave of depression and desperation occurs in such individuals. The individual's relation to the world may become impaired resulting in greater preoccupation with fantasies (e.g., "a new undreamt-of world of stars"). The fantasies are far beyond the grievous earth for the individual. Ultimately, however, in some individuals the snap results in *the* end of his relation to the world and, Jung notes, that such a break may be very sudden, as evident in a case of Bleuler's that Jung (1902) cites. The case involved a middle-aged epileptic man who, without prodromal symptoms (such as depression), attempted to kill himself on a holiday. In a twilight state, he threw himself in a river. Jung (1904) cites another case to illustrate his point; a man in desperation becomes dissociated and attempts to bash his head in, but subsequently has no conscious recall of the incident.

In suicide, one's inherent reasonableness is prevented from being conscious, and illogical and irrational characteristics arise that are clearly related to the self-destruction. Thus, although the person usually experiences a traumatic event before the suicide, it is his *weak nature* that drives him to suicide. The trauma results in a hurt in an individual whose conscious and unconscious are in disharmony. It is the destructive character in such an individual, who is unable to meet the challenge, that leads to the death.

Central to Jung's formulations regarding suicide and personality functioning in general, as noted previously, are the two "realities," the world of the conscious and the unconscious. He notes that today we (people in general) doubt the latter's reality and it is this doubt and denial that results not only in personal conflict and destruction, but also in world division and the ultimate possibility of the world's suicide. Jung (1961) states:

> Man is bound to follow the exploits of his scientific and inventive mind and to admire himself for his splendid achievement. At the same time, he cannot help admitting that his genius shows an uncanny tendency to invent things that became more and more dangerous, because they represent better and better means for wholesale suicide. (p. 260)

Jung stresses that we not only deny our individual unconscious but also our "primordial images", the *archetypes.* Important archetypes in suicide are the Shadow (which serves as the focus for material that is repressed from consciousness including, but not limited to, our own self-destruction) and the Anima and Animus (which represent the unrecognized contra-sexual parts of man and woman). According to Jung (1961), these archetypes are "living entities that make up a great part of the human psyche," but are unrecognized. The Shadow, however, can be easily recognized in the destructiveness itself. The Anima-Animus can be recognized in the following manner. In the male who kills himself, there are traits (sentimentality, emotional weakness) that were stereotypically characterized in the individual (and our culture in general) as *female* traits. These traits had been vigorously repressed in that same individual's unconscious, until a wave of destructiveness occurred. In the female who kills herself, there are traits (argumentation, rationalization) that were overly characterized in the individual as *male* traits and a similar pattern developed as in the male. The repression of such traits or any other denial or repression results in an imbalance, conflict, and disharmony.

In the case of the youth cited earlier, the youth's "love" symbolized his Anima and his destructiveness symbolized his Shadow. These living archetypes and other unconscious forces ultimately unite in the youth as "all these pairs of lovers" when the youth is at the river and his unconscious pours out as "untold riches," symbolizing the central archetype of the Self. In this case and other cases of suicide and attempted suicide, an open conflict had occurred between the physical (material) and spiritual aspects of the individual. During such an open conflict, the person experiences a wave of pain and desperation. The unconscious forces pour out in the individual, who is *constitutionally* unable to meet the challenge, resulting in destructiveness and, in certain cases, suicide.

Given his formulations regarding destructiveness, Jung emphasizes that we—each individual—must establish a state of harmony between his conscious and unconscious. We can obtain this balance by, for example, listening to our dreams. Dreams, according to Jung, are the unquestionable products of unconscious psychic activity from which one can "draw trustworthy conclusions." A case of Jung's (1928) of a fifty-year-old man highlights not only the importance of dreams, but that they are in "the best position to tell us something" about suicide. The man had the following dream:

> He was alone in the mountains, and wanted to climb a very high, steep mountain which he could see towering in front of him. At first the ascent was laborious, but then it seemed to him that the higher he climbed the more he felt himself being drawn toward the summit. Faster and faster he climbed, and gradually a sort of ecstasy came over him. He felt he was actually soaring upon wings, and when he

> reached the top he seemed to weigh nothing at all, and stepped lightly off into empty space. Here he awoke. (p. 60–61)

The man, who Jung occasionally met, was an ardent mountain climber. During a conversation with Jung, the man associated to the dream that he was fascinated with dangerous tours, "apparently with almost morbid enjoyment." He further noted to Jung that death in the mountains would be something "very beautiful," suggesting to Jung and the man himself, that the man was looking for danger, "possibly with the unavowed idea of suicide." The man, however, acknowledged that he would never "give up his mountains," for he needed them to get away from his family and city, suggesting to Jung a "deeper reason" for the man's passion. He was experiencing a number of traumatic events (a failing marriage, disgust with his work), which had been intolerable to him, resulting in his escape to the mountains. Privately, Jung further interpreted that the dream was expressing the destructive forces within the man; a clear disharmony was evident. In the dream, the man, surrendering himself to his passion, climbed "lightly off into empty space," meaning, according to Jung, "death in the mountains". Jung communicated some of these thoughts, but the man stated, "On the contrary, I am seeking my health in the mountains." Six months later, he "literally stepped off into space" during the descent of a very dangerous peak, killing himself and a companion who had been standing on a ledge below.

Protocol Sentences

The following 10 protocol sentences were derived from Jung's formulations regarding suicide:

In the suicide note:

1. A "complex" is evident, i.e., something discordant, unassimilated, and antagonistic exists (e.g., symptoms, ideas), perhaps as an obstacle, pointing to unresolved problems in the individual.

2. Unresolved problems in the individual are evident, where he has suffered defeat, at least for the time being, and where there is something he cannot evade or overcome. His weak spots are evident.
3. A clash is evident between a demand of adaptation and the individual's constitutional inability to meet the challenge.
4. Suppressions of infantile and primitive demands for cultural reasons are evident.
5. At least symbolically, there is a distance, a lack of balance, a lack of harmony between the conscious and unconscious attitudes, impulses, etc., resulting in a conflict and the individual's destructive character.
6. The person communicates the existence of a traumatic event (e.g., an unmet love, a failing marriage, disgust with one's work) that results in a deep hurt, being desperate and, ultimately, the suicide itself.
7. It appears that a wave of depression and desperation snaps the individual's link with his relation to the world, resulting in fantasies ("a new undreamt-of world of stars") that for the individual is far beyond the grievous earth.
8. There is an open conflict between the physical (material) and the spiritual aspects of the individual.
9. If written by a male, there is evidence for the existence of feminine (anima) traits (e.g., sentimentality, emotional weakness). If the note was written by a female, there is evidence for the existence of masculine (animus) traits (e.g., argumentation, rationalization).
10. It appears that inherent reasonableness was prevented from being conscious; rather, illogical and irrational characteristics are evident that are related to the self-destruction.

FINDINGS

No protocol sentences were verified significantly more often within the genuine notes as compared with the simulated notes.

Sentences 1, 2, 3, and 6 were observed at the critical level of verification count (i.e., at least ⅔ of the time). These very common sentences were related to the following classifications: the existence of something discordant, unassimilated, and antagonistic in the person; unresolved problems are evident in a person, who has suffered defeat; a clash is evident between the need for adaptation and the person's inability to meet that challenge; and there is the reported experience of a traumatic event.

Bibliography

Jung, C. G. (1974). A medical opinion on a case of simulated insanity (R. Hull, Trans.). In H. Read, M. Fordam, & G. Adler (Eds.), *The collected works of C. G. Jung, Vol. I*. London: Routledge and Kegan Paul. (Original published in 1904).

Jung, C. G. (1974). The psychological diagnosis of evidence. *Ibid., Vol. II*. (Original published in 1906).

Jung, C. G. (1974). Psychological types. *Ibid., Vol. VI*. (Original published in 1921).

Jung, C. G. (1974). The relations between the ego and the unconscious. *Ibid., Vol. VII*. (Original published in 1928).

Jung, C. G. (1974). On the nature of dreams. *Ibid., Vol. VIII*. (Original published in 1945/1948).

Jung, C. G. (1974). Basic postulates of analytic psychology. *Ibid., Vol. VIII*. (Original published in 1931).

Jung, C. G. (1974). Mind and earth. *Ibid., Vol. X*. (Original published in 1927/31).

Jung, C. G. (1974). Problems of modern psychotherapy. *Ibid., Vol. XVI*. (Original published in 1929).

Jung, C. G. (1974). Child development and education. *Ibid., Vol. XVII*. (Original published in 1928).

Jung, C. G. (1974). The development of personality. *Ibid., Vol. XVII*. (Original published in 1934).

Jung, C. G. (1977). Symbols and the interpretation of dreams. *Ibid., Vol. XVIII*. (Original published in 1961).

Chapter 8

GEORGE A. KELLY

Personal History

George A. Kelly was born (an only child) to a farming family near Perth, Kansas on April 26, 1905.[1] The generally acknowledged key influence on Kelly during his early years was this isolated but warm farming community. Kelly attended a number of different colleges in the Middle West (Friends University in Kansas; Park College in Missouri, University of Kansas, and University of Minnesota) and spent an exchange year during his graduate studies in Edinburgh, studying physics, mathematics, education, and a little psychology. He completed his Ph.D. at Iowa State University in 1931; his dissertation was on physiological disorders, specifically speech disorders. His first publication, "The Sincere Motive" was published in 1924 in *Messenger of Peace*. During his studies, he was directly influenced by B. Travis, his doctoral advisor; S.G. Thompson, a sociologist at

---

[1]For this section, the author gratefully acknowledges the assistance and cooperation of Mrs. George Kelly and Dr. Jack Adams-Webber.

Edinburgh; and Cyril Burt, a specialist on intelligence. He was extremely impressed with the works of Galton and Dewey and was influenced by the writings of Freud; in fact, Kelly, for a long time, saw himself as wishing to do psychoanalytic therapy.

In the fall of 1931, Kelly became a faculty member (and later director of the clinic) at Fort Hays, Kansas State College. Here, practical psychological needs postponed his interest in experimental work on perception. Kelly remained at Fort Hays for 13 years, developing his clinical skills during the years of the Dust Bowl and Great Depression. His primary work occurred in travelling clinics, where he was actively involved in testing, diagnosing and remediation of school children. Here he began to develop his central ideas about how problems where related to the construction of events (e.g., the teacher's of the students), refusing to accept things as black-and-white but open to alternative constructions. He produced a series of handbooks (e.g., *Handbook of Clinical Practice,* 1943) and published a number of practical papers; for example, on personality, intelligence, reading and speech disabilities, the importance of the idiographic approach in psychology, the role of the psychologist in school systems, and the utility of practical rather than ideal recommendations. In these papers, Kelly moved away from his early psychoanalytic modality of treatment to a more cognitive, "educative" approach, which later developed into *Fixed Role Therapy.* Kelly's early testing program also produced precursors to his idiographic case study approaches to people, that were later incorporated into the Role Construct Repertory Grid (REP) Test.

With the beginning of World War II, Kelly left Fort Hays and served as an aviation psychologist in the U.S. Navy. Here, he turned to the application of his clinical skills to Navy personnel (e.g., pilots) as well as the application of his experimental training (notably on perception) to areas such as the design of aircraft instrument panels. After the war, Kelly took a job at the University of Maryland, but in 1946, with the encouragement of Carl Seashore, who had significant influence on Kelly, he accepted the position of professor and director of clinical psychology at Ohio State University. Here, along with other psychologists (e.g., Julian Rotter), Kelly developed a practical clinical program, especially influenced by W. Johnson, a philosopher of science.

With this background, Kelly began to crystallize his constructions, based on the notion that each man is a scientist who anticipates, predicts, and controls his environment. This work culminated in the 1955 two-volume book, *The Psychology of Personal Constructs,* as well as a number of papers that were edited, in 1969, under the title, *Clinical Psychology and Personality: The Selected Papers of George Kelly.* He also applied his formulations to suicide in a paper, "Suicide: The Personal Construct Point of View" which was published in *The Cry for Help,* edited by N. Farberow and E. Shneidman in 1961. During 1960–1961, travelling around the world, he delivered a number of interesting papers, especially one in Moscow entitled, "A Mathematical Approach to Psychology." Kelly's works have also influenced a number of other psychologists; e.g., J. Adams-Webber, D. Bannister, J. Benjafield, and F. Fransella.

Kelly was a charter member of the American Board of Examiners in Professional Psychology, its first vice president and later president. He was also a president of the Clinical and Consulting Divisions of the American Psychological Association. In 1965 Kelly accepted a post at Brandeis University, Boston, where he continued his academic work. He died March 6, 1967, in Boston.

THEORY OF SUICIDE

Kelly's formulations regarding suicide are presented in the paper, "Suicide: The Personal Construct Point of View," although a few references are made elsewhere in his 1955 volumes. In these writings, Kelly presents his perspective that man is a construer of events; events are open to a host of alternative constructions. Man must make sense out of whatever happens, even when facing suicide. This idea is stated best in his fundamental postulate: "A person's processes are psychologically channelized by the ways in which he anticipates events." To illustrate this formulation in relation to suicide, Kelly utilizes the case of A.S.

(a twenty-three-year-old, white, Protestant, single male college student) who attempted to kill himself; the case is outlined in detail in *The Cry for Help.* Briefly, A.S. related his attempt to the following:

> Well, it all goes back to before I went into the Army. I had a girlfriend then, Mary (who was of South American-Spanish descent)—she was a wonderful girl." He repeated this several times. "I loved her, and she loved me. She was intelligent and gracious, and I really wanted to marry her. But my folks were against it and I couldn't understand it. It was the first time they had ever crossed me. . . .

Kelly begins by asking, 'What truths did A.S. invent?' Suicide, according to Kelly, is best understood if we look at the act and what it accomplishes or validates. There are two general possibilities: A person may kill himself because his worst anticipations (expectations) are coming true; alternatively, his anticipations about himself, others, or the world are *not* coming true. The latter refer to a time when everything seems utterly unpredictable. Essentially, a suicide or suicide attempt can be regarded as an act designed to *validate* one's life; for example, A.S. arrived at his suicide attempt as the result of a series of perceived relationships, where suicide was "the most obvious thing to do." The suicide was designed, in a sense, to validate A.S.'s choice.

In Kelly's formulations, more traditional concepts, such as hostility, impulsivity, guilt, etc., play only a secondary role. Constructs of feelings, emotions, needs, psychodynamics, motivations, learning, reinforcement, stimulus, cognition, irrationality, and disorganization drop out of the formulations. Rather, the emphasis in the formulations is "placed on the use of the axes of reference that are abstract; i.e., mathematical in the broad sense," to provide a more meaningful construction of the event, suicide, than the more traditional concepts will allow. Kelly looks at suicide anew, with his own frame of reference.

In search of personal constructs upon which to base one's anticipations, a person sometimes broadens his world (dilation) and sometimes shrinks his world. According to Kelly suicide is almost always the latter, a constrictive gesture. The person may anticipate or expect less and less from himself, others, and the world, finding himself helpless in understanding an unpredictable and senseless world. This results, according to Kelly, in anxiety. In the case of A.S., we find A.S. tending toward the predicted direction of constriction, shutting himself off from his life. However, as is usually the case in constriction, this brought him more chaos, helplessness, and a state of anxiety. Anxiety here is not defined in traditional terms, but that one is aware that events with which one is confronted lie mostly outside the range of one's constructs. One is confronted with events for which one's constructs are not applicable.

Thus, in the case of A.S., we find him aware of events (rejection at home, conflict at school, unemployment) that did not make adequate sense to him, resulting in what Kelly termed an invalidation (notably, by his mother who had always been his primary source of validation) of the basic constructs he used to make sense of events. A.S. was anxious, and this was more related, according to Kelly, to the loss at home, i.e., his mother, than the loss of Mary. A.S.'s mother had always been his ground, his source for constructing the world. With the loss of his mother, his validation, A.S. felt that the events with which he was confronted did not make sense. He did not know how to anticipate events, himself, others, and/or the world.

In addition to anxiety, Kelly notes that threat may also occur in suicide. A person is threatened when he needs to change himself in order to handle forthcoming events in a way that seems to be impossible for that person. Threat implies the need to change one's core construct system—or formulations referring to the "self"—how one evaluates oneself, one's issues, one's anticipations. Threat is comprehensive. Threat is more comprehensive than a fear, fear being only an awareness of an incidental change. Threat is awareness of a comprehensive change and thus should never be overlooked in suicide.

Kelly's basic postulate is, as we noted, that the person's processes are psychologically channeled by ways in which he anticipates events. Constructs are the way we anticipate events; a personal construct is a sort of representational scheme which the individual himself creates and into which he then attempts to fit events from a changing environment. Kelly notes that we have psychological choice in how we anticipate the environment. The environment is open to alternative constructions. Our constructs are how we anticipate events, how we *construct* events. For most of us, our constructions are validated by events; but sometimes hostility occurs in these constructions. One can be hostile in one's choice of anticipating the environment; one can try to make people or events fit with what one *expects* is the right thing. If one cannot revise the very formulations of one's construct system, the way one anticipates events, one may, as a last resort, force events to prove one right, by a misleading manipulation of the data—the environment. Hostility is especially evident in suicide, including hostility towards oneself (although this should not be construed as the same as Stekel's 1910 statement that suicide is aggression turned inward). For Kelly, hostility is an artificial validation of one's construction of life. Kelly states that too often the suicidal person, as in the case of A.S., "uses both his verbal warning and his actual suicide attempt to extort validating evidence from those upon whom he has come to depend for confirmation of his social outlook."

According to Kelly, the suicidal person may also exhibit guilt which refers to the need to change his role. He regulates his behavior in reference to significant others; he does what others expect, which is his role. In suicide, however, the person finds that he does not seem to fit into or be able to do what other people expect of him. His role has been lost, he is socially excommunicated. This was evident in A.S. when he neglected his mother's sisters when she was ill and died. A.S. had remained at this time with Mary, the person whom the mother did not like. This resulted in breaking off with Mary. A.S.'s guilt required a change in reference to A.S.'s mother; A.S. had deserted his mother. Or, more accurately, A.S. had not done what his mother had *expected* of him. The mother rejected him and A.S. *lost his source for anticipating the world.*

Ultimately, this series of psychological events resulted in A.S.'s attempting to kill himself because he saw no alternative to this. He saw the suicide as giving some meaning to his life. There was nothing in life to validate him. A.S. attempted to die in relation to his personal construction of life and truth. A.S.'s anticipations were validated by the suicide attempt itself. He made his choice. Kelly (1965) concludes:

> . . . we are apt to say that a person committed a mere suicide . . . when it seems clear by our lights that the problem he faced had a better solution. We think we would have known better. Perhaps so. Nevertheless, the fact remains that none of the alternatives that beckon so clearly in our minds was quite so visible in his. So the suicide makes *his* choice, and not *ours*. (p. 259)

PROTOCOL SENTENCES

The following 10 protocol sentences were derived from Kelly's formulations regarding suicide.

In the suicide note:

1. The person communicates that his suicide is an attempt to make sense out of whatever has happened to him.
2. The person communicates that he is killing himself because his worst expectations are coming true.
3. The person communicates that his expectations/anticipations about himself, others, and/or the world are not coming true.
4. The person communicates that he is expecting less and less from himself, others, and/or the world.
5. The person communicates that he is helpless in understanding an unpredictable and senseless world.
6. The person communicates that he is aware of events that don't make adequate sense to him.
7. The person communicates that he needs to change himself in order to handle forthcoming events in a way that seems to be impossible to himself.
8. The person communicates that he has been trying or is trying to make people or events fit with what he expects is the right thing.
9. The person communicates that he does not seem to fit into or be able to do what other people expect of him.
10. The person communicates that he is killing himself because he sees no alternative to this action and he sees the suicide as giving him some meaning in his life.

FINDINGS

No significant discriminations or verification counts were observed. These findings, however, do not necessarily suggest that various factors *explained* by Kelly do not occur in suicide. For example, other judges trained in Kelly's formulations may well verify some (or all) of Kelly's protocol sentences in the notes—an observation, of course, that can be made about all 10 suicidologists. Furthermore, it should be noted that Kelly's formulations in general were the initial basis, structure for the protocol method. The method can be seen as a constructive alternative to the Repertory Grid Test.

BIBLIOGRAPHY

Kelly, G. (1955) *The psychology of personal constructs* (Vols. 1 & 2). New York: Norton.

Kelly, G. (1961) Suicide: The personal construct point of view. In N. Farberow & E. Shneidman (Eds.), *The cry for help*. New York: McGraw-Hill.

Kelly, G. (1969) A mathematical approach to psychology. In B. Maher (Ed.), *Clinical psychology and personality*. New York: Wiley.

Kelly, G. (1977) Confusion and the clock. In F. Fransella (Ed.), *Personal construct psychology*. London: Academic Press.

Chapter 9

KARL A. MENNINGER

Personal History

Karl A. Menninger was born on July 22, 1893 in Topeka, Kansas, into a family that became well-known in medicine (notably, his father, Charles, and his brother, William). Menninger received his medical degree at Harvard University in 1917. He interned at Kansas City General Hospital, focusing on neurology and psychiatry and continued his work at Boston Psychopathic Hospital. In Boston, he worked under Elmer Southard, who, according to Menninger himself, was the most notable influence in his early theoretical and research development. He was also influenced by the work of Freud and Adolf Meyer. He took his psychoanalytic training at the Chicago Institute for Psychoanalysis, holding the first certificate of training there. In 1919, he returned to Topeka and in 1925, with his family, established the Menninger Clinic and the Menninger Psychiatric Hospital, utilizing Freud's psychoanalytic principles as the framework for these institutions. These psychoanalytic concepts were also later expanded to other areas such as research and education by Menninger.

Menninger's first major work, *The Human Mind,* was published in 1930, largely reflecting the influence of Freud's concepts as, indeed, is found in his later works. On September 7, 1932 his paper entitled, "Psychoanalytic Aspects of Suicide" was read in absentia at the Twelfth International Psycho-Analytic Congress, Weisbaden, Germany. Herein, Menninger gave his first public presentation of his views on suicide, which he later published in his famous book, *Man Against Himself* (1938). In 1942, he wrote *Love Against Hate,* where he turned to more constructive life aspects of man. In the same year, he cofounded the Topeka Institute of Psychoanalysis and the year following, the Menninger School of Psychiatry. He widely influenced the psychiatric training of numerous physicians and served as president of the American Psychiatric Association. His later books include *Theory of Psychoanalytic Techniques* (1958) and *The Vital Balance* (1963). This work led him to greater emphasis on preventing destruction and mistreatment, promoting mental health for all. In later years, he also became very active in establishing mental health facilities; for example, in 1963, he established The Village Inc., a home for abused and abandoned children. Although less active at this writing—in his nineties—than in his earlier years, Menninger continues to work and serves as the Chairman of the Board of Trustees of the Menninger Foundation in Topeka, Kansas.

THEORY OF SUICIDE

According to Menninger (1933), "Psychological suicide is a very complex act, and not a simple, incidental, isolated act of impulsion either logical or unexplicable" (p. 377). Suicide is not simply a consequence of (or escape from) ill health, financial reverses, or unrequited love; in fact, Menninger (1938) notes that such explanations "do not explain anything." Suicide is not *only* determined from without; rather, it is largely determined from within. We create our situation, evidenced by the fact that "for some persons no reality, however terrible, is unbearable." The suicidal person, in some largely unconscious way, helps to *create* the very thing that he tries to escape.

According to Menninger, there are three critical elements

(or wishes) in the act of suicide: the element of dying; the element of killing; and the element of being killed. Each of these is an act for which there are motives, conscious and unconscious. Menninger focuses on the latter "because the former is usually evident enough." Furthermore, in understanding the suicide, the unconscious purpose is very significant whereas the conscious ones cannot be relied upon. A case that Menninger (1938) offers illustrates this assumption.

A quiet, friendly, and generally trusted cashier in a small bank, one day, after banking hours, shoots himself. People were perplexed as to why such a friendly man would kill himself. Subsequently, a cash shortfall was discovered, providing the explanation; he killed himself because he had stolen during a sudden irrational moment and then succumbed to remorse to which the suicide was the tragic consequence. However, a few weeks later, it was found that he had an "affair," providing the next ready "real" explanation; when a respectable married man has an affair, he needs money to support the woman, resulting in this case, out of remorse, in his death. Others had another explanation, while a few knew that the marriage was unhappy, providing the "real" reason. The family physician knew that for 20 years the wife had been frigid, another "real" explanation. Still others knew that his mother had been a cold and hard woman, providing *the* explanation. This chain of explanations show that the man "took the pistol in his hand long before he took the money"—but Menninger concludes that we still fall short of explaining this man's suicide. We only have more obvious external data, not the full explanation.

According to Menninger, "the destructive instinct" slumbers in all of us, even the young child. The wish to kill—eliminating, driving away, disposing of, annihilating—is evident in all; but under ordinary circumstances, internal and external, the constructive and creative aspects of life inhibit this wish. If the destructive tendencies are, however, not "neutralized" by the "life instinct," destruction and, ultimately, in an "ebbing flow of aggressiveness," suicide may occur. Such a process is illustrated by the series of events and the ultimate death of the defaulting bank cashier. Menninger (1938) also illustrates this view with the following case:

> A man, being angry with his brother, thought of killing him; however, he restrained himself, suffering deep remorse. Subsequently, the man attempted, unsuccessfully, to kill himself several times; began to drive his car recklessly, causing several accidents; began to expose himself to some diseases, including syphilis; turned to alcohol; lost his job and argued and exasperated his wife, ultimately telling her that he did not love her. The list, hence, of this man's self-directed aggressiveness is long; fortunately he did not kill himself and, ultimately, was able to return to his wife and obtain a new position. (p. 30)

Positive attachment to objects (notably people) in the environment result in constructive impulses in man. Under certain traumatic circumstances these attachments break, resulting in a need for readjustment which most people can handle, after a temporary period of grief and anxiety. Most people attach themselves to a new object; however, in certain individuals this does not happen. Instead, an ebbing flow of aggressiveness overwhelms the individual; the life instinct is inhibited, giving rise to the wish to kill. This wish to kill, which is unexpectedly robbed of external opportunities (possibly unconscious) is then turned back upon oneself and carried into effect as suicide, corresponding to three facts: if there are 1) destructive tendencies toward oneself; 2) high ambivalence in attachment to people; 3) sudden interruption in these attachments.

Menninger (1945) noted:

> Suicide is a combination of hate, rage, revenge, a sense of guilt, and a feeling of unbearable frustration. Meeting with reverses, irritations, or disappointments too great for his personality to absorb or to deal with rationally, the suicide solves them by a flight from reality. (p. 124)

The person thus vents hostilities in bitter reproach and attacks toward another person by expressing *toward himself* the resentment and hostilities—he kills himself. Menninger does note, however, that the suicide does indirectly accomplish one purpose—it does hurt "the other fellow"—although in a childishly dramatic way.

How is it possible to treat oneself as an external object? How does one carry out the aggressiveness towards oneself? Menninger believes that identification, or more accurately, introjection, accounts for this process. One identifies oneself with the other person. One introjects the other person into the self, allowing any wish towards that person now to be carried out upon oneself.

A case example may illustrate these formulations: A young boy, scolded by his father, hangs himself, thus having a sort of revenge; that is, the boy sacrifices himself by turning the death wish on himself. This boy and other individuals who kill themselves have an immature personality makeup, being incapable of adjusting to sharp disappointments, frustrations, or reverses. They are incapable of forming attachments to people without a high degree of ambivalence and are, therefore, at "the mercy of circumstances" if there is a sudden interruption in their attachments. The circumstances may be severe or seem trivial but must be put in the context of a long list of precipitating events as well as the person's history of maladjustment.

To summarize, Menninger notes that one element in suicide is the wish to kill, evidenced by the *fact* that "the man who kills himself has, after all, killed something." The wish to kill (arising from primitive destructiveness) invested with weak neutralization in one or several people, whose sudden removal or faithlessness dislodges the attachment, dilutes the emotional bond and allows the murderous impulse, now freed, to be turned toward the wisher himself as a substitute person, thus accomplishing what might be called a displaced murder.

The second element is suicide is the wish to be killed. Being killed is the extreme form of submission. "Why does anyone wish to be killed—to submit in such an extreme?" Menninger notes that suicide is a form of masochism. Masochism is the enjoyment of submission, pain, defeat, even ending in death. Menninger notes that some people, for example, like to be beaten for the accompanying erotic enjoyment. Some individuals push this to extremes, like "Nancy" (in Dickens's *Oliver Twist*) who pushed the pleasure of pain to the ultimate by remaining with Bill Sykes who beats her to death. Still others kill themselves to achieve satisfaction, enjoyment.

But, why is satisfaction achieved by punishment in these individuals? Menninger provides several case illustrations. One patient who had survived a serious suicide attempt, believing he had a bad heart, then entered athletics vigorously. Despite his conscious intention, the man found himself successful in sports, resulting in his quickly giving them up. Menninger explains that insight into such cases and masochism in general can be found in the nature of conscience. Conscience, defined as an internal psychological representation of authority, originally and mainly parental authority but fused in later life with prevalent ethical, religous, and social standards, is one's guide; but it may be a bad guide. It is a sort of internal judge or king, a part of which is unconscious. Conscience has its own rules. One universal law of conscience is that the person (ego) "must suffer in direct proportion to externally directed destructiveness" (Menninger, 1938, p. 52). If one attacks someone in the environment, then conscience (or superego) directs an attack of the same nature on oneself (ego).

Stated differently, the individual's attack (such as murderous wishes) upon some person in the environment are directed as a attack of the same sort upon oneself (as punishment). One cannot placate the conscience in such circumstances—the person's conscience demands an extreme submission, such as a wish to suffer and to submit to pain and even death. Another law of the conscience, according to Menninger (1938), is that "in the unconscious a wish to destroy is quite equivalent to the actual destruction" (p. 54). This point is illustrated, for example, by Dmitri in *The Brothers Karamazov,* who did not kill his father but only wished for his father's death. Dmitri, because of this wish, subsequently seemed to demand a punishment, permitting himself to be imprisoned for life. The wish was enough to require the punishment. Although *The Brothers Karamazov* is a novel, Freud had earlier pointed out that these events paralled the life of Dostoyevsky, who after the death of his father, suffered greatly and permitted himself to be sentenced to prison for a crime that he did not commit.

Many suicides are disguised murders, according to Menninger, following Stekel's original formulation. In the suicide, the person strikes an impulsive blow at himself, thereby expressing toward himself the resentment he feels toward something or someone (that had been incorporated into his personality) in his environment. Simultaneously, he exhibits a dramatic submission to punishment. The suicide is the punishment for the wish to kill. One wishes to be killed as a submission to conscience for the wish to kill someone else. Menninger (1938) provides the following suggestive illustration to highlight these ideas.

Mrs. Z., following (as always), her autocratic father's demands, married an elderly, terminally ill man. Fifteen months later, the man died, resulting in the severe depression, "illness," and an attempt at suicide on the part of Mrs. Z. Recovering, she married another friend of her father's, but Mrs. Z.'s father died shortly afterwards. Again, Mrs. Z. became depressed and attempted to kill herself. Careful study of the facts revealed that Mrs. Z. had "killed" her first husband, for she had wished him dead, fortified by "a deeper, more ancient death wish" towards her father. A wish being unconsciously equivalent to the act, determined the conscience to demand, consciously or unconsciously, action. Her father's death again renewed these reactions, which had been temporarily submerged (undoing) by the second marriage to another father substitute. The loss of her father robbed her not only of the person who, although an ambivalent one, was the source of gratification for Mrs. Z., but also revived her destructive wishes for him. Her attempt at self-inflicted execution was her punishment.

The above case also illustrates the fact that unconscious death wishes reach their highest intensity towards members of one's family. If a member of a family dies (or kills himself), the death wish of others is unexpectedly satisfied, producing a sudden and often overpowering reaction in the conscience—guilt. The conscience then, according to Menninger, demands an equally extreme submission for the wish, which may occur in dreams of being killed, an actual death sentence. These observations are not only important to highlight Menninger's formulations, but also are critical in comprehending multiple familial suicide, since it is not heredity that explains suicides in a family.

The third and final element in suicide is the wish to die.

The wish to die, however, is a "hypothesis" in contrast to the other two elements that have been proven. Menninger (1938) illustrates this concept with the following:

> Anyone who has sat by the bedside of a patient dying from a self-inflicted wound and listened to pleadings that the physician save a life, the destruction of which had only a few hours or minutes before been attempted, must have been impressed by the paradox that one who has wished to kill himself does not wish to die. (p. 71)

Menninger has stressed that we must distinguish between the conscious wish to die (or wish not to die) and the unconscious wish to die (or the unconscious wish not to die). One must look at all four possible vectors. The unconscious wish not to die—the absence of the wish to die—is frequently exhibited in individuals who utilize faulty methods in their attempt or attempts. They may attempt to kill themselves, but unconsciously they do not wish to die. For example, Menninger (1938) offers the following case, among many others, from a newspaper:

> Mr. Q.R.S. of Los Angeles, first tried "to hang himself from a chandelier. The chandelier came down. He cut his throat and still lived. He slashed his wrists and still lived. He opened veins at his elbows. When two detectives and a doctor came he was pronounced dead. Then Q.R.S. jumped out of bed, began fighting all three.
>
> *Time*, Nov. 17, 1930.

The wish to die is, however, exceedingly widespread, even in those who state they do not wish to die while others "marshal almost unanswerable arguments for the desirability of dying." This latter group argues, with passionate eloquence and with flawless logic (from their perspective) that life is hard, bitter, futile, and hopeless; that it entails more pain than pleasure; that there is for them no profit or purpose in it and no conceivable justification for living on. One patient of Menninger's stated this as: "Do not ask me why I should like to die. In a more energetic mood I would defy you to tell me why I should live, but now I only wonder, and even wonder is difficult when one has a preconceived conviction in favor of death."

The death instinct, according to Menninger, is more evident in daredevils, mountain climbers, and others who expose themselves to unnecessary danger than in most other people. However, it is in the suicide where one sees a conscious and unconscious wish to die. The suicide is accomplished due to some relative weakness in the capacity for developing constructive tendencies (e.g., attachment, love). Love usually converts destructive tendencies into measures of self-defense and useful adjustment. "Love against hate"; but, in suicide, it is hate against love.

The suicide may communicate one of the following: flight from pain, incurable disease, the threat of helpless senility, a violent death at the gallows. It may be a flight from anticipated rejection or result from fear of becoming dependent. Or it may be a flight from self-depreciation, feelings of sexual or general inadequacy, humiliation, unknown danger. *However,* the suicide is not caused *only* by such a single thing; *other* motives (elements, wishes) appear to be evident. According to Menninger (1938), there appear in suicide the following elements:

> 1. impulses derived from the primary aggressiveness crystalyzed as a wish to kill,
> 2. impulses derived from modification of the primitive aggressiveness, the conscience, crystalyzed as the wish to be killed, and
> 3. I believe there is evidence that some of the original self-directed aggressiveness, the wish to die, join hands with the more sophisticated motives and all to the total vectorial force which impels the precipitate self-destruction. (p. 82)

Protocol Sentences

The following 10 protocol sentences were derived from Menninger's formulations regarding suicide:

In the suicide note:

1. The following three elements (or wishes) are evident: the element of dying, the element of killing, and the element of being killed.
2. The communications indicate that the wish to kill, which is unexpectedly robbed of external opportunities (possibly unconscious), is turned back upon oneself and carried into effect as suicide, corresponding to 3 facts: if there are 1) destructive tendencies toward oneself; 2) high ambivalence in attachment to people; 3) sudden interruption in these attachments.
3. The person, meeting with reverses, irritations, or disappointments with a beloved person too great for him to absorb or to deal with rationally, vents hostilities (hate, rage, revenge) in bitter reproaches and attacks toward that person.
4. There is evidence for a wish to kill (arising from primitive destructiveness) invested with weak neutralization in one or several people whose sudden removal or faithlessness dislodges the attachment, defuses the element of emotional bond, and allows the murderous impulse, now freed, to be turned toward the wisher himself as a substitute person, thus accomplishing what might be called a displaced murder.
5. The communications indicate that the person's conscience (defined as an internal, psychological representation of authority, originally and mainly parental authority but fused in later life with prevalent ethical, religious, and social standards) demands an extreme submission—a wish to suffer and to submit to pain and even death.
6. The person strikes an impulsive blow at himself, thereby expressing toward himself the resentment he feels toward something or someone (that had been incorporated into his personality) in his environment and simultaneously exhibits a dramatic submission to punishment.
7. It appears that the individual's attack of a certain nature (such as murderous wishes) upon some person in the environment are directed as an attack of the same sort upon oneself (as punishment).

8. The person points out, with passionate eloquence and with flawless logic (from his perspective) that life is hard, bitter, futile, and hopeless; that it entails more pain than pleasure; that there is no profit or purpose in it for him and no conceivable justification for living on.
9. The communications indicate that the person wishes to die; i.e., the suicide is accomplished due to some relative weakness in the capacity for developing constructive tendencies (e.g., attachment, love).
10. The person communicates flight from one of the following: pain, incurable disease, the threat of helpless senility, a violent death; from anticipated rejection, or fear of becoming dependent; or from self-depreciation, feelings of sexual or general inadequacy, humiliation, unknown danger. *However,* the suicide does not appear to be caused only by such a single thing; other motives (elements, wishes) appear to be evident.

FINDINGS

The protocol sentences that were verified significantly more often within the genuine notes (as compared with the simulated notes) were the following: (9) the person, who wishes to die, exhibits a weakness in constructive tendencies (X^2 (1,N=66) = 6.67, $p < .01$); and (10) although the person communicates a single thing that caused the suicide, other motives appear evident (X^2 (1,N=66) = 5.14, $p < .05$). In the actual notes, the weakness in constructive tendencies (e.g., attachment, love) was evident in those cases previously reported regarding loss and rejection, cited in the discussion on Freud. A few further examples follow. One person wrote: "I have only hurt everyone." Another stated: "I'll always love you with all my heart and soul. It could have been so simple if you had given me the help that you alone knew I needed." The person in the notes frequently stated that he wishes to die. As one individual noted: "I don't want to go but there is nothing else to do." Another person, exemplifying the findings, stated: "You still refuse to have me when you as well as I know that I can't do it by myself, then there's only one thing to do."

Of course, that one thing is to die—to be dead. Here too, one can see the person preoccupied with or focused on a single thing that he believes caused the suicide. As in many notes the single thing was a lost love. In one specific note, the writer to his parents communicated one thing—"a jam"—but even in his own statements he noted that, and hoped that his father drowns in alcohol ("if you ever take a drink I hope you drown yourself with it"). Clearly as in most suicide notes, other motives (elements, wishes, needs) appear evident.

Sentences 8 and 10 were observed at least 22 out of 33 times (i.e., the level of critical verification count). These sentences were the following: arguing that, from his perspective, life is hard, bitter, futile, painful, unjustified and hopeless; and the suicide appears to be motivated by more than what the person manifestly communicates. Thus, sentence 10 appears to be a very significant protocol sentence, being highly predictive of the content of suicide notes and also discriminating between genuine and simulated notes. This suggests that the suicidal person is relatively fixated on one thing that he reports caused the suicide. The "thing" may vary (e.g., pain, incurable disease, the threat of helpless senility, anticipated rejection, fear of becoming dependent, self-depreciation, feelings of sexual or general inadequacy, humiliation, unknown danger). A single "thing," according to the person himself, caused the suicide. Yet, the judges would suggest that the suicidal person is severely constricted and focused on only this one "thing," while they, the judges, verified other motives (elements, wishes) in the notes.

Bibliography

Menninger, K. (1933) Psychoanalytic aspects of suicide. *The International Journal of Psycho-analysis, 14,* 376–390.

Menninger, K. (1938) *Man against himself.* New York: Harcourt, Brace & Co.

Menninger, K. (1945) *The human mind.* New York: Alfred A. Knopf.

Menninger, K. (1963) *The vital balance.* New York: Viking Press.

Menninger, K. (1969) Expressions and punishment. In E. Shneidman (Ed.) *On the nature of suicide.* San Francisco: Jossey-Bass.

Chapter 10

HENRY A. MURRAY

PERSONAL HISTORY

Henry Murray was born on May 13, 1893 in New York City. His early scholastic records, according to Murray himself, were not indicative of special intellectual interests or aptitudes. Nevertheless he entered Harvard and received his B.A. in 1915 in History. Subsequently (1919), he obtained his M.D. from Columbia University—where he received straight A's except for a B in biochemistry—and did a surgical internship at Presbyterian Hospital, New York City. He received a Ph.D. in biochemistry from Cambridge in 1926. From 1926–1927, he undertook embryological research, publishing numerous articles, at The Rockfeller Institute for Medical Research. Two books which were especially influential were Herman Melville's *Moby Dick* and Carl Jung's *Psychological Types.* Two giants of psychoanalysis, Freud and Jung, were important influences on him, especially Jung whom he met in Zurich for the first time in 1926. Murray himself has said that from this explosive experience (of meeting Jung) he emerged "a reborn man." Melville had also a somewhat magical influence on Murray. Murray, in fact, wrote several profound papers on Melville including one on suicide entitled, "Dead to the World: The Passions of Herman Melville."

In 1927, Murray began his academic career at Harvard. Two years later, on the death of Morton Prince, he became director of the Harvard Psychological Clinic. In 1935, Murray and Christiana Morgan published a paper entitled "A Method of Investigating Fantasies," which introduced the *Thematic Apperception Test* (TAT). In 1938, Murray and several of his colleagues published, *Explorations in Personality.* In this work, Murray introduced his personality theory, termed *personology.* Personology is defined as the "study of human beings and the factors that influence their course."

From 1942–1946, Murray served in the Armed Forces as one of the directors of the Office of Strategic Service (OSS). In 1948, he became Professor of Clinical Psychology at Harvard and published *Assessment of Men* and *Personality in Nature, Society, and Culture* (with Clyde Kluckhohn). In 1962, he became Emeritus Professor of Clinical Psychology at Harvard. An edited book, *Endeavors In Psychology* (1981) presents a collection of his writings. In 1979, the Henry A. Murray Research Center for the Study of Lives was established at Radcliffe College. Murray, at this writing, in his nineties, continues his work, notably on Herman Melville.

Theory of Suicide

If one studies the functions of personality, one quickly realizes, according to Murray, that the *actual* effects of these processes are not necessarily functional. Often they do not lead to satisfaction, happiness, and survival but instead to pain and suffering, even to suicide. The suicide is, in fact, a form of "relief for intolerable suffering." Thus, although the suicide does not have *adaptive* (survival) value, it does have *adjustive* value for that individual. The suicide is *functional,* because it abolishes painful tension for the individual; it provides relief from intolerable suffering. The "purpose" of the act is a conscious fact, but—and this is critical—the person "does not recognize the need that prompted the resolution" (Murray, 1981, p. 216). Usually, there are a number of needs related to the act and the individual is generally aware of only those he will acknowledge. Murray (1981) states:

> In any case, the goal, or purpose, towards which he strives is founded on nothing more solid than faith, conscious or unconscious, that its realization will serve to appease the existing tension. Actually the effective goal may be something else. Thus it is often difficult to determine either by questioning or by observation precisely which needs are operating at a given moment. (p. 216)

The needs may include those—to use Murray's terms—of achievement, affiliation, aggression, autonomy, dominance, inviolacy, nurturance, order, sentience, succorance, or a host of others and/or a combination of these needs. The suicidal act is clearly related to unsatisfied or frustrated needs.

In addition to these unsatisfied or frustrated needs, there are intolerable affects present in suicide. Suicide is frequently, according to Murray, an action to interrupt or put an end to these unbearable affects. Stated in another way, Murray stresses that the person may attempt a partial interruption of consciousness or may act to interrupt the whole of consciousness. He may be socially "dead to the world" or actually dead. Therefore, it would appear to be critical to understand these affects and related reactions. In one paper, Murray (1967) provides such a study, by way of an analogous study of the work and life of Herman Melville.

First, in suicide the following emotional states are evident: pitiful forlornness, deprivation, distress, and grief. The expressive prototype of utter destitution of hope is the first cry of the baby at birth and is subsequently evident in other helpless states, where one is deprived and alone. One has no contact, no love in this state. When one is helpless, a gradation of feelings may arise from pitiful forlornness to grief or woe. Grief is especially notable in such a state, defined by Murray as "an accentuation, deepening, and prolongation of deprivation distress." Melville provides a description of such an emotional state in *Redburn,* when the hero leaves home to go to sea. Perhaps his mother, Redburn tells us,

> thought me an erring and willful boy, and perhaps I was; but if I was, it had been a hard-hearted world, and hard times that and made me so . . . cold, bitter cold as December, and bleak as its blasts, seemed the world then to me; there is no misanthrope like a boy disappointed; and such was I, with the warm soul of me flogged out by adversity.

In *Moby Dick* too, we find Ahab in a state of woe—"woe that is madness"—which relates to Murray's second category in suicide, namely *extrapunitiveness* (blaming others), anger, hate, and/or physical aggression. The prototype of this category is the newborn child who when hungry cries in an angry protest or furious complaint about its helplessness. Likewise in suicide, affect, words, and acts of blaming others, anger, hate or physical aggressiveness are evident, and follow, or even accompany, feeling of pitiful forlornness, deprivation, distress, and grief. At such a time, the person is essentially ruled by a grief-rage, a consolidated, all-pervasive tragic state, coupled with dedicated vengeful hatred. A conation (i.e., a persisting effort, intention, volition, act of willing) to attain a specific goal is strikingly present during this grief-rage stage. These conations, perhaps a long series of them, "derive their force from one or more needs." The general motivating factor is the unsatisfied or frustrated needs whereas the conation (in the suicide) directs the vengeful hatred.

Captain Ahab exhibited this grief-rage to an irrational degree as an intense, all-embracing global emotion. The hatred directed the personality of Ahab, for whom all evil was:

> . . . . visibly personified and made practically assailable in Moby Dick. He piled upon the whale's white hump the sum of all the general rage and hate felt by his whole race from Adam down; and then, as if his chest had been a mortar, he burst his hot heart's shell upon it.

Murray, further, illustrates these formulations by noting that Melville's work was a consequence of Melville's own trauma—a rejecting mother and a punishing father. In Ahab, we see the man reacting with fury because the white whale had severed his leg. Melville too, according to Murray, suffered from an "Oedipus complex." Melville was deprived by his mother, and his father, for whom he felt ambivalent (love and hate), was a source of punitive conscience. Similarly, Murray speculates that in suicide too there is evidence for historical painful antecedents; e.g., a rejecting mother, a punishing father, which beset the individual in his current reaction (affect, words, and act).

The third state that is evident in suicide is the following: intrapunitiveness (blaming oneself), remorse, guilt, depression, bad conscience, and need for punishment. This state generally refers to any kind or degree of self-punishment, subsequent to an actual or imagined execution of an act. In Melville's *Mardi*, for example, we find an analogy where the hero murders a warlike old priest to free a captive maiden who, according to the hero, was to be sacrificed to the gods. The hero, who consciously initially believed his own act to be virtuous, later suspecting his real motive, is struck with remorse. The hero is thus pursued by the Furies, personified as the three sons of the old priest. Murray further notes that this allegorical tale is derived from Melville's own oedipal fantasy. Similar analogies are provided in other works of Melville, such as *Pierre* and in the "return of the repressed" in *Moby Dick*. These writings illustrate how, as in suicide, we find all three categories that have been discussed. For instance, Ahab's moody melancholy was a combination of grief (category 1), rage (category 2) and a bad conscience (category 3).

Murray relates, in suicide, the idea of being killed and killing, exemplified, for example, in Melville's *White Jacket:*

> The privilege, inborn and inalienable, that every man has, of dying himself, and inflicting death upon another, was not given to us without a purpose. These are the last resources of an insulted and unendurable existence.

Thus we see how all three categories are related to the ultimate suicide, bringing us to the fourth category, *egression.* In suicide, there is an egression (defined as a person's intended departure from a region of distress, chiefly the aim of terminating, with relief, the pain he has been suffering) and desertion—desertion, for example, from the suicide's closest bonded person.

Conation may result in action; action may be attraction or repulsion. The latter is egression. For example, in Ishmael in *Moby Dick,* we find the hope of terminating homicidal rage and suicidal depression by going on a long whaling journey. These writings, according to Murray, reflect Melville's own departure from his distressing home, when he left his widowed mother on several occasions, and other stresses at school, job, country, and ships. Such egression, as is evident also in suicide as well as in Melville himself, usually involves breaking expected familial or social boundaries, resulting, in the egression, in possible punishment, ostracism, somebody's disapproval and guilt. The prototype of this state is the child who runs away from home. Such desertion of a closely attached person usually calls for excuses—as seeing the priest in *Mardi* as an intended aggresser and the hero himself as innocent in saving the maiden or, as in the malice of Ahab because of the symbolic castration, or as in the mother who was rejecting and affectless to the son. Murray notes that such action is *rushed through conscience;* then, when the deed is done, we see as in Melville, desolation and inconsolable misery. The person thus intends to depart from the region of distress, the pain and suffering. He egresses, being "as good as dead in his affections," which is Murray's final category: a state of affectlessness; e.g., withdrawal, emotional dissociation, everything being seen as meaningless and purposeless, "a death to the world."

In Melville's short story, *Bartleby, the Scrivener,* we find this hollowness, this affectlessness described as a "burnt-out crater." Here a forlorn young man, whose spirit is vacant, is nearly immobile and speechless, only uttering "I would prefer not to" to questions put to him by his employer. And so "it goes until the very end when Bartleby dies with reticence unconquered and his privacy intact." The prototype of this condition is the morose, unresponsive apathy of the institutionalized child, the failing-tothrive child. Likewise, in the suicide, there is an affectlessness—"a dead(ness) to the world." Thus, as in Melville and his writings, we find in the suicide: "piteous forlornness, desolation, grief-rage, fantasies of suicidal homicide, suicidal depression, egression as a substitute for suicide, egression as an intentional social suicide and eventually after several cycles of these grievous dispositions, a burnt-out crater, dead inside as well as outside" (Murray, 1967, p. 25). The final act is exemplified by Murray in a number of Melville's statements reflecting psychological stages of Melville's own course through life:

> "May my annihilation be complete; all or nothing!"
> "I forsee my annihilation."
> "I am on the verge of annihilation but I can't make up my mind to."
> "I accept my annihilation."

Protocol Sentences

The following 10 protocol sentences were derived from Murray's formulations regarding suicide.

In the suicide note:

1. It appears that although the suicide act does not have adaptive (survival) value, the suicide does have adjustive value for the individual. The suicide is functional because it abolishes painful tension for the individual; it provides relief from intolerable suffering.
2. The suicide appears to be related to unsatisfied or frustrated needs, e.g., achievement, affiliation, autonomy, dominance, etc., although it may be difficult to determine precisely which needs are operating at the time the note was written.
3. The following emotional states are evident: pitiful forlornness, deprivation, distress, and/or grief.
4. The following emotional states are evident: extrapunitiveness (blaming others), anger, hate, and/or physical aggression.

5. Affect, words and/or acts of blaming others, anger, hate and/or physical aggressiveness follow, or even accompany, feelings of pitiful forlornness, deprivation, distress and/or grief. The grief-rage stage has become a consolidated, all-pervasive tragic state, coupled with dedicated vengeful hatred that is ruling the personality.
6. A conation, i.e., a persisting effort (intention, volition, act of willing) to attain a specific goal is evident in the individual's communication.
7. There is evidence of historical painful antecedents, e.g., a rejecting mother, a punishing father, which beset the individual in his current reaction (affect, words, and/or act).
8. The following states are evident: intrapunitiveness (blaming oneself), remorse, guilt, depression, bad conscience and need for punishment. This state generally refers to any kind or degree of self-punishment subsequent to actual or imagined execution of an act.
9. There is evidence for egression (defined as a person's intended departure from a region of distress, chiefly with the aim of terminating, with relief of, the pain he has been suffering) and desertion (e.g., from the suicide's closest bonded person).
10. A state of affectlessness (e.g., withdrawal, emotional dissocation, everything being seen as meaningless and purposeless, "a death to the world") is evident.

FINDINGS

The protocol sentence that was verified significantly more often within the genuine notes (as compared with the simulated notes) was the following: (3) the emotional state of pitiful forlornness, deprivation, distress and/or grief is evident (X^2 (1,N-66) = 5.81, $p < .05$). In the actual notes, this emotional state is often evident, as can be seen in the cases previously cited. One person in his suicide note wrote about this state in the words, "I can't find my place in life." Another individual, who communicated in his note that he tried his best, but found himself and his wife in a trauma due to his "poor judgment," noted that he "bit off more than I could chew." The note clearly exemplifies a state of devastating gloom, distress, deprivation, and grief. The man ends his note: "God bless them all and forgive me—Goodbye darling and God bless you all. Your loving husband always."

Sentences 1, 2, 3, and 9 were evident in almost all of the genuine suicide notes—well above the critical cutoff point. These latter sentences were related to the following: The suicide is functional for the person for it abolishes pain and intolerable suffering; the suicide appears to be related to unsatisfied needs; feelings of inconsolable misery, deprivation, distress, and/or grief are evident; and there is evidence for egression. Thus, sentence 3 appears to be a critical common factor in suicide, both as a discriminator and predictor. In suicide, the following emotional states are not only very often evident but discriminate the state of the suicide from one who merely simulates the state: pitiful forlornness, deprivation, distress and/or grief. The person is in a helpless state, there is no contact, no love, etc. Murray has suggested that grief especially may be evident, a deep, prolonged distress related to some deprivation—a lack, a loss, a trauma of some type.

Bibliography

Murray, H.A. (1938) *Explorations in personality.* New York: Oxford University Press.

Murray, H.A. (1967) Death to the World: The passions of Herman Melville. In E. Shneidman (Ed), *Essays in self destruction.* New York: Science House, Inc.

Murray, H.A. (1981) *Endeavors in psychology: Selections from the personology of Henry A. Murray.* E. Shneidman (Ed). New York: Harper & Row.

Chapter 11

EDWIN S. SHNEIDMAN

Personal History

Edwin S. Shneidman was born on May 13, 1918 in York, Pennsylvania. He attended the University of California at Los Angeles (B.A., 1938) and, after World War II, received his Ph.D. in 1948 from the University of Southern California. His dissertation was entitled "A Study of Certain Formal Psychosocial Aspects of Fantasy Productions in Schizophrenia as Revealed by Performance on the Make-a-Picture Story (MAPS) Test"—a test which he developed. In 1951, he followed this work with an edited book, *Thematic Test Analysis.* Early on his work was influenced by Bruno Klopfer. His work has also been especially influenced by the writings of Henry A. Murray and Herman Melville, the latter being a subject of considerable interest. In 1981, he edited a book of Murray's writing entitled, *Endeavors in Psychology: Selections from the Personology of Henry A. Murray.*

From 1947–1950, Shneidman worked at a V.A. Center in Los Angeles as a psychologist and later (1950–1953) as the chief for research. From 1953–1955, beginning his work on suicide, he was codirector at the V.A. Central Research Unit for Study of Unpredicted Deaths. In 1958, along with Norman Farberow, he founded the Suicide Prevention Center in Los Angeles, a model crisis intervention center; he was codirector there until 1966 when he became the first Chief of the Center for the Study of Suicide Prevention at the National Institute of Mental Health in Bethesda, MD, remaining there until 1969. He has been on the faculty as well as a visiting professor at a number of universities, including Harvard, Johns Hopkins, George Washington, and the Ben-Gurion University of Negev, and was a Fellow at the Center for Advanced Study of the Behavioral Sciences at Stanford. In 1970 he joined the faculty at the University of California, Los Angeles, and since 1975 has held the title there of Professor of Thanatology.

He has authored, edited, or coedited over 165 publications and books on suicide, including articles for the *Encyclopedia Britannica* and *The Comprehensive Textbook of Psychiatry*. His edited books include *Clues to Suicide,* 1957 (with N. Farberow); *The Cry for Help,* 1961 (with N. Farberow); *Essays in Self-Destruction,* 1967; *On the Nature of Suicide,* 1969; *Psychology of Suicide* (with N. Farberow & R. Litman), 1970; *Death and the College Student,* 1972; *Death: Current Perspectives,* 1976; *Suicidology: Contemporary Development,* 1976; and *Suicide Thoughts and Reflections,* 1981. He is the author of *Deaths of Man* (1973), nominated for a National Book Award, *Voices of Death* (1980), and *Definition of Suicide* (1985).

He is the founder and past president of the American Association of Suicidology, (A.A.S.) which he established in 1968. He is the founding editor of two journals on suicide, the former *Bulletin of Suicidology* and *Suicide and Life-Threatening Behavior.* He has been president of the Clinical and Public Service Divisions of the American Psychological Association. In 1988 he is active at UCLA.

Theory of Suicide

Shneidman (1985) begins his formulations regarding suicide with the question, What are the interesting common psychological dimensions of committed suicide?—*not* what *kind* of people commit suicide (cf. Zilboorg). This question, according to Shneidman, is critical; for they (the common dimensions) are what suicide is. Not necessarily the universal, but certainly the most frequent or common characteristics provide us with a meaningful conceptualization regarding suicide. (According to Shneidman, there are no universals in suicide.) We will outline these formulations in this chapter and illustrate them with selected excerpts from two cases, two women in their twenties: one who fortunately survived a suicide attempt, jumping from a fifth-floor balcony (Case 1); the other, who had survived an attempt at immolating herself, dying 3 years later of congestive heart failure while hospitalized for acute tonsillitis (Case 2).

Most frequently, nonprofessionals identify external causes (e.g., ill health, being left by a lover, losing one's fortune, etc.) as what is common in suicide. A *recent downhill course* (e.g., drop in income, sudden acute alcoholism, a change in work, and divorce or separation) can, indeed, be identified in suicide. However, although there are always situational aspects in every suicidal act, these are only the precipitating events, whereas *the* common stimulus in suicide is *unendurable psychological pain.* Shneidman (1985) stated:

> Pain is what the suicidal person is seeking to escape. In any close analysis, suicide is best understood as a combined movement toward cessation of consciousness and as a movement away from intolerable emotion, the wish or need to effect a cessation of consciousness because of the pain. No one commits suicide out of joy; no suicide is born out of exultation. The enemy of life is pain. It is psychological pain of which we are speaking; mental pain; the pain of feeling pain. (p. 124)

The person, just before his suicidal act, is in a state of high and dangerous lethality. He is in an acute crisis that is experienced as intolerable pain, unendurable hurt, unacceptable anguish. Shneidman notes that the suicide betokens a genuine crisis and reflects considerable inner psychological disturbance. It is the pain of feeling pain. The person, at least inwardly, and usually outwardly, is in a state of heightened perturbation; he is disturbed, anxious, perhaps depressed or agitated. The person is focused almost entirely on his unbearable emotion, and especially one specific (and arbitrarily selected) way to escape from it. It is not pain itself precisely, but rather, *the desire to stop the pain.* For the individual, feelings, things, etc., are getting out of control; he is experiencing a reverberating crisis with its *own autonomy.* Life is not going well in terms of felt pressures (physical health, rejection, inner feeling of failure) and the person is not handling those pressures and pain. His abilities are not the best; thus, he makes a judgment—this far and no further. The pain is felt to be above a threshold that is tolerable to that individual and he becomes focused on the one way to escape from it.

The fear in suicide is of something far worse in life. The fear is of more pain, more degradation, more tension, more shame, more guilt, more terror, more hopelessness. The fear is that the trauma, the crisis, is bottomless—an *eternal* suffering.

Case I .... and I was not functioning at all and these people are going to throw me into the street. And I didn't want to go to a psychiatric ward because I was really frightened that I would wind up—that I would possibly have a psychiatric episode or something like that.

Case II I was just feeling very bad and sad for myself and very sorry for myself. It was like the straw that broke the camel's back. I sort of had had enough piled up on me that I really couldn't handle it.

In suicide, the person's psychological needs are frustrated, exemplified in the trauma itself (e.g., poor health, rejection by the spouse, being married to an indifferent or competing spouse). In the face of such a trauma, the suicide is not felt as an unreasonable act. The suicide is *logical;* it is committed because of thwarted or unfulfilled needs; needs that parallel general human needs—health, acceptance, love, etc.,—needs that became frustrated in the trauma.

Case II Well, then. . . . things weren't going well for me; job, social life, personal life, and there was some precipitating facts .... (she next discusses a deteriorative relationship with a friend and unsatisfactory relationship with her own mother).

It is obvious that there are conative aspects to suicide. Suicide is an "intentional" act of self-destruction. Some *willing*, some formed purpose, some conceptualized goal, some striving in relation to some trauma is evident in suicide. A frequent purpose of suicide is to seek a solution to the conflict. The solution permits one to resolve the unbearable state of disturbance and isolation. The idea of cessation (death, stopping, or eternal cessation) provides the solution for this desperate person. Shneidman (1985) stated: "Suicide is not a random act. It is never done pointlessly or without purpose. It is a way out of a problem, dilemma, bind, challenge, difficulty, crisis, or unbearable solution" (p. 129).

Suicide has its own logic and impetus. It is an answer to the question, How to get out of this? The answer, however, appears in a special state of mind, a state of relatively fixed purpose and of relative constriction of the mind. In the face of shame, loss of face, disgrace, dereliction of duty, or something that is unique for that individual, a possible solution becomes *the* solution. The suicide has its purpose—the seeking of a solution to some perceived problem. The person, believing he is failing and not wishing to accommodate to a new (less effective) image of himself, does not wish to let "it" happen to him. He wants to play a *role* in its occurrence—he has his solution.

> Case II . . . . I was hurting very badly inside and it just, just was an overwhelming desire, I guess, to die. And I know I debated about death, I'm sure, around two to three months, if I recall. I had planned and planned and planned . . . what was going through my mind is that I would burn myself.

The common goal of suicide is cessation of consciousness. Shneidman (1985) stated:

> In a curious and paradoxical way, suicide is both a moving toward and a moving away from something; the something that it is moving toward, the common practical goal of suicide, is the stopping of the painful flow of consciousness. (p. 129)

Before his act, the person usually verbalizes, or expresses in some other fashion, his wish for ending all conscious experience, and behaves, with the act itself, to achieve this end. His behavior is *intentional;* the individual plays a direct, conscious role in his own death. The idea of cessation—the idea of death, of being dead, eternal nothingness, being out of it, stopping the pain—is the spark that ignites the explosive mixture of heightened inimicality—perturbation—constriction. The complete stopping of consciousness is seen by the individual as "a solution, indeed, the perfect solution" to his painful trauma.

> Case I I was so desperate, I felt, My God, I can't face this thing, going out, and being thrown out in the street. And everything was like a terrible sort of whirlpool of confusion. And I thought to myself—there's *only* one thing I can do, I just have to lose consciousness. That's the *only* way to get away from it. The *only* way to lose consciousness, I thought, was to jump off something good and high.

In suicide, there are many emotions: hostility, despair, shame, guilt, dependency, hopelessness, ennui. The person is in a state of heightened disturbance; e.g., he feels acutely boxed in, rejected, harassed, unsuccessful, hopeless, and helpless. Indeed, the common emotion in suicide is hopelessness—helplessness, not aggression turned inward, as stated by Stekel in 1910. "Although aggression is evident in suicide, other deep basic emotions are equally evident. But, underlying all of these," asserted Shneidman (1985), "is that emotion of impotence, the feeling of hopelessness—helplessness." The person feels helpless and confused emotionally and feels pessimistic about any possibility of making meaningful interpersonal relations. The person states, "There is nothing that I can do," and "There is no one who can help me," and, when talking to someone (spouse, friend, therapist), "Not even you."

> Case II I seemed to be able to get out of depression off and on but I really didn't feel any happiness or any good feelings about myself.

The internal state, conflict, and attitude toward suicide is frequently ambivalence, according to Shneidman. Freud was the first to recognize that something could be psychologically both A and non-A. We can both hate and love, like or dislike the same person. Ambivalence, e.g., complications, concomitant contradictory feelings, attitudes, and thrusts, for example, towards the same person, is common in suicide. One can frequently see the simultaneous presence of both love and hate as well as other emotions. However, it may not only be ambivalence towards someone, but may also be conflict between survival and unbearable pain. Indeed, ambivalence may even be evident in the simultaneous yearning for rescue-and-intervention at the very moment of killing oneself.

> Case II I have to discuss more the way my father died and how I was involved in it. I saw a psychiatrist and it all came out that I really did love my father. I really thought I hated him. I was very upset with him but he was dead and it came out, I really do think I loved him.
>
> My roomate and I were living together and I left this note saying, Don't look for me, come into the bedroom later on in the evening and there will be a surprise for you. And I remember that she came into the bedroom, obviously because she was enticed to do so and of course, I wasn't dead, I was only very ill . . . (here, the woman discusses an earlier suicide attempt with pills).

Reason is as much a part of suicide as emotion, according to Shneidman. The reason is, however, "not logical," i.e., the person's reasoning is not as logical as the logic of a person who does not kill himself or who merely speculates about being suicidal. The person is not only relatively "intoxicated" by his overpowering emotions but also by his constricted reasoning and perception. Indeed, the common cognitive state in suicide is constriction. Synonymous with constriction of intellectual focus is tunnel vision, a narrowing of the mind's eye. There is a narrowing of the range of perception and of options that occur to the suicidal mind. There is a penchant for dichotomous thinking. The range of choices is narrowed only to *two*—an "either/or" thinking. Everything is divided into two (and only two) parts; it might be good/bad, or love/hate, or a desired life/a necessary death. This is, as Shneidman (1985) noted, not very much of a range. In suicide, we find the person abandoning life's continuum, instead using words like "always," "either/or," "never," "forever," and especially "only" in his verbalizations or personal documents. Examples: "He will always hate me," "Either I'll kill my brother or myself," "I will never be happy," "It will be forever," "It was the only answer." "He was the only one for me." "That's the only way to get away from it." "It is the only thing I can do."

The person plainly lacks clear insight and useful communication; his state of mind is incompatible with discerning recitation of what is going on. Indeed, the constriction is one of the most dangerous aspects of the suicidal state. As Shneidman (1985) has noted:

> Adjustment lies in the fundamental abilities to make subtle discriminations and distinctions, to wink at disparities, to sense what is appropriate to the moment, and on occasion to do what one thinks is right rather than to act on one's principles. . . . (p. 140)

There is no single suicidal logic; nevertheless, the reasoning is full of errors, notably semantic errors; e.g., "If anybody kills himself then he will get attention. I will kill myself. Therefore I will then get attention." Yet, to the individual, this logic seems reasonable. It may even be formally logical, but the person starts off in a disastrous direction. As in the above example, the fallacy is concealed in the concept "I;" specifically, the person confuses the self as it is experienced by himself and the self as he feels himself thought of or experienced by others. After suicide, there will not *be* "I" to get attention. He confuses the "I" and the "me."

Shneidman has further isolated a number of other fallacies that may occur in some suicides; for example, the suicide wants to effect his own termination and cessation but wishes to continue to exist in some manner or other. The person does not understand death. Sometimes, the person confuses the real world—our *only* world—with a possible hereafter. The person's cultural or religious beliefs, especially about the hereafter, thus permit him to view suicide not as death, but as a transition to another life. Suicide is a focused, narrowed, desperate, violent act of stopping unbearable pain, the pain of this world.

> Case I I just walked around until I found this open staircase. As soon as I saw it, I just made a beeline right up it. And then I got to the fifth floor and everything just got very dark all of a sudden, and all I could see was this balcony. Everything around it just blacked out. It was just a circle. That was all I could see, just the balcony . . . and I went over it.
>
> Case II This was all I could take. It was just enough. There was no more that I wanted to hear. There was no more that I wanted to see. There was no more that I wanted to live and I knew that my only way out was death. And at this time I made the decision, that evening about six o'clock. I was making these decisions and I don't remember things going through my mind or even thinking of my sadness or the things that were breaking my heart. It was kind of like the end of things that I was thinking about, that I would be no more. It was going to be good, it was going to be something that was going to fulfill me. I was going to be strong and able to perform something.

Suicide is often a dyadic event between two people, two unhappy people. The suicide is a two-person event (e.g., spouse, parent and child, lover and lover). Frequently, a calamitous relationship has prevailed; e.g., rejecting father, hostile mother, spiteful aunt, exploiting lover, unloving husband, unresponsive friend, disapproving employer, or some other relationship. The other—the significant other—plays a crucial role in dooming the suicide to his outcome; e.g., the suicide sees his spouse as hostile, belittling, disloyal, and nonsupportive. Very frequently, an element in the self-destruction is the sense of total rejection in a personality that already depreciates itself. The withdrawal, rejection, etc., plunges the individual into even deeper despair and pain; i.e., the pain in the dyadic trauma becomes intolerable.

Case I There was some question about my husband letting me return home. And everything was just all up in the air—it was sort of like, well, you go and find a place to stay, and there was no place for me to stay. I don't know anyone here. All of a sudden there I was in the middle of nowhere without any money, and my husband wasn't going to let me come back to the house and I was desperate.

Case II I think that I should mention that my father died. He was accidently shot in the chest when I was sixteen and I found him. He died instantly, from what we understand from the coroner's report, and it was proven that it was not suicide. However, he had threatened suicide and he had talked about it with my aunt, his sister, and with my mother, and we were all quite aware of it, so my mother was quite sure that he had committed suicide. Well, my aunt who lives very close, my father's sister, she came down and was with us at that time. She stood there and told me that I had killed my father, that he had committed suicide because of me.

Others also, as can be noted in the other formulations in this book, have highlighted the common relational aspect of suicide, but Shneidman (1985) has further noted that "what we have not looked at so carefully are the common relational aspects of suicide other than specific psychodynamic or emotional states" (p. 143). Shneidman (1985) has presented two such common aspects. First, the common interpersonal act in suicide is *communication of intention*. Second, the common action in suicide is *egression,* leaving the scene.

With regard to the first, approximately eight out of ten people who kill themselves give clues; they emit signals. Shneidman (1985) stated:

> Individuals intent on committing suicide, albeit ambivalently minded about it, consciously or unconsciously, emit signals of distress, indications of helplessness, pleas for response, and opportunities for rescue in the usually dyadic interplay. (p. 144)

Communication of intention is the most common interpersonal factor, not rage or destruction. The suicide note itself is one such example. The communication may be a cry, but not always. The communication may be for help, for autonomy, or for any number of needs. Thus suicide may not only be a cry for help.

> Case II Well, on the day I don't recall . . . I had collected the things that were meaningful to me. . . . I had an electric toaster that I had to return to some friends' house which was a few blocks away . . . I remember just walking in and walking through the house and by this time I was sobbing again and not one word was said to me by these people. I think there were around four people in the house. And I just walked through the house and put the toaster in the kitchen table and walked right out. Nobody touched my arm, nobody said what's wrong, nobody even gestured, and I think it upset me even more that this was sort of the end. Nobody really reached out for me in any way and I think at that time I really must have been reaching out. I must have been saying, You know I am really upset. I am really having problems. But at that moment nobody responded.

The second relational aspect not usually examined is egression. Egression means to leave, exit or escape. One egresses by running away from home, quitting a job, deserting an army, leaving a family—and killing oneself. The suicide, according to Shneidman, needs or wishes to egress. He wants to leave (the scene), to exit, to get out, to get away, to be gone, not to be around, to be "elsewhere" . . . not to be. But, as Shneidman has frequently noted, suicide is a *radical* egression. It is a *permanent* change of scene. It is irreversibly *not to be.*

> Case II I had no interruptions. There was nobody to hold me back in any way, that I would change my mind that this is what I had to do. . . .

When one looks at only the external cause, one forgets that the individual has a history. The suicide has a history. The common consistency in suicide is with *lifelong coping patterns.* Shneidman (1985) stated:

> In suicide, we are initially thrown off the scent because suicide is an act which, by definition, that individual has never done before—so there is no precedent. And yet there are deep consistencies with lifelong coping patterns. We must look to previous episodes of disturbance, to capacity to endure psychological pain, or to be penchant for constriction and dichotomous thinking, for earlier paradigms of egression. (p. 148)

People show enormous *consistency with themselves,* a steadiness over time, and adherence to certain internal principles of behavior. So do suicides. They show patterns of behavior that diminish and truncate life; patterns that in fact, subtract from life's length or reduce its scope. The very life-style demeans his life; he lives an inimical life and, at times, he may exhibit long-term instability (e.g., psychiatric hospitalization, alcoholism, multiple divorces). Frequently, trauma or stress may have been evident in early life, such as death of a parent, separation or divorce of parents, lack of familial support, stress (either overt and subtle) between the parents, or rejection by either parent. Such trauma may not only occur in childhood but also during adolescence and later life.

The common consistency in suicide is the life-long coping patterns to the trauma or stress: indeed, an inimical repetitive life-style of purposes, goals, stimuli, stresses, emotions, internal attitudes, cognitive states, interpersonal aspects, and actions. We may not *see* the consistency, only the precipitating event. Likewise, the suicide himself will likely not see the consistency, only the trauma. Yet, the consistencies exist. Furthermore, the person's behavior, communications, etc., have not only conscious implications; but unconscious psychodynamic implications—which we must address if we are to answer the question, What is common in suicide?—are also clearly evident.

> Case II (The woman discusses a consistency of lifelong coping patterns; here is one example among many:) I considered him my boyfriend and somebody that I thought I cared a whole lot about and worried a whole lot about and wanted him to love me ever so badly, but he didn't. He was twenty-six years old at the time. I was nineteen. He was going to school full-time along with working a full-time job. And he more or less played me for laughs, had used me, had taken advantage of me sexually and otherwise. I thought I had been good to him and I had given him all, all my feelings, all my hopes, all my desires, all my dreams and yet he sort of laughed at it. He sort of took advantage of it and walked away, like, well, that's how it is, sweetie, that's how life is. Some people are takers and some people are givers and you're a giver and I'm a taker. At that time I didn't really know how to cope with it.

Protocol Sentences

The following 10 protocol sentences were derived from Shneidman's formulations regarding suicide.

In the suicide note:

1. The person is focused almost entirely on an unbearable emotion (pain), and especially, one specific (an arbitrarily selected) way to escape from it.
2. The person communicates evidence of adult trauma (e.g., poor health, rejection by the spouse, being married to a competing spouse).

3. The person communicates that the idea of cessation (death, stopping, or eternal sleep) provides the solution for a desperate person. It permits him to resolve the unbearable state of self-destructiveness, disturbance, and isolation.
4. The person verbalizes his wish for an ending to all conscious experience and behaves in order to achieve this end.
5. The person is in a state of heightened disturbance (perturbation), e.g., he feels boxed in, rejected, harassed, unsuccessful, and especially hopeless and helpless.
6. The person communicates ambivalence; e.g., complications, concomitant contradictory feelings, attitudes, and/or thrusts.
7. The person appears to be figuratively intoxicated or drugged by his overpowering emotions and constricted logic and perception.
8. The person communicates the need or wish to "egress," that is, to leave (the scene), to exit, to get out, to get away, to be gone, not to be around, to be "elsewhere" . . . not to be.
9. The person communicates patterns of behavior which diminish or truncate the individual's life, which subtract from its length or reduce its scope.
10. In the suicide note, the person's communications appear to have unconscious psychodynamic implications.

FINDINGS

The protocol sentence that was verified significantly more often within the simulated notes (as compared with the genuine notes) was the following: (1) the person communicating the need or wish to "egress" (X^2 (1, N=66) = 8.76, p < .01). Whereas, the protocol sentences that were verified significantly more often within the genuine notes (as compared with the simulated notes) were the following: (2) the reported experience of adult trauma (X^2 (1, N=66) = 5.32, p < .05); (6) the reported feelings, attitudes and/or thrusts of ambivalence (X^2 (1, N=66) 7.34, p <

.01); (7) the suicidal person appearing to be relatively intoxicated by his overpowering emotions and constricted logic and perception (X^2 (1, N=66) = 7.85, $p < .01$); and (10) the person's communications appearing to have unconscious psychodynamic implications (X^2 (1, N=66 = 6.27, $p < .01$).

Shneidman (1980) and others (e.g., Freud) have indicated that the most frequent trauma in a suicide is a loss in a dyadic relationship (e.g., husband-wife, parent-child). A calamitous relationship is frequently cited in suicide notes, one that led to a deep frustration of needs. The person finds himself, as noted previously, in a deep state of despair; one person, in response to such an interpersonal trauma, wrote; "This is the last note I shall ever write. No one should feel bad about my going as I am not worth it. I don't want to go but there is nothing else to do."

Compared to loss in a dyadic relationship, other adult trauma, such as poor health or chronic illness, are much less frequently cited but evident in some of the notes. For example, one person stated; "This is to say good-bye; I have not told you because I did not want you to worry, but I have been feeling bad for two years, with my heart." Job loss, social disgrace, and alcoholism are also cited.

People in suicide notes express many emotions, including the simultaneous presence of conflicting emotions, such as love and hate. As noted previously in the chapter on Freud, the person in his note appears to be ambivalent. For example, in one note the writer stated: "I'm sorry, honey, but please believe me, this is the only way out for me as long as you feel as you do."

Our findings also suggest that not only is the person overpowered by his emotions, he also appears to be drugged by constricted logic and perception. His reasoning is less logical than that of a nonsuicidal individual who merely simulates the state of being suicidal. This intoxication is conveyed in the actual notes as "I am taking the only way out." In another note, the person writes "Mary, darling. It's all my fault. I've thought this over a million times and this seems to be the only way I can settle all the trouble I've caused you and others. This is only a sample of how sorry I am." Finally, the judges noted the presence of unconscious dynamics in this person's writing; an observation that can be made quite frequently in suicide notes; but what these latent meanings might be directly related to in the manifest content is difficult to show concretely. It refers to what is written *and more.*

Sentences 2, 5, and 6 were perceived to occur at least ⅔ of the time (i.e., the critical frequency). These latter common sentences were the following: evidence of adult trauma; feeling boxed in, harassed, unsuccessful, and especially hopeless and helpless; and the person communicating ambivalence. It should be noted that the protocol sentence regarding the suicide appearing to be related to unsatisfied needs in Murray's formulations is equally applicable to Shneidman's. Of course, similar statements could be made about some other theorists—this is where the suicidologists agree. Indeed, this is a weakness of the protocol method—the theory is *not* just the 10 sentences.

Interestingly, sentences 2 and 6 are thus not only good discriminators but also sound predictors of suicide. Adult trauma (e.g., poor health, rejection by the spouse, being married to a critical and nonsupportive spouse) appears to be an ominous common clue to suicide. This echoes a similar observation made by Menninger and clearly supports the notion that the suicide is related to a situation that somehow—unlike for most other people—was too much to bear; too many needs were frustrated. The trauma resulted in unbearable pain for that person. The practical implication is important: The way to save a would-be suicide is to reduce the felt pain. In addition, the current findings suggest that an additional common critical factor in suicide is ambivalence, the simultaneous presence of A and not-A. It may be a *feeling* of ambivalence, it may be *attitudes* that are ambivalent. It may be ambivalent thrusts. Frequently, such concomitant contradictory feelings, attitudes, and/or thrusts are toward a person; but it may be a conflict between survival and unbearable pain or a yearning for rescue while about to kill oneself or seeing hope when one is dead.

BIBLIOGRAPHY

Shneidman, E. (1967). Sleep and self-destruction: A phenomenological approach. In E. Shneidman (Ed.), *Essays in self-destruction.* New York: Science House.

Shneidman, E. (1973). Suicide. *Encyclopedia Britannica.* Chicago: William Benton.

Shneidman, E. (1980). *Voices of death.* New York: Harper & Row.

Shneidman, E. (1981). *Suicide thoughts and reflections: 1960–1980.* New York: Human Sciences Press.

Shneidman, E. (1982). The suicidal logic of Cesare Pavese. *Journal of the American Academy of Psychoanalysis, 10,* 547–563.

Shneidman, E. (1985). *Definition of suicide.* New York: John Wiley & Sons.

Shneidman, E. (1987). A psychological approach to suicide. In G. Vanden Bos & B. Bryant (Eds.), *Cataclysms, crisis, and catastrophes: Psychology in action.* Washington, D.C.: American Psychological Association.

Chapter 12

HARRY STACK SULLIVAN

Personal History

Harry Stack Sullivan was born on February 21, 1892 in Norwick, New York to a family of Irish ancestry. He was the only child in the Sullivan family (although others had died in infancy), resulting in isolated early years. Childhood and adolescence were traumatic. His companions were horses, which Sullivan later adopted as his personal symbol. In 1908, he attended Cornell at Ithaca, New York to study physics, but in his second term he left for personal reasons. A few years later (1909), he entered the Chicago College of Medicine and Surgery and graduated in 1917 (although his actual studies were completed in 1915). After his graduation, he worked for the National Guard and several insurance companies. He joined the Medical Corps during World War I and, after the war, continued to work with veterans, developing procedures for assisting disabled soldiers who were suffering from neuropsychiatric conditions. In 1922–1923 he worked for the Veterans Administration at Saint Elizabeth's—his first education and experience in psychiatry—where he met William Alanson White. With White's support, Sullivan undertook some of his classical work with schizophrenics. In 1923, Sullivan went to work, under Ross McC. Chapman, at Sheppard-Pratt Hospital at Towson, Maryland. Key influential people, by this time, as well as later in Sullivan's career, were Alexander, Ferenczi, Hedley, Horney, Meyer, and Thompson (his first analyst).

In 1924, Sullivan published his first papers on schizophrenia in the *American Journal of Psychiatry*, entitled "The Oral Complex" and "Schizophrenia, Its Constructive and Malignant Features." Subsequently, these and other papers were published under the title, *Schizophrenia as a Human Process* (1962). In 1925, he became research director at Sheppard-Pratt; established a model project in a six-bed ward to treat young male schizophrenics; and became a professor of psychiatry at the University of Maryland. By this time, he also developed his active social interests, focusing on physicians' misconceptions of psychiatric principles, as well as writing, with H. Lasswell, the political scientist, on the relation of psychiatry to the social sciences. In 1930, he set up practice in New York, developing his views in a number of papers on the interpersonal theory of psychiatry, which were never intended for publication, but were subsequently published under the title, *Personal Psychopathology* (1972). He founded a journal in 1938, *Psychiatry*, which he utilized to publish papers on his views. In 1938 he began his active social concerns on the international scene, espousing his increasingly non-Freudian perspective (which had become more apparent in the 1930s). In 1940, Sullivan returned to government service, working on procedures for psychiatric screening and examination. In 1946 he aided in the establishment in New York of the William Alanson White Institute of Psychiatry, Psychoanalysis and Psychology in New York. Here he continued to present papers on his point of view, including work on his interpersonal perspective of suicide.

Sullivan struggled with emotional problems and interpersonal difficulties (e.g., homosexuality, alcoholism) throughout his life. In early January 1949 he went to Europe to attend a meeting of the World Federation of Mental Health in the hope of achieving international acceptance of his interpersonal views. Frustration of this wish brought him considerable discouragement. He travelled to Paris, where on January 14, 1949 he died alone in his hotel room.

Theory of Suicide

Sullivan notes that it is quite common to contemplate suicide. It is not unusual to follow a train of reverie in which one destroys oneself, although he further notes that in some it would indeed be strange. The goal of such thoughts, he adds, is not self-destruction; but one usually drifts from the worthlessness of life to thoughts of the world after one's death, and then drops the daydreaming. According to Sullivan, the fit of musing is functional. It is likely a discharge of the suicidal impulses to a constructive end; the reverie of *most* people serves not to destroy the self but, on the contrary, to prevent the hostile-destructive act. In others, it may lead to a much less destructive end than death, but in a few it may lead to an unsuccessful attempt, and in even fewer, self-destruction. In all, the reverie is the exteriorization of a derogatory and hostile attitude, which is assumed to have been acquired in infancy and childhood—particularly childhood—which the individual continues to entertain, resulting in a focusing effect on the individual's self and manifested towards other people.

Whereas for most, when one calculates the outcome of the act during the fit of musing, one concludes that the self-destruction would not achieve the desired effect, in a few the self-destruction is seen as achieving it. Their derogation and hostile attitude, which is directed towards the outer world, is thus directed with full force towards the self. However, if one looks carefully at the act, the suicide is "hatefully conceived and executed," namely "destroying oneself in order to strike at some other person" (Sullivan 1940, Vol. 1, p. 25). Although this may not be evident to the individual directly, there is evidence that a particular, significant other person(s), who was a destructive influence in the individual's past, is the target of the self-destruction. Self-destruction may not have been the only goal of the individual. The individual may well have calculated that the act would have a prolonged evil effect on an other person(s).

The suicide inflicts an unhealing wound on the enemy although the suicide himself may be unaware of this process and this target. He is likely, in fact, not to agree with any of these formulations. Yet Sullivan (1956) notes "all my observations indicate quite conclusively that the depressive always hits the target and does this, unhappily by self-destruction" (Vol. 2, p. 298). The intent is, as noted above, that the target shall suffer the rest of his life, by destroying oneself. Such an end or conclusion to the reverie is clearly related to a so-called poverty of thought. The individual expresses only permutations and combinations of grief-provoking thought and, unlike most others, he does not get very far away from it.

In the suicide, we have "instance of a part of personality working in dissociation, but working very powerfully, more powerfully than all the motives that one channelled through the self" (Sullivan, 1940, Vol. 1, p. 28). The dissociation part, according to Sullivan, of such individuals, is the experience of human warmth and friendliness, resulting in this critical group of processes not preventing the suicide. Typically, it is one's warm relations that stop destruction and any form of psychiatric disturbance. It stops the "reverie" in most of us. But, in the suicide, the person's field of interpersonal relations is very disturbed. The person, in addition, is under the considerable stress of a situational factor, which *changes* a relatively *unvarying* disturbance in such interpersonal relations to one that is relatively persisting to a traumatic degree. The suicide thus is determined by the present interpersonal situation and his own history. Sullivan (1940) stated:

> The disturbance are ways of meeting the necessities of life as they are determined by one's history and the present interpersonal situation. The past conditions the particular events which precipitated the episode of mental disorder and, with the foresight of the patient, which is itself a function of the past determines the type of disorder in interpersonal relations. (p. 174)

The limited anticipatory foresight of the suicide closes all the possibilities. He is closed to the possibilities for further development of the personality and movements towards mental health. Only a positive development in the disturbed relations was held as the possible way to go on living, but such development was seen as not forthcoming by the suicide himself. The person is separated from life; the suicide ends all. Unlike most of us, his daydreaming of self-destruction leads to destruction, not construction.

Sullivan, regrettably, provides no individual case illustrations of suicide; rather, he provides differential diagnosis, general classification, and descriptions of people who commit suicide. Consistent with the general trend in his writings are the following:

(a) Diagnosis of the "down phase" of a manic-depressive disorder. Critical symptoms include, for example, a sort of all-embracing (grandiose) negative self-appraisal—he is no good, has never been any good, and has caused everyone else a great deal of trouble, which can only be ended by destroying oneself.

(b) Diagnosis of schizophrenia. Critical symptoms include, for example, that the schizophrenic ends his life quite incidentally to some fantastic procedure for the remedy of his distress: to be reborn, to protect others from some delusional contamination, to save the world, to demonstrate omnipotence and the like.

(c) Diagnosis of obsessive-compulsive disorder. Critical symptoms include, for example, exhibiting obsessional characteristics, such as overwhelming suicidal thoughts with unlimited attention to the detail of such an act.

(d) Diagnosis of psychopathic disorder. Critical symptoms include, for example, utilizing the suicide as a tool for ensuring attention of others, but the act itself was likely an accidental misjudgment—too great a dose of poison, too long a delay in calling for help, and so forth.

(e) Diagnosis of depressive disorder. Critical symptoms include, for example, exhibiting a "reverie" of self-depreciating statements and appearing to be very restrictive in thoughts and actions.

(f) Diagnosis of no serious specific disorder, but the act appears to be undertaken by an individual who is so baffled in his attempt to subjugate his interests, that a paralysis of interest in others and in future possibilities of self has progressed to the point that life has become colorless and completely wholly unattractive.

Protocol Sentences

The following 10 protocol sentences were developed from Sullivan's formulations regarding suicide:

In the suicide note:

1. The communication allows one to conclude that the suicide appeared to be determined by the individual's history and the present interpersonal situation.
2. The person appears to be under the stress of a situational factor which changes a relatively unvarying disturbance in interpersonal relations to one that is relatively persisting to a traumatic degree.
3. The person appears to close the possibilities for further development of the personality and movements towards mental health.
4. There is a poverty of thought exhibited by the individual expressing only permutations and combinations of grief-provoking content.
5. The person's communications indicate that his field of interpersonal relations are disturbed. A positive development in those same disturbed relations was held as the only possible way to go on living, but such development was seen as not forthcoming.
6. The experience of human warmth and friendliness is dissociated from oneself, resulting in this group of processes not preventing the suicide.
7. Although the person may not state this directly, there is evidence that a particular, significant other person(s), who was a destructive influence in the individual's past, is the target of the self-destruction. Self-destruction may not have been the only goal of the individual; the individual may well have calculated that the act would have a prolonged evil effect on this other person(s).
8. A derogatory and hostile attitude is evident, which ordinarily directed towards the outer world, is directed with full force towards the self.
9. There is a hostile, derogatory attitude, which is assumed to have been acquired in infancy and childhood, par-

ticularly childhood, which the individual continues to entertain, resulting in a focusing effect on the individual's self and to be manifested toward other people.

10. There is evidence of *one* of the following serious disorders of social behavior:

    (a) There is evidence consistent with the down phase of a manic-depressive disorder. For example, there is a sort of all-embracing (grandiose) negative self-appraisal-he is no good, has never been any good, and has caused everyone else a great deal of trouble, which can only be ended by destroying oneself.
    (b) There is evidence consistent with a diagnosis of schizophrenia. For example, the schizophrenic ends his life quite incidentally to some fantastic procedure for the remedy of his distress: to be reborn, to protect others from some delusional contamination, to save the world, to demonstrate omnipotence, and the like.
    (c) There is evidence consistent with the diagnosis of obsessive-compulsive disorder. For example, the individual exhibits obsessional characteristics such as overwhelming suicidal thoughts with unlimited attention to the detail of such an act.
    (d) There is evidence consistent with a diagnosis of psychopathic disorder. For example, the note is a tool for ensuring attention of others, but the act itself was likely an accidental misjudgment—too great a dose of poison, too long a delay in calling for help, and so forth.
    (e) There is evidence consistent with a diagnosis of depressive disorder. For example, the person exhibits a "reverie" of self-depreciating statements and appears to be very restrictive in thoughts and actions.
    (f) There is no evidence of a serious specific disorder but the note appears to be written by an individual who is so baffled in his attempt to subjugate his

interests that a paralysis of interest in others and in future possibilities of self has progressed to the point that life has become colorless and wholly unattractive.

FINDINGS

The protocol sentence that was verified significantly more often within the genuine notes (as compared with the simulated notes) was the following: (4) the person's thoughts exhibiting only permutations and combinations of grief-provoking content (X^2 (1, N=66) = 4.01, $p < .05$). The observation of Sullivan that the suicidal person's thoughts exhibit only permutations and combinations of grief-provoking content is like Shneidman's observation that the suicidal person is constricted in his perceptions and logic. The case illustrations in the chapter on Shneidman clearly illustrate this tendency of the suicide only to generate permutations and combinations of one thing, related to a loss, rejection, or other trauma. To further illustrate Sullivan's point, the following case is cited: "I cannot endure this situation any longer. I cannot believe I have been so bad a husband to merit this. Something is certainly wrong." The person is clearly grieving; indeed, he added: "I honestly don't know what it is." The person, as noted also by Menninger, never discusses anything else, only this one thing—only permutations and combinations of one thing.

Sentences 1, 2, 5, 7, and 10 were observed at the critical frequency level. These common classifications were the following: the suicide appears to be determined by both the person's history and the present situation; the person is under stress to a traumatic degree; a disturbance exists in interpersonal relations; self-destruction may not have been the only goal of the person; i.e., destruction of others may also have been intended; and a serious disorder of social behavior is evident. Sentence 10, which was related to various serious disorders, was verified most frequently in relation to "f"—no specific disorder, but the communication appearing to be consistent with an individual who is so baffled and paralyzed that his life is completely unattractive. Sentence

10 was verified 24 times; half of these were related to this classification, i.e., "f." Four were related to classification "a"—the down phase of a manic-depressive disorder. One was related to "c"—an obsessive-compulsive disorder. Three were related to "d"—a psychopathic disorder. Four were related to "e"—a depressive disorder. None was related to "b"—schizophrenia (although this may be related to the fact that this group rarely leaves a note when they are in a psychotic state). These results also support the position that depressives are not the only ones who kill themselves—a point made by a number of the 10 suicidologists. Finally, it suggests that the suicide may not fit *best* any specific nosological classification (although clearly some do if one wished to use such a system for classifying suicide).

BIBLIOGRAPHY

Sullivan, H.S. (1940). Conceptions of modern psychiatry. In H. Perry & M. Gawell (Eds.), *The collected works of Harry Stack Sullivan, Vol. I*. New York: W.W. Norton.

Sullivan, H.S. (1956). Clinical studies in psychiatry. In H. Perry, M. Gawell, & M. Gibben (Eds.), *The collected works of Harry Stack Sullivan, Vol. II*. New York: W.W. Norton.

Sullivan, H.S. (1962). Schizophrenia as a human process. *Ibid, Vol. II*.

Sullivan, H.S. (1964). The fusion of psychiatry and social science. *Ibid, Vol. II*.

Chapter 13

GREGORY ZILBOORG

Personal History

Gregory Zilboorg was born on December 25, 1890 in Kiev, Russia. His Orthodox Jewish upbringing has been generally seen to have been a key influence in his early years as well as later, although then, when he was in the U.S., he became a Quaker, and later, a Roman Catholic. In 1917, he received his medical degree from the Psychoneurological Institute, St. Petersburg. At the Institute, he studied under Vladimir Bekhterev, a notable critic of Pavlov's approach to psychiatry. From Bekhterev, Zilboorg learned to look at patients as whole human beings, not as items of behavior. After graduating, he served in a military hospital and in the army itself. He participated in the first post-Tsar government in 1917 in Petrograd and joined the government of Lvov and Kerensky as the secretary to the Ministry of Labor. Zilboorg publicly espoused strong views against the Communists and as the Communists established control, he fled to Kiev, which was occupied at that time by the Germans. In Kiev he worked with Marc Slonin to edit a newspaper that was critical of Germans, resulting in his having to flee again.

In 1919, he emigrated to the U.S. and came to New York, where, after learning English, he engaged in lecturing and journalism, obtaining some prestige as a translator of Russian plays. In 1926 he obtained his second medical degree from the (Columbia) College of Physicians and Surgeons. He began his practice at this time at Bloomingdale Psychiatric Hospital and also underwent psychoanalysis by Franz Alexander. Zilboorg was strongly influenced in his views by Freud, and in his lectures and papers he generally expounded psychoanalytic themes. However, in new areas of research, including suicide, he was somewhat critical of some of these. In 1951 Zilboorg published a book on Freud's life, titled *Sigmund Freud: His Exploration of the Mind of Man.* In 1931 he began private practice in New York, which he continued until his death. He lectured at numerous universities, including California and Yale, and held academic positions at New York State University and Fordham. He also served on a few key international and national committees related to public mental health, most notably in criminology, alcoholism, and suicide.

Zilboorg published extensively during his life, including in such journals as *The Nation* and *The Atlantic Monthly.* He wrote about numerous psychiatric topics such as psychosis (especially treatment), loneliness, aggression, and suicide. His studies of suicide were uniquely highlighted by investigations of "primitive races." His papers on suicide are the following; "Differential Diagnostic Types of Suicide," "Suicide among Civilized and Primitive Races," and "Considerations on Suicide, with Particular Reference to That of the Young." In 1941 Zilboorg published (with George Henry) *A History of Medical Psychology,* which presents biographies of great figures in psychological medicine, a book generally regarded by many (e.g., Karl Menninger) as a highly significant historical document. The major book on his theoretical views, which contains a few passages on suicide, was *Mind, Medicine and Man* (1943). He also published a book in 1954 on criminology entitled *The Psychology of the Criminal Act and Punishment.* Zilboorg died September 17, 1959 at Mt. Kisco, New York.

Theory of Suicide

Zilboorg asks, What kind of persons are likely to commit suicide? He notes that frequently people simply point out a self-evident motivation for the act, such as a man's despair over a disappointment, a loss, old age, or illness. This, according to Zilboorg (1937), testifies to human superficiality "which springs from universal human anxiety and leads man to grasp at any straw of external plausibility, when faced with the discomfort of looking closer and deeper into the problems of death and life" (p. 16). Popular attitudes are not only superficial but contradictory, frequently, for example, formulating incorrectly that the act was caused by mental disease. Statistical studies of suicide too are "well-nigh useless," deindividualizing the person and leading to misconceptions. Likewise, common theoretical formulations are seen as misleading; for example, the popular notion that suicide is agression turned inward and thus occurring only in the depressive person. Zilboorg notes that depressives "have more or less monopolized the clinical right to commit suicide." These formulations, usually ascribed to Freud, can be capitulated briefly as following, according to Zilboorg (1936a):

> In the case of pathologic depression, the patient, through identification with a person toward whom his feelings have always been highly ambivalent, loves and hates himself. Since his own ego has become his love object, he feels detached from reality and therefore experiences a sense of poverty of the ego. The unconscious sadism originally directed against the object reinforced by a sense of guilt, produces the singular phenomenon of the person's becoming sadistic toward himself. (p. 275)

Zilboorg (1936a) provides a number of cases to illustrate that these processes indeed occur in the depressive. For example:

> A physician, aged 36, had a particularly great fear of increasing the size of his family and thus the burden of his financial obligations. Being a Catholic, he was equally fearful of the use of contraceptives, and the fecundity of his wife

> served constantly to deepen and sharpen the conflict. One day, one of his little sons died of acute illness. He was sad, but his unconscious attitude was betrayed when one day the following exclamation inadvertently slipped from his tongue: "One less mouth to feed." From that time he fell into a typical suicidal depression. He hanged himself and was revived with difficulty. (p. 277)

In cases of depression one thus finds evidence for the postulate of aggression turned inward. Tradition, however, has overemphasized that depression means suicide, according to Zilboorg. Traditionally it was believed that if one committed suicide, and depression had not been diagnosed, it had been merely overlooked. Zilboorg argued that this formulation may be of real value, but the suicidal drive is more complex. "It is not only depressives who commit suicide—hysterias, compulsion, neurosis, obsessional neurosis, and some types of schizophrenia all contribute to the toll" (1936b). Zilboorg (1936a) provides a case of a thirty-one-year-old man, who indulged in tearless catatonic whining, ceaseless shouting, scattered and fragmented thought, and other symptoms usually ascribed to a schizophrenia, but also exhibited constant vigorous and impulsive self-destructive acts. Another patient, suffering from paranoid psychosis, during a period of appearing more serene, hanged himself with a necktie tied to his bed. Zilboorg provides other cases that fit different diagnoses, such as that of a woman who exhibited a compulsive neurosis. This woman, who was prone to bitter outbursts, failing one day to obtain attention from a physician, killed herself. She thus exhibited the well-known spiteful childish fantasy, "When I am dead, they will be sorry." Adolescents, Zilboorg notes, also frequently exhibit such an impulsive characteristic—they kill themselves because mother forbade them to go to a party, or for some other reason that seems trivial compared to the act of killing oneself. Zilboorg thus concludes that no single clinical entity is immune to the suicide drive. The presence or absence of the mechanisms in depression cannot serve as the reliable diagnostic criteria.

Returning to the why of suicide, according to Zilboorg, a study of the deeper layers of the suicidal person reveals the universality of the "death drive;" yet much of the puzzle remains unsolved. A few observations can be made, however; such as that frequently the suicide experienced the death of a parent or a sibling during a formative period (between the ages of four and six or at puberty). Zilboorg (1937) offers the following case illustration: A girl of twenty-two, on a day when she appeared cheerful, jumped to her death. The day before, she had gone shopping for a complete outfit that she wore on the day of her death. No motive appeared immediately evident, but on further inquiry it was found that when she was eight, her mother had died. Subsequently the girl had exhibited depression around the date of her mother's death; in fact, the day of her suicide was the anniversary of her mother's death. Zilboorg further notes that buying the new clothes supports the relation, since such an act is a primitive custom seen in other cultures—to dress in one's best for one's suicide.

This case and others also support a number of further critical observations that can be made, according to Zilboorg. There is a strong identification with a loss, not necessarily an actual loss of a relative or a friend (father, mother, psychological surrogate), but alternatively, a *fantasized* loss. There is direct or indirect evidence or inference of too great an attachment and too intimate (and primitive) a relationship, no matter how conventionally correct, in suicide to another person (e.g., a family member). Zilboorg adds that such an attachment actually keeps a person under the constant strain of having wishes (e.g., for closeness, incestuous) stimulated and inhibited at one and the same time. This relationship becomes frustrated. Suicide in fact is more frequently a primitive and impulsive and semiceremonial outcome of frustrated closeness wishes than of aggressive wishes or of spite. And finally, the person frequently, before the act, experiences a form of primitive mourning—a regression to the primitive impulses, so that in acting out his mourning, he actually joined the loss (e.g., a dead parent) by killing himself. Alternatively, the latter point is simple and more basically stated as "joining one's dead."

Zilboorg notes that a key to suicide lies in the suicide of children, adolescents, and especially the primitives, rooting suicide deeply in the "ontogenetic and phylogenetic point of view." For example, the ceremonial quality of many suicides offers a psychological link with the suicides among the primitive races. The primitive worldview has not been abandoned in the suicide. The suicide's ego (personality) organization is, indeed, primitive, weak, not adequately developed, and narcissistic. Not only is the suicide related to the act of the primitive, but also, according to Zilboorg, the act of certain animals; for instance, dogs or monkeys that refuse food and die when they have been mistreated or abandoned.

Zilboorg (1937) stated:

> Suicide . . . is most probably a universal phenomenon, more biological than purely sociological. This statement, general as it is, has a practical methodological value, for should suicide prove to be a complex biological phenomenon, the clue to the pathogenesis of suicide might rightfully be sought in the instinctual life of man among primitive people and children. (p. 24)

In children and adolescents, we frequently observe that they prefer death to pain, illness, or punishment. For example, the child who is late getting home, fearing punishment, prefers death. In primitive races, one frequently observes a similar phenomenon. A minor offense, even a remark misconstrued, initiates the act. It is sufficient reason in a person with a weak and not adequately developed personality to kill himself. Anger, spite, unwillingness to submit, love, fidelity, devotion to the dead, incest are all possible motivations, according to Zilboorg. One can observe in such people a number of reactions such as agitation, sarcasm, and a mild panicky state, tinged with aggression and reactions of fear (e.g., illness, pain, etc.) as well as hate and spite (toward a parent, a friend, or someone else). Ultimately, however, the person is unwilling to accept sickness, old age, or too many painful emotions, and accepts death willingly, even seeks it. One's ideal in such cases is projected beyond life, where life is eternal and forever devoid of any discomfort, regardless of the nature of the discomfort. For example, there will be no punishment from the parent for being late. The majority of primitive races in fact idealize suicide. The primitive is frequently not afraid to die. Suicide for them may indeed be a desirable end to existence on earth.

Although the data are not substantial, Zilboorg does offer some intriguing case illustrations from primitive races to highlight his point of view:

For example, Zilboorg cites the following case, found in Seligman (1929):

> A girl of Southern Massim prefers the Kanioga root to any other food; her mother and aunt twice ate the Kanioga she had collected for herself. When they asked her to come with them to collect more of the desired root, she refuses; then she laid out all her ornaments and finery and put them on, necklaces of shell heads and quill shell armlets, anklets and a new grass petticoat; then taking her pet dog in her arms she began to sing slowly: "Because the lily root, because the lily root I am going." Presently she went into the bush weeping. . . . When the girl came to a lofty wakola tree which was easy to climb, she climbed it, and her mother, running up, saw her: "Come down, dear, come down," she said, but the girl answered: "No, no, too late," and then looking down, she saw a crocodile in the sea close beneath her. . . . She took off her ornaments one by one and threw them to the crocodile who snapped them hungrily, she then threw her dog, and finally her petticoat until, when naked, she threw herself down and the crocodile took her.

This case, according to Zilboorg (1936a), is "a good symbolic summary" of the suicidal act today. It illustrates, for example, the ritualistic quality, hints of the deeper dynamics regarding the wish for death, loss, or some other discomfort as a perceived psychological stress, frustration, and rejection in a important relationship, impulsive-like reactions, the reaction of anger, and turning one's aggression on oneself. All this and more—and this is crucial—occurs in a weak and primitive individual.

In another case which Zilboorg (1936a) cites, related in Malinowski (1926), a sixteen-year-old boy of Kima'i had a forbidden (taboo) incestuous relation with a girl cousin:

> This had been known and generally disapproved of but nothing was done until the girl's discarded lover, who had wanted to marry her, took the initiative. . . . Then, one evening, he insulted the culprit in public, accusing him in the hearing of the whole public community of incest and hurling at him a certain expression intolerable to a native. For this there was only one remedy; only one means of escape remained to the unfortunate youth. Next morning he put on his festive attire and ornamentations, climbed a coconut palm, and addressed the community speaking from among the palm leaves and bidding them farewell. He explained the reason for his desperate deed and also launched forth a veiled accusation against the man who had driven him to his death, upon which it became the duty of his clansmen to avenge him. Then he wailed about, as is the custom, jumped from the palm some sixty feet high, and was killed on the spot. There followed a fight within the village in which the rival was wounded and the quarrel was repeated during the funeral.

The unwillingness of the primitive man, as in any suicide, to accept sickness, old age, accusations, loss, or too many painful emotions, not only makes it possible for the individual to accept death willingly, even to seek it, but it also generally led him to project the ideal beyond life. The suicide prefers death rather than relinquish his ideal of what life should be. For example, the Micronesian women prefer to join their husband in death than to remain behind. The Eskimo in Hudson Bay, when old, chooses to die. These individuals, like all suicides, simply want to lie down and wait for death to come, expressing the most primitive attitude towards one's own death.

Zilboorg (1937) provides a rich number of other cases from primitive races to illustrate his formulations; to cite a few:

> A young lad, wounding a comrade, hangs himself out of fear of the elder brother of the comrade.
>
> A New Zealand man, suffering from a toothache for two days, cuts his throat.

> Young people of the Pelee Islands, when a love affair is unhappy, refuse to eat, or kill themselves on the spot.
>
> A Melanesian girl hanged herself when the mother of the boy she was romantically involved with scolded her. The boy, hearing this, climbed a coconut tree, stated that his mother would not lose much by the death, and killed himself.
>
> A girl, having had a sexual relation with her father, tells the villagers, and takes poison. The father, hearing this, takes poison too.

Zilboorg (1936a, 1936b, and 1937) also provides a number of cases from our own culture that illustrate the same processes; for example (1937):

> A youth named Hessler lived in a small New Jersey town; he was killed by the brother of the sixteen-year-old girl whom he courted. The case was in the hands of the prosecuting attorney, when the following note was discovered among the dead boy's clothing: "To whoever finds this note give it to Miss (here follows the girl's name), the girl I love, to whom I am now giving my life for. I cannot have her so life is not worth living. I know this is a bad thing to do but I don't think God will hold me responsible. So good-bye. I love her. I always keep promises." What happened is not clear. All we know is that Hessler called on his girl and was shot by her brother who claimed self-defense. A psychologically trained mind cannot dispose of such a murder and suicidal note as mere coincidence. (p. 29–30)

To conclude, Zilboorg notes that although his formulations regarding suicide, illustrated dramatically by cases from primitive races, give us some hypotheses about what kind of people kill themselves, a larger number of other elements still need to be found.

Protocol Sentences

The following 10 protocol sentences were derived from Zilboorg's formulations regarding suicide.

In the suicide note:

1. The communications suggest that the person's personality (ego) organization is not adequately developed ("primitive," "weak") and narcissistic.
2. One can observe agitation, sarcasm, and a mild panicky state, definitely tinged with strong aggression and reactions of fear (e.g., of illness, pain, punishment, etc.) as well as hate and spite (toward a parent, friend, or someone else).
3. An unwillingness to accept sickness, old age, or too many painful emotions, not only made it possible for the suicide to accept death willingly, even to seek it, but it also generally led him to project his ideal beyond life (e.g., in a hereafter) where life is eternal and forever devoid of any discomfort.
4. The person communicates that he prefers death rather than relinquish his ideal of what life should be.
5. The communications indicate that the suicide is a primitive and impulsive and semiceremonial outcome more of frustrated closeness wishes than of aggressive wishes or of spite.
6. There is direct or indirect evidence or inference of too great an attachment and too intimate (and primitive) a relationship, no matter how conventionally correct, of the suicide to another person (e.g., family member), keeping him under the constant strain of having wishes (e.g., for closeness, incestuous) stimulated and inhibited at one and the same time.
7. The person communicates that he had experienced the death of a parent or a sibling during a formative period (between the ages of four and six and/or at puberty).
8. The person communicates a strong identification with a loss of a relative or friend (father, mother, or psychological surrogate) or, alternatively, a fantasized loss.
9. The communications indicate that the person experienced a form of primitive mourning—a regression to the primitive impulses so that in acting out his mourning, he actually joined the loss (e.g., a dead parent,

health) by killing himself (alternatively stated as "joining one's dead").

10. The person communicates that he simply wants to lie down and wait for death to come.

Findings

The protocol sentences that were verified significantly more often within the genuine notes (as compared with the simulated notes) were the following: (1) the person's ego organization is primitive, weak, not adequately developed, and narcissistic (X^2 $(1, N=66) = 11.52$, $p < .01$); (3) suicide being accepted by the person as an alternative to sickness, old age, or too many painful emotions (X^2 $(1, N=66) = 12.32$, $p < .01$); (5) the suicide appearing to be more related to frustrated closeness wishes than aggressive wishes or spite (X^2 $(1, N=66) = 9.98$, $p < .01$) and (6) evidence, direct or indirect, of too great an attachment to a person that had resulted in both stimulation and inhibition of wishes (X^2 $(1, N=66) = 5.07$, $p < .05$).

These findings clearly suggest that it is the person himself who contributes to the suicide. It is not just the situation. The judges observed the variable regarding a weak ego in most of the previous cited cases. Of course, this observation is more of an inference, such as the presence of unconscious dynamics, than many more manifest related statements. The writer of the note may not—indeed he is not likely to—state such weaknesses directly. He sees himself as acting intelligently; others, however, note something more—for example, a weak, not well developed personality (ego).

The suicide is unwilling to accept sickness, old age, or too many painful emotions. The person seeks or projects his ideal beyond life. He wills only comfort—but in death. In the actual notes, one person put it in these words: "Don't think too badly of me for taking this way but I can't take much more pain." Another person wrote: "I am very sorry but it is just too hard to breathe." Often, as noted over and over, this pain is related to frustrated closeness wishes. Indeed, although aggressive wishes or spite are often evident, frustrated closeness wishes appear to be noted even more frequently, and are clearly evident. One person wrote: "The only thing you never called me was crazy. Now you can do that. I loved you so." Another: "I didn't know you felt the way you did about everything. I really thought we were the 'happily married couple.' Too bad you just keep everything inside you." Often in these notes one can observe too great an attachment where wishes are simultaneously stimulated and inhibited. In the last case, for example, the person continued his note, "For the first time in my life I was really in love and I thought you were. I had hopes that you would forget your feelings and we would try to be happy together." Earlier in the same note, this man wrote about love and understanding in his marriage, a marriage that from his view was initially happy but now frustrating. Of course, in this example, one can observe indirect aggression, not only closeness wishes. Indeed, other frustrated needs are very frequently cited in suicide notes as noted previously, for example, by Murray.

Only sentence 1, which is related to the indication that the note was written by a person with a "weak personality," was observed at the critical frequency level. Sentence 1 thus is our last critical highly predictive and discriminative variable. This factor is indeed very important. It suggests that a common element in suicide, beyond the trauma, is the individual himself. The person's personality (ego) organization is primitive, weak, not adequately developed, and narcissistic. Not everyone kills themselves in face of a trauma; only a few do. All 10 suicidologists, despite various terms, concepts, ideas, etc. would agree about this: that the person himself—his psychological traits, dynamics, needs—play a critical role in the suicide. *The situation alone does not cause suicide.*

Bibliography

Zilboorg, G. (1936a) Differential diagnostic types of suicide. *Archives of Neurology and Psychiatry, 35,* 270–291.

Zilboorg, G. (1936b) Suicide among civilized and primitive races. *American Journal of Psychiatry,* 92, 1347–1369.

Zilboorg, G. (1937) Considerations on suicide, with particular reference to that of the young. *American Journal of Orthopsychiatry, 7,* 15–31.

Zilboorg, G. (1943) *Mind, medicine and man.* New York: Harcourt, Brace.

Part III

IMPLICATIONS AND APPLICATIONS

Part III consists of four sections, all focused on clarifying a definition of suicide in terms of suicide notes: A summary of the findings regarding the investigations of all 10 suicidologists with synthesis; a brief section on the differences and similarities of suicide notes from 1945–1954 and 1983–1984; some observations on age and sex; and some comments on suicide notes as the penultimate act of an unhappy life.

Chapter 14

SUMMARY AND SYNTHESIS

Fundamentally, each of the 10 suicidologists provides a perspective on suicide. The intent here is to take the empirically supported formulations (based on our operational definition) and to provide a perspective in both nomothethic and idiographic terms. It bears on two questions: Why do people kill themselves? and Why did that individual kill himself?

Frank (cited and summarized by Adams-Webber, 1985, and Berlyne, 1971) speaks of two kinds of information. One type is that which occurs most frequently. This is the common and highly predictive information about suicide *in general.* Another form or type of information is that which differentiates or *stands out,* especially if put against a background of the commonplace. This information is salient, for it maximizes the differences between the suicide and nonsuicide. Obviously, the suicidal person is in many ways like the nonsuicidal counterpart, but "something" happens as the suicidal state develops and as the suicidal person falls into an abyss. It is this schema that will be used in reporting what is frequently observed in suicide notes and what information distinguishes genuine suicide notes from simulated notes.

SUMMARY

Twenty-three out of 100 protocol sentences, derived from the 10 suicidologists, were found to occur in at least two-thirds of the genuine suicide notes (or, at least, one standard deviation above the mean of all frequency counts). These are the common characteristics of suicide notes and are, by implication, highly predictive of suicide. Table 14-1 reproduces these 23 sentences with reference to each theorist.

Table 14-1 Protocol Sentences Derived From 10 Suicidologists That Were Verified at A High Common Frequency Level (i.e., at least ⅔ of the time)

In the suicide note:

1) The person who appears to have arrived at the end of his limited social interest sees his suicide as a solution for an urgent problem and/or the injustices of life (Adler).
2) The individual considers himself too weak to overcome his personal difficulties and therefore (in revenge) rejects everything with one full swoop in order to escape the feeling of inferiority, and/or to act intelligent according to his goal of coping with the difficulties of life (with disregard to the community—a beloved person, a teacher, society, or the world at large) (Adler).
3) It appears that the unconscious has created a situation in which death is desired, partly in order to hurt/attack someone else, or as an act of revenge towards someone who has slighted him. One can conclude that the person, by attacking himself, is likely attacking another person (Adler).
4) The individual's aggression appears to have been turned inward. Themes of humility, submission, and devotion, subordination, flagellation, or masochism are evident (Adler).
5) A "complex" is evident, i.e., something discordant, unassimilated, and antagonistic exists (e.g., symptoms, ideas), perhaps as an obstacle, pointing to unresolved problems in the individual (Jung).
6) Unresolved problems in the individual are evident, where he has suffered defeat, at least for the time being, and where there is something he cannot evade or overcome. His weak spots in every sense of the word are evident (Jung).

7) A clash is evident between a demand for adaptation and the individual's constitutional inability to meet the challenge (Jung).
8) The person communicates the existence of a traumatic event (e.g., an unmet love, a failing marriage, disgust with one's work) that results in a deep hurt, being desperate, and, ultimately, the suicide itself (Jung).
9) The person points out, with passionate eloquence and with flawless logic (from his perspective) that life is hard, bitter, futile, and hopeless; that it entails more pain than pleasure; that there is no profit or purpose in it for him and no conceivable justification for living on (Menninger).
10) The person communicates flight from one of the following: pain, incurable disease, the threat of helpless senility, a violent death; from anticipated rejection or from fear of becoming dependent; or from self-depreciation, feelings of sexual or general inadequacy, humiliation, unknown danger. *However,* the suicide does not appear to be caused only by such a single thing; other motives (elements, wishes) appear to be evident (Menninger).
11) It appears that although the suicide act does not have adaptive (survival) value, the suicide does have adjustive value for the individual. The suicide is functional because it abolishes painful tension for the individual; it provides relief from intolerable suffering (Murray).
12) The suicide appears to be related to unsatisfied or frustrated needs, e.g., achievement, affiliation, autonomy, dominance, etc., although it may be difficult to determine precisely which needs are operating at the time the note was written (Murray).
13) The following emotional states are evident: pitiful forlornness, deprivation, distress, and/or grief (Murray).
14) There is evidence for egression (defined as a person's intended departure from a region of distress, chiefly with the aim of terminating, with relief, of the pain he has been suffering) and desertion (e.g., from the suicide's closest bonded person) (Murray).
15) The person communicated evidence of adult trauma (e.g., poor health, rejection by the spouse, being married to a competing spouse) (Shneidman).
16) The person is in a state of heightened disturbance (perturbation); e.g., he feels boxed in, rejected, harassed, unsuccessful, and especially, hopeless and helpless (Shneidman).

Table 14-1 (*continued*)

17) The person communicates ambivalence; e.g., complications, concomitant contradictory feelings, attitudes, and/or thrusts (Shneidman).
18) The communication allows one to conclude that the suicide appeared to be determined by the individual's history and the present interpersonal situation (Sullivan).
19) The person appears to be under the stress of a situational factor which changes a relatively unvarying disturbance in interpersonal relations to one that is relatively persisting to a traumatic degree (Sullivan).
20) The person's communications indicate that his field of interpersonal relations is disturbed. A positive development in those same disturbed relations was held as the only possible way to go on living, but such development was seen as not forthcoming (Sullivan).
21) Although the person may not state this directly, there is evidence that a particular, significant other person(s), who was a destructive influence in the individual's past, is the target of the self-destruction. Self-destruction may not have been the only goal of the individual; the individual may well have calculated that the act would have a prolonged evil effect on this other person(s) (Sullivan).
22) There is evidence of *one* of the following serious disorders of social behavior:
    (a) the down phase of a manic-depressive disorder. For example, there is a sort of all-embracing (grandiose) negative self appraisal—he is no good, has never been any good, and has caused everyone else a great deal of trouble, which can only be ended by destroying oneself.
    (b) a diagnosis of schizophrenia. For example, the schizophrenic ends his life quite incidentally to some fantastic procedure for the remedy of his distress: to be reborn, to protect others from some delusional contamination, to save the world, to demonstrate omnipotence, and the like.
    (c) the diagnosis of obsessive-compulsive disorder. For example, the individual exhibits obsessional characteristics such as overwhelming suicidal thoughts with unlimited attention to the detail of such an act.

Table 14-1 (*continued*)

(d) a diagnosis of psychopathic disorder. For example, the note is a tool for ensuring attention of others, but the act itself was likely an accidental misjudgment—too great a dose of poison, too long a delay in calling for help, and so forth.

(e) a diagnosis of depressive disorder. For example, the person exhibits a "reverie" of self-depreciating statements and appears to be very restrictive in thoughts and actions.

Or:

(f) There is no evidence of a serious specific disorder, but the note appears to be written by an individual who is so baffled in his attempt to subjugate his interests, that a paralysis of interest in others and in future possibilities of self has progressed to the point that life has become colorless and completely, wholly unattractive (Sullivan).

23) The communications suggest that the person's personality (ego) organization is not adequately developed ("primitive," "weak") and narcissistic (Zilboorg).

Eighteen out of the same 100 protocol sentences were found to appear significantly more often in the genuine suicide notes as compared with the simulated notes. It is the information that maximizes the salient features that differentiate, by implication, the suicidal person from the nonsuicidal person. Table 14-2 reproduces these sentences with reference to the theorist.

The data that provide the greatest informational value are those which are *both* highly predictive and differentiating. Only five protocol sentences both highly predicted the content and discriminated the content in suicide notes. These five sentences are:

1. In the suicide note, the person communicates flight from one of following: pain, incurable disease, the threat of helplessness, senility, a violent death; from anticipated rejection or fear of becoming dependent; or from self-depreciation, feelings of sexual or general inadequacy, humiliation, unknown danger. *However,* the suicide does

Table 14-2 Protocol Sentences Derived From 10 Suicidologists That Were Verified Significantly More Often Within the Genuine Suicide Notes as Compared with the Simulated Notes.

In the suicide note:

1) The person communicates that he is preoccupied with a person he had lost or who had rejected him (Freud).
2) The person communicates that he is feeling quite ambivalent; i.e., affectionate and hostile towards a lost or rejecting person (Freud).
3) The person communicates that he is in some direct or indirect fashion identifying with a rejecting or lost person (Freud).
4) The person communicates feelings and/or ideas of vengefulness and aggression towards himself; however, he appears to be angry towards someone else (Freud).
5) The person communicates that he is turning back upon himself murderous impulses that had been directed against someone else (Freud).
6) The person communicates that his suicide is a fulfillment of punishment, i.e., self-punishment (Freud).
7) The communications indicate that the person wished to die; i.e., the suicide is accomplished due to some relative weakness in the capacity for developing constructive tendencies (e.g., attachment, love) (Menninger).
8) The person communicates flight from one of the following: pain, incurable disease, the threat of helpless senility, a violent death; from anticipated rejection, or fear of becoming dependent; or from self-depreciation, feelings of sexual or general inadequacy, humiliation, unknown danger. *However,* the suicide does not appear to be caused only by such a single thing; other motives (elements, wishes) appear to be evident (Menninger).
9) In the suicide note, the following emotional states are evident: pitiful forlornness, deprivation, distress, and/or grief (Murray).
10) The person communicates evidence of adult trauma (e.g., poor health, rejection by the spouse, being married to a competing spouse) (Shneidman).
11) The person communicates ambivalence; e.g., complications, concomitant contradictory feelings, attitudes, and/or thrusts (Shneidman).

12) The person appears to be figuratively intoxicated or drugged by overpowering emotions and constricted logic and perception (Shneidman).
13) The person's communications appear to have unconscious psychodynamic implications (Shneidman).
14) There is a poverty of thought, exhibited by the individual expressing only permutations and combinations of grief-provoking content (Sullivan).
15) The communications suggest that the person's personality (ego) organization is not adequately developed ("primitive," "weak") and narcissistic (Zilboorg).
16) An unwillingness to accept sickness, old age, or too many painful emotions, not only made it possible for the suicide to accept death willingly, even to seek it, but it also generally led him to project his ideal beyond life (e.g., in a hereafter) where life is eternal and forever devoid of any discomfort (Zilboorg).
17) The communications indicate that the suicide is a primitive and impulsive and semiceremonial outcome more of frustrated closeness wishes than of aggressive wishes or of spite (Zilboorg).
18) There is direct or indirect evidence or inference of too great an attachment and too intimate (and primitive) a relationship, no matter how conventionally correct, of the suicide to any other person (e.g., family member), keeping him under the constant strain of having wishes (e.g., for closeness, incestuous) stimulated and inhibited at one and the same time (Zilboorg).

---

not appear to be caused only by such a single thing; other motives (elements, wishes) appear to be evident (Menninger).

2. In the suicide note, the following emotional states are evident: pitiful forlornness, deprivation, distress and/or grief (Murray).
3. In the suicide note, the person communicates evidence of adult trauma (e.g., poor health, rejection by the spouse, being married to a competing spouse) (Shneidman).

4. In the suicide note, the person communicates ambivalence; e.g., complications, concomitant contradictory feelings, attitudes and/or thrusts (Shneidman).
5. In the suicide note, the communications suggest that the person's personality (ego) organization is not adequately developed ("primitive," "weak") and narcissistic (Zilboorg).

SYNTHESIS

Taken as a whole, the various formulations regarding suicide presented in this volume provide considerable diversity. We are obligated to attempt to integrate and synthesize the findings. The proposed scheme will follow the outline in the Chapter, "Previous Studies of Suicide Notes" (with one addition). The categories are not distinct, "except in the mind," to borrow from Aristotle, since we are attempting to understand a unity—a person.

The problem of synthesizing a number of different evaluations about the same subject, here, suicide notes (and, by inference, suicide) is one the clinician faces constantly. He may have different reports—a nurse's, a teacher's, a lawyer's, a social worker's—reflecting different perspectives and data. All the reports may be "true" (i.e., meaningful and useful), yet not one is really like the other (with, of course, some similarities). Even with the same data considered—a suicide note—each suicidologist approaches the individual and the suicide with theoretical biases. Our method of protocol analyses does exactly that—it construes a suicide note with constructs derived from different points of view.

There is a number of possible modes of investigation in such a situation. The approach decided upon, following Carnap, for determining the synthesis was making inductions from the verified singular protocol sentence and applying a series of meaningful categories. These categories or subheadings are as follows: Situation; Relationship; Emotional State; and Cognitive State. Our findings, however, require one additional subheading: Ego. A later chapter will address the demographic variables of age and sex. Each verified protocol sentence might be considered a separate explanatory or descriptive item about suicide that can be categorized. We will present under each category three sections as follows: A) common elements; B) differentiating elements; and C) illustration.

The following emerged from both the predictive and discriminative data that were derived from the 10 suicidologists. Some redundancy will be evident where the common and discriminative overlap. The scheme will be illustrated, following an earlier plan in the review chapter, with an actual case. Here we have chosen Shneidman's "Natalie" (1980), a forty-year-old woman who killed herself. The reason for choosing this case is that it provides a relatively full case study, through the use of not only suicide notes, but also other documents, including early school records, teacher's notes to her parents, school physicians' reports, school evaluations, college records, several psychological tests, numerous questionnaires, dozens of her letters, and miscellaneous personal documents. Let us begin with Natalie's five suicide notes cited verbatim:

1. To her adult friend:
   Rosalyn—Get Eastern Steel Co.—Tell them and they will find Bob right away. Papa is at his business. Betty is at the Smiths—Would you ask Helene to keep her until her Daddy comes—so she won't know until he comes for her. You have been so good—I love you—Please keep in touch with Betty—Natalie.
2. To her eldest daughter:
   Betty, go over to Rosalyn's right away—Get in touch with Papa.
3. To her ex-husband, from whom she was recently divorced:
   Bob—I'm making all kinds of mistakes with our girls—They have to have a leader and everyday the job seems more enormous—You couldn't have been a better Daddy to Nancy and they do love you—Nancy misses you so and she doesn't know what's the matter—I know you've built a whole new life for yourself but make room for the girls and keep them with you—Take them where you go—It's only for just a few years—Betty is almost

ready to stand on her own two feet—But Nancy needs you desperately. Nancy needs help—She really thinks you didn't love her—and she's got to be made to do her part for her own self-respect—Nancy hasn't been hurt much yet—but ah! the future if they keep on the way I've been going lately—Barbara sounds warm and friendly and relaxed and I pray to God she will understand just a little and be good to my girls—They need two happy people—not a sick mixed-up mother—There will be a little money to help with extras—It had better go that way than for more pills and more doctor bills—I wish to God it had been different but be happy—but please—stay by your girls—And just one thing—be kind to Papa (his father)—He's done everything he could to try to help me—He loves the girls dearly and it's right that they should see him often—Natalie

Bob—this afternoon Betty and Nancy had such a horrible fight it scares me. Do you suppose Gladys and Orville would take Betty for this school year? She should be away from Nancy for a little while—in a calm atmosphere.

4. To her ex-father-in-law:

   Papa—no one could have been more kind or generous than you have been to me—I know you couldn't understand this—and forgive me—(The lawyer) has copy of my will—Everything equal—the few personal things I have of value—the bracelet to Nancy and my wedding ring to Betty—But I would like Betty to have Nana's diamond—have them appraised and give Betty and Nancy each half of the diamonds in the band. Please have somebody come in and clean—Have Bob take the girls away immediately—I don't want them to have to stay around—You're so good Papa dear—

5. To her two children:

   My dearest ones—You two have been the most wonderful things in my life—Try to forgive me for what I've done—Your father would be so much better for you. It will be harder for you for awhile—but so much easier in the long run—I'm getting you all mixed up—

> Respect and love are almost the same—Remember that—and the most important thing is to respect yourself—The only way you can do that is by doing your share and learning to stand on your own two feet—Betty, try to remember the happy times—and be good to Nancy. Promise me you will look after your sister's welfare—I love you very much—but I can't face what the future will bring.

SITUATION

Suicide notes are a communication, but much more than "everyday talk." They are a note about a *situation,* about events, people, oneself. The following are some common and differentiating elements in the situation of the suicide that we have learned from Jung, Murray, Shneidman, Sullivan, and Zilboorg.

A) *The common elements in the situation:* The person very frequently before his death "finds" himself in a situation that, according to Jung and Shneidman, is *perceived* as a trauma (an unmet love, poor health, a rejection, a failing marriage, disgust with one's work, etc.). It is critical to understand that the situation is *perceived* to be a trauma; *the* situation for most of us would not be seen in the same light—indeed, it *may* be seen *from our view* as trivial. Case examples include a competing spouse, a scratch on a prized car, the death of a pet, loss of a fantasized love. The stress, according to Murray and Shneidman, is provided by unsatisfied or frustrated needs. The need or combination of needs might be affiliation, autonomy, achievement, dominance, etc. (Murray, 1938). This results in a deep hurt, unbearable anguish, and a state of desperation. The individual wants to egress, to depart from the region of distress and pain. Indeed, according to Shneidman, the most frequent stimulus in suicide is intolerable psychological pain. The situation changed from a relatively persisting disturbance to a traumatic and unbearable one. It was too stressful, too traumatic, too painful for that person. However, all 10 suicidologists have stressed that the suicide is not just a response to *a* situation; rather, there are abundant precursors. The suicidal person is a person with a history.

A final common element of the suicidal situation, which was derived initially from Murray's formulations, is that it appears that although the suicidal act does not have *adaptive* (survival) value, the suicide does have *adjustive* value for that individual. The suicide is functional in that it abolishes pain and provides relief from an intolerable situation.

B) *The differentiating elements in the situation:* There are a number of discriminating clues about the situation that appear to be salient in suicide (based on the studies of the genuine and simulated suicide notes). First, a situation is *perceived* to be too traumatic. The existence, especially the perception of trauma, appears to be not only a predictive characteristic but also a differentiating characteristic of the suicidal person. The present situation is seen as a trauma, or catastrophic or cataclysmic (Shneidman, 1987). The situation may be about any thing, most often a disturbed relationship, and the suicidal person is unwilling to accept the disturbance, the sickness, old age, rejection. Indeed, what differentiates the suicide is that the pain is too much for that individual to bear (Shneidman, 1985). It is this pain—*the pain of feeling pain*—that makes it possible for the suicidal person to accept death willingly and, according to Zilboorg, also to project his only ideal beyond life.

C) *An illustration:* In her notes, Natalie seems pushed, weary, harried, and beaten by life. Her personal documents clearly give evidence of trauma; even her everyday life was described as too "enormous." She noted that life was too painful. She wanted immediate relief. She wanted to depart from her distress. To her children she wrote, *I can't face what the future will bring.* For her, suicide had adjustive value. It provided relief from intolerable suffering.

Natalie's father had reported the following to the police:

> Undersigned spoke to (name and address), who stated he was victim's father. He further said that approximately two weeks ago, victim told him that she was going to commit suicide. He said he talked her out of the notion at that time, and did not figure she would make any further attempt on her life. He further said victim had been in ill health since her divorce and had been treated by a psychiatrist, address

unknown; also that the victim had filed a will which is currently in the possession of her attorney."

To put the situation into the appropriate historical context (something that a suicide note does not provide but may be essential in understanding the suicidal person), the following brief synopsis of Natalie's life is provided from Shneidman's more detailed history (1980): The conditions of Natalie's birth and early years were noted as normal. When Natalie was six, her mother wrote to a friend; "I have tried to use a lot of common sense and have answered every question to the best of my ability because she is an understanding child and will listen to reason. I have not had to stimulate a desire to learn because she always wanted to know everything her older playmates knew and she would try to learn voluntarily." She had a brother, who was 8 years older than she. Later she would say about him that "he could never make a living."

When Natalie was six years old, in the first grade, she was given an individual intelligence test, scoring in the extremely superior category. Curiously, one of the few items that she missed on the test was this one: "Yesterday the police found the body of a girl cut into 18 pieces. They believe that she killed herself. What is foolish about that?" Her nonprophetic answer, as Shneidman described it, was "She wouldn't kill herself."

A very important event occurred in Natalie's life when she was seven: her father deserted her mother. Later in her life, she noted, with obvious sadness, that "My father never came to see me except once."

The records of her childhood are interesting. One, written by a school physician when she was eight, states that she was "somewhat nervous, bordering on irritability." A school record when she was eleven notes that her last name had been changed to reflect the fact that her mother had divorced and remarried. All of the above point to an early stressful life. At age twelve there were several items of interest. She suffered from numerous headaches and had glasses prescribed but she still reported disturbed eyestrain. She experienced her menarche; she was a straight-A student (in the seventh grade) and indicated that she wanted to go to college and that she would also like to be a dancer.

A hearing loss had been diagnosed earlier but was now assessed to have increased and she was somewhat sensitive about it; she would not admit this difficulty to any of her teachers. Her main teacher reported that although Natalie was extremely bright, she "shrinks from opportunities for leadership."

She finished high school and went on to college for 3 years but did not graduate. At the age of twenty-five, having been, in her own words, "an unsuccessful secretary," her "ultimate goal [was to] be a successful homemaker." She married and in the next 2 years lived in five different cities. Understandably, she wrote that "it is hard to develop interests in any one place." She became pregnant almost immediately after getting married.

There is a gap in the records for 5 years. By age thirty she had two children and reported a "great tendency to worry and extreme nervousness." Her marriage was not peaceful. Her husband was drinking rather heavily. There was a dramatic change in her own physical and psychological state. She reported that she was "too tired even to wash the windows."

RELATIONSHIP

As noted above, the suicidal person frequently writes (in the suicide note) about an interpersonal relationship that was too traumatic and too painful to bear. Indeed, the lack of success in establishing a satisfying relationship, or, conversely, experiencing a broken relationship (with spouse, friend, patrons, others) is *the* most frequently cited event in suicide notes. Adler, Freud, Shneidman, Sullivan, and Zilboorg have given us the following insights into the dyadic nature of suicide.

A) *The common elements of the relationship:* Suicide is related to the person's interpersonal situation *and* the individual's history. A common reality for the suicidal person is that his interpersonal relations are disturbing. A dramatic improvement, according to Sullivan, in those troubled relations was seen as the *only* possible way to go on living. However, such development is seen as never forthcoming. The suicides' social aspirations are lacking; they have arrived at what Adler terms the end of personal and social interest. Suicide is the suicidal person's solution to these disturbing relations or injustices.

B) *The differentiating elements of the relationship:* Suicide is, as all 10 suicidologists have noted, most often a dyadic event. However, according to Freud, the differentiating relationship in the suicide is one of loss and rejection. Freud has asserted that the suicidal person is often singly preoccupied with a person who has gone or who rejected him. Freud further noted that the suicidal person is overly attached or identified to this same person (object). Indeed, what differentiates the suicidal person is that there is, directly or indirectly, too great an attachment and too intimate a relationship, no matter how conventionally correct, of the suicidal person to any other person (such as a family member). This kept him under constant pressures of having wishes or needs (e.g., closeness, incestuous) stimulated and inhibited at one and the same time. From Zilboorg we have, indeed, learned that suicide is more often an outcome of frustrated closeness wishes (or needs) than aggressive wishes or spite.

C) *An illustration:* What is clearly evident from the documents related to Natalie's life is that her interpersonal relationships were disturbing. She had experienced considerable loss and rejection, not only from her ex-husband but also (and deeper) from her father. In a letter about her troubled life, Natalie said this about her father: "I adored my father from afar. Our occasional meetings were unsatisfactory—my father is a very brilliant man—however, he has little use for me—he lives 20 minutes away but has been in our home only once for a few minutes in the past two years." Natalie clearly identifies with her father in these words; she is and wants to be attached to him. Her relationship with her father, as with her ex-husband, was, however, under a constant strain—her wishes, needs, etc., were unsatisfied and frustrated. Here is part of a letter she sent her favorite college professor, written when she was about thirty-five:

> . . . Until I was 25 I didn't know there were such things as problems in this world, but since then with the exception of my two lovely children and my perfect relationship with my mother, I've had just one struggle after another, made

> one blunder after another. My husband and I bicker constantly. I've wanted to divorce him a thousand times and still I know that is not the solution. We were both raised in broken homes and we both love our children too much. He comes home drunk at night far too often. He can't afford it. He refuses to look at the bills and says "Why haven't you saved money?" I have no one to talk to. I feel like I'm cornered . . . My mother's youngest brother and my nearest neighbor both committed suicide in one month (about a year before).

Here is another such letter regarding her relation to her children:

> Our little ones are nice, but the eldest still bites her fingernails and fights constantly with her younger sister. She is the result of my selfishness . . . Well, I've poured out my heart and I'm a little ashamed. In my heart I've never doubted that I can be a happy, relaxed, useful human being, but it's taking such a long time to get there.

When Natalie was thirty-nine, she and her husband separated because of "his violent temper, his selfishness and his drinking." Nine months later she was divorced. Four months after the divorce was final (and he had already remarried), she was dead. At the end, according to Shneidman, Natalie was frantic to achieve a satisfying relation, "the feeling of childhood love." This love was expressed in one of her suicide notes to her ex-father-in-law, "You're so good Papa dear." But to her own father (and mother), there was no note. Shneidman summarized the relationships thus (1980):

> In her suicide she reenacted her own earlier life drama—the yearning for her parents to be together—and in this misdirected symbolic sacrifice, instead of giving her children a (seemingly) united home, she, in the most traumatic way possible, deprived them of their own mother. Her aspirations—to be her father's favorite, to be accepted and not abandoned, to care for and not reject her own children (as she had been rejected and not cared for), to be symbolically

> reunited with her father in a happy home, to sacrifice herself so that some of the problems of her children might be solved—were no better realized in her death than they were in her life. (p. 66)

EMOTIONAL STATE

Many emotions are present in suicide: hostility, despair, shame, guilt, despondency, hopelessness, and/or ennui (Leenaars et al., 1985). Our current findings, derived from Adler, Freud, Murray, Shneidman, and Sullivan, suggest that the following predictive and discriminative emotional states appear to occur in suicide.

A) *The common elements of the emotional state:* A common emotional state in the suicidal person is pitiful forlornness, deprivation, distress and/or grief (Murray, 1967). The suicidal person is in a state of heightened disturbance, i.e., perturbation (Shneidman, 1985). The person especially feels hopeless and helpless, which is a very important common emotion in suicide (Shneidman, 1985). The suicidal person feels boxed in, rejected, harassed, unsuccessful,—and helpless to cope with these overpowering emotions. He believes that there is nothing he can do and that there is nothing anyone else can do to help him.

Another common emotion in suicide is anger turned inward, as noted by Adler, Freud, and Sullivan. Themes of humility, submission, devotion, subordination, abasement, flagellation, or masochism are often evident in the suicidal person. Self-destruction may be a goal of suicide but not the *only* one. Frequently, according to Freud and Sullivan, the target of the suicide is a particular significant other person, a person in the suicidal person's disturbing relationship. The suicide *may,* according to Sullivan, even have calculated the act to have a prolonged deleterious effect on this person. The suicide, partially unconscious, creates a situation in which death is desired partly in order to hurt or attack someone else, or as an act of revenge towards someone who had slighted him. The person, by attacking himself, may be attacking another person (or company, or ideal, or lack of recognition).

B) *The differentiating elements of the emotional state:* Not only is the emotional state of inconsolable misery, deprivation, distress, and/or grief common in the suicide, but it is also a differentiating clue in the suicide. In addition, according to Freud, an emotional state (with concomitant ideation) that differentiates the suicide from other emotional states is vengefulness and aggression. The suicide may exhibit feelings (and/or ideas) of aggression towards himself, but this appears primarly to be aggression turned inward. Freud has noted that murderous impulses (or wishes) directed against someone else are critical in understanding the deeper interpretation of suicide. However, aggression, whether expressed outwardly or inwardly, is not the only differentiating emotion, as documented by both Murray and Shneidman.

A further differentiating aspect of the emotional state, noted by Freud and Shneidman, is that the suicide feels ambivalent, much more deeply than is common in all of us. Not only is he angry, distressed, and grieving but he also simultaneously expresses affectionate feelings, often towards a person in a disturbing relationship. He communicates both love and hate in his note. More importantly, what differentiates the suicidal person is that the emotional state (regardless of the specific nature of the emotion) is overpowering; the emotions *"intoxicate"* the suicidal person (Shneidman, 1985).

C) *An illustration:* Natalie exhibited many emotions. Her personal documents are filled with overpowering emotions. She was frantic. Pitiful forlornness, deprivation, distress, and grief were all evident in this "emotional intoxication." Feelings (and ideas) of vengefulness and aggression toward herself appear to be evident—especially submission. Her note to her husband is manifestly a painful mea culpa. She took all the blame. She punished herself. She was passive, fearing aggression and violence. All of the feelings are expressed overtly in her final letters. It is easy to read the anger towards her ex-husband and her father. She also exhibited love, concern, etc. towards others (her ex-father-in-law, her children). Her notes and other documents are marked by ambivalence—love and hate. At the end, Natalie was boxed in, passive, rejected, and especially helpless and hopeless.

COGNITIVE STATE

The suicide exhibits unusual and lethal modes of reasoning. Our studies of Menninger, Shneidman, and Sullivan suggest the following aspects of the suicidal person's cognitive state.

A) *The common elements of the cognitive state:* A very frequent aspect of the cognitive state in the suicidal person is that *the person himself* believes that his suicide was caused by *a single thing* (Menninger, 1938). It might be flight from pain, incurable disease, the threat of senility, anticipated rejection, dependency, self-depreciation, feelings of inadequacy, humiliation, or even something unknown. However, a common "thing" in suicide is that it is *not only* caused by one thing. Other motives (elements, wishes, needs) appear to be evident in suicide notes.

Menninger has, however, noted that the person points out, with passionate eloquence and with seemingly logical insistence, that it is *this* one thing that caused the suicide. Menninger, Shneidman, and Sullivan suggest that the person anticipates more pain than pleasure. The suicidal person says something like this: "Life is this way and it will always be this way." He sees no profit or purpose in life, no justification for living on. From the outside, we who read his note see more, and we see the constriction of suicidal thinking.

B) *The differentiating elements of the cognitive state:* Not only is the emotional state overpowering, but what also differentiates the suicidal person from others is that the person is *simultaneously* "intoxicated" by his own constricted logic and perception. The discriminating cognitive state in suicide is constriction (Shneidman, 1985). The suicidal person exhibits a much greater poverty of thought than other people, even when they imagine being suicidal. The suicidal person, according to Sullivan, expresses only permutations and combinations of grief-provoking thought. Not only is it very common for the suicide to be preoccupied with one thing that he believes led to his suicidal solution, but this characteristic also differentiates the suicidal person from the nonsuicidal person.

The suicidal person's cognitive state also exhibits complications, contradictory thoughts and attitudes. Shneidman has characterized this state as an ambivalent "internal attitude." This attitude is not only observed frequently in suicide notes but also differentiates the suicidal person.

C) *An illustration:* Natalie was not only figuratively overcome by her emotions but also by her perception and ideas. Her notes are full of permutations and combinations of grief-provoking content (despite the ever-present thrust of ambivalence). She believed that her life was hard, futile. She was occupied with the following: "I can't face what the future brings." She said that she was "making all kinds of mistakes." She clearly believed, with flawless logic from her perspective, that once she was dead it would be "so much easier" for her children, her ex-husband, herself—everybody. She almost stated the following prototypical sentences in the documents: "Everyone will be much better off when I'm dead. Everything will be much better when I'm dead."

Natalie's suicide, from our perspective, is much less logical than she believed. Here, for example, is some of Shneidman's analysis of the content in her notes in relation to cognition (1980):

> Natalie's suicide note to her children is filled with contradictions and inconsistencies. (We remember that when she was tested as a child, the psychologist called her extremely logical.) In the suicide note, the implicit logical arguments flow back and forth, between assertion and counterassertion, never with any resolution. Here are some examples: She says, in effect, you will stay with your father, you should love your father, I know that you cannot love your father but at least you must respect him. She then almost free-associates to the word "respect" and argues, rather lamely, that love and respect are almost the same anyway, and in case that argument is not persuasive (which it is not), then one should, at least, respect one's self. The logic wanders.
>
> Another sad example: She says to her children, You must stand on your own two feet, but she also implies that the point of her removing herself from their lives is so that they can be reunited with their father—as, probably, she unconsciously yearns to be reunited with her father.
>
> To tell one's children in a suicide note to remember the happy times certainly has some contradictory element

> in it, on the very face of it. I love you so much, she says, but the end result of her actions is to make them orphans. She adds, I can't face what the future will bring, but she then takes her life largely because of the haunting, inescapable past. And finally, there is her statement, "I'm getting you all mixed up," which obviously betokens the confusion not in their minds but in her own. (p. 66–67)

EGO

The title for this subsection appears to be the best fit with the data—softer data, less observable than the previous sections—that emerged regarding the fact that suicide is not just related to a situation and a state. It is also related to the fact that the person himself is a critical common and differentiating aspect in the suicidal act, based on the formulations of Adler, Jung, Freud, Murray, Menninger, Shneidman, Sullivan, and Zilboorg.

A) *The common elements of the ego:* The suicide's ego organization is, according to Zilboorg, "weak," "primitive," and not adequately developed. Jung has noted that something discordant, unassimilated, and antagonistic is frequently evident in the suicidal person. We believe that both these variables, but especially Zilboorg's, are misleading. The central question in defining suicide is what are the commonalities in suicidal people, not what kinds of persons kill themselves. Even Zilboorg's terms are discriminatory and dated. Zilboorg calls other cultures weak and primitive and then makes a statement about how suicidal people are similar to suicidal people in these primitive cultures. No anthropologist today would call another culture (or race) weak, primitive, etc. We believe that such descriptions have no utility; in addition, if one returns to the actual data where Zilboorg's (and Jung's) protocol sentence was verified, one can readily transpose these observations into more accurate descriptions.

The suicidal person does not communicate that he is weak or primitive; he is more likely to say that he *feels* weak, that he is experiencing something discordant or antagonistic in himself, that he is defeated and cannot go on, that he has always experienced problems, etc. Our findings more accurately allow us to conclude that the person has not only suffered a trauma, but he is not capable, given his emotional and cognitive states, to cope with the trauma. The situation demands adaptation but the person sees himself defeated and unable to meet the challenge. The person, seeking to cope intelligently—what Adler calls the suicidal person's own inferiority—with the difficulties of life, kills himself.

The person may be seen by others as exhibiting a social disorder (if one wishes to use such words), usually a nonspecific disorder. The person, according to Sullivan, is baffled and paralyzed. His life is so disordered that it is colorless and completely, wholly unattractive. What is important is that various disorders, not just depression, may be evident in suicide. Sullivan suggested the following: the down phase of a manic-depressive disorder, a schizophrenic disorder, an obsessive—compulsive disorder, a psychopathic disorder.

B) *The differentiating elements of the ego:* What differentiates the suicidal person, according to Menninger, is his relative weakness in the capacity for developing *constructive tendencies* (e.g., attachment, love). Indeed, the suicidal person sees, expresses, communicates, etc., that the act itself is a fulfillment of punishment (i.e., self-punishment). This self-punishment is directly related to the emotional state, especially the emotions of aggression and grief. According to Freud's formulation, from which this element was derived, this aspect of suicide is related to a conflict or clash between contradictory impulses, wishes or needs in one's conscience (superego). It is these aspects of personality that allow the person to wish to die *and* to kill himself.

Finally, what differentiates the suicidal person from others is the appearance of critical unconscious psychodynamic implications in his communication, behaviors, etc. However, what these latent implications might be appears to be difficult to isolate at this time. All 10 suicidologists reported in this book would cite different factors. Freud, for example, would cite intense identification with a lost or rejecting object *and* aggression turned inward. Shneidman, for another example, would cite intense (unbearable) psychological pain, with accompanying constriction, hopelessness, push for egression, etc.—sparked underneath by dramatically frustrated needs. To begin empirically to investigate the nature of the latent implications in suicide, the following study of suicide notes was undertaken (Leenaars, 1986a).

Two individuals, who had served as the initial judges of this variable, were asked to rescore the same protocol sentence in the same sample of suicide notes a year later. Specifically, the following sentence was investigated: "In the suicide note, the person's communications appear to have unconscious psychodynamic implications." The judges were also asked to provide concluding statements about what these unconscious implications might be in such personal documents. The results indicated significant test-retest reliability ($p < .01$). Regrettably, the judges did not agree about what the latent implications might be. One judge cited psychoanalytic defense mechanisms, whereas the other cited concepts that were generally derived from Shneidman's work. Our own preliminary empirical investigation indicated that these forces may be most associated with the relational nature of suicide (Leenaars, 1986a); however, further research is needed into this very important determinant of suicide.

C) *An illustration:* One can conclude that Natalie was emotionally perturbed; but it would be wrong, based on her personal documents, to call her weak or not adequately developed. Natalie's history, however, does attest to the fact that she had difficulties developing constructive and loving attachments. She had suffered defeat which, at the time of her death, she felt she could not overcome. The active withdrawal by key significant others plunged Natalie into despair, grief, hopelessness, and helplessness. She was not able to go on; she described herself as "a sick mixed-up mother." Indeed, her notes suggest that she was figuratively "drugged" by overpowering emotions and constricted perceptions. Her history was full of these "mixed-up" states, which one of her doctors described as "neurotic tendencies." Life, she said, "seems so enormous." She had a great tendency to worry and was extremely nervous. In the end, Natalie appeared to have been so preoccupied with her trauma that she was unaware of how to adjust and she chose cessation. We would here follow Shneidman's belief that: "Each individual tends to die as he or she has lived, especially as he or she has previously reacted in periods of threat, stress, failure, challenge, shock and loss." Finally, it is likely that unconscious dynamics were the major determinants of her suicide.

Chapter 15

SUICIDE NOTES, 1945–1954 AND 1983–1984

Differences and Similarities

An historical review of suicide will show that people's conceptions about suicide have changed over time. In this chapter, we shall address the question of changes in the recent past by asking a question that relates to the predictive and discriminative clues to suicide. Has suicide changed or remained constant, specifically between 1945–1954 and 1983–1984?

An essential element in suicide is a *psychological* one, a view espoused by all 10 suicidologists discussed in this volume. In this regard, Shneidman (1985) has explicated the meaning of suicide beyond the traditional definition (presented in Chapter 1) and defined suicide as follows:

> Currently, in the Western world, suicide is a conscious act of self-induced annihilation, best understood as a multidimensional malaise in a needful individual who defines an issue for which the suicide is perceived as the best solution. (p. 203)

Suicide is a psychological state of existence, a human malaise. Rarely has it been asked—and never in studies on suicide notes—

whether this state is different or similar during different recent periods of time. Many previous studies have utilized the collection of suicides notes (published by Shneidman and Farberow) written between 1945–1954. Fortunately, we now have a collection of notes from 1983–1984, which were obtained from the Los Angeles Coroner's Office by Shneidman. The 1945–1954 published sample consisted of 33 genuine suicide notes. Thirty-three notes from the 1983–1984 sample were matched on age range and sex with the 1945–1954 sample. These two samples will allow us to investigate the question about the general nature of suicide over this 40-year period, a period of considerable turmoil in our history, from World War II through Vietnam. (Examples of suicide notes are presented in the Appendices).

We can now ask, Did the 1960s and 1970s—computers, space travel, media, terrorism, etc.—make a difference in suicide in the Western world? Even more specifically, since both samples came from the United States, we can ask: Did the Vietnam War, the assassination of Martin Luther King, the forced resignation of Richard Nixon, etc., make any difference in the quality of suicide? Also, what about shifts in social attitudes? For instance, in a much publicized case of the 1940s, a sixteen-year-old New York couple made a suicide pact. (In the event, it was a manslaughter—he shot her—she was pregnant—but not himself). Was illegitimate pregnancy more "suicide-worthy" then, than now? Or would this couple have been suicidal over another issue? Have shifts in social attitudes made a difference?

Method: We cannot readily review the results of the previous studies on suicide notes—now over 60 in number—nor can we easily undertake a study of all 100 protocol sentences that were derived from the 10 suicidologists in this volume. We have thus decided to undertake two critical investigations: First, all 23 protocol sentences that were verified at the high frequency—common—level were investigated. (These sentences are reproduced in Table 14-1). Second, all 18 protocol sentences that were verified significantly more often in the genuine suicide notes than the simulated suicide notes were also investigated. (These sentences are reproduced in Table 14-2).

Findings: Our results suggest that our predictive and discriminative clues to suicide are generally ubiquitous across time—

at least, these 40 years in the United States. The "reasons" for suicide have been generally the same. There have not been many differences in "I love you," "I am in pain," "I am sick," "This is the only thing I can do."

Among the 23 highly predictive sentences, only two significant discriminations were noted, both being observed more frequently in the notes of 1945–1954. The findings were sentences 17 and 21 in Table 14-1. These statements were the following: (17) the reported feelings, attitudes, and/or thrusts of ambivalence ($X^2(1,N=66) = 7.34, p < .01$); and (21) self-destruction may not have been the only goal of the person, i.e., destruction of others may also have been intended ($X^2(1,N=66) = 8.73, p < .01$). In addition, both these sentences in the 1983–1984 notes were observed well below the critical frequency level of at least two-thirds; indeed, they were observed below one-third of the time.

Speculating, it appears that people in the 1940s and 1950s expressed more ambivalences and concomitant contradictory feelings. These attitudes were more frequently verified in their suicide notes than in notes written by people from the 1980s. This aspect of our findings, based on the 1940s–1950s sample, was not only highly predictive of the content in suicide notes but also discriminated genuine notes from simulated notes in this era.

Suicides from the 1980s are also less likely to indicate or communicate that their act was intended to destroy or hurt someone else. There appears to be a less frequent calculation of the act to have a prolonged evil effect on others. However, this does not imply that the suicide by attacking himself is not attacking someone else. A number of predictive sentences verified in both eras attest to this; it may be that the conscious interpersonal intent per se is reported less today. Furthermore, the various classifications on aggression turned inward still discriminated; no differences were found on such factors between the 1945–1954 and 1983–1984 samples.

In the 18 sentences that discriminated genuine suicide notes from simulated suicide notes, two significant observations were made. The variable that ambivalence may no longer be a good discriminator has already been discussed. The other sentence that discriminated the two samples in the direction of the 1980s was sentence 14 in Table 14-2. This sentence was: (14) the person's thoughts exhibits only permutations and combinations of grief-provoking content ($X^2(1,N=66) = 7.39, p < .01$). Suicidal people in the 1980s, by implication, appear to be more often constricted. One other sentence related to mental constriction or tunnel vision—sentence 12 in Table 14-2—was verified in a similar direction, but it was significant only at a borderline level. Both these sentences—12 and 14—in the notes of the 1980s not only discriminated suicide notes from control data but also highly predicted the content in suicide notes; thus, both can now in the 1980's be perceived as very critical factors in defining suicide. An additional statement—sentence 7 in Table 14-2—was in the 1980s' sample also observed to be not only a discriminating factor but also a predictive factor. In the 1945–1954, this sentence was observed just below the critical frequency value of 22.

Our final list of the sentences that are highly predictive of the content of suicide notes and also discriminated between genuine and simulated notes for both 1945–1954 *and* 1983–1984 were:

In the suicide note:

1. The communications indicate the person wishes to die; i.e., the suicide is accomplished due to some relative weakness in the capacity for developing constructive tendencies (e.g., attachment, love) (Menninger).
2. The person communicates flight from one of the following: pain, incurable disease, the threat of helpless senility, a violent death; from anticipated rejection, or fear of becoming dependent; or from self-depreciation, feelings of sexual or general inadequacy, humiliation, unknown danger. *However,* the suicide does not appear to be caused only by such a single thing; other motives (elements, wishes) appear to be evident (Menninger).
3. The following emotional states are evident: pitiful forlornness, deprivation, distress and/or grief (Murray).
4. The person communicates evidence of adult trauma (e.g., poor health), rejection by the spouse, being married to a competing spouse) (Shneidman).

5. The person appears to be figuratively intoxicated or drugged by one's overpowering emotions and constricted logic and perception (Shneidman).
6. There is a poverty of thought, exhibited by the individual expressing only permutations and combinations of grief-provoking content (Sullivan).
7. The communications suggest that the person's personality (ego) organization is not adequately developed ("primitive," "weak") and narcissistic (Zilboorg).

We can conclude that over the past 40 years, the psychological state of the suicide—a human malaise—has been relatively constant. There are only a few differences: suicidal people in the 1940s–1950s were more ambivalent and suicidal people today are more constricted—observations that are not necessarily mutually exclusive. Generally, however, we believe that our findings regarding suicide, outlined in Chapter 14, are as applicable today as they were 40 years ago.

Chapter 16

SOME OBSERVATIONS ON AGE AND SEX

The first formal study of suicide notes (Shneidman & Farberow, 1957) indicated that the dynamics or reaction patterns might vary with the demographic variables of age. Few subsequent studies on suicide notes have examined such variables. The present observations were undertaken to examine the demographic variables of age and sex. We decided, as in the previous chapter, to undertake a critical investigation of all 23 original classifications that were observed at the high frequency—at least, two-thirds—level and all original 18 classifications that were significantly verified more often in the genuine notes than the simulated notes. (The protocol sentences are reproduced in Tables 14-1 and 14-2). This study will investigate whether our findings of the 10 suicidologists, summarized in Chapter 14, can be transposed across sex and the adult life span.

Age

Previous research on age was summarized in Chapter 2. Briefly, this research (Darbonne, 1969; Farberow & Shneidman, 1957; Leenaars & Balance, 1984c; Lester & Hummel, 1980; Lester & Reeve, 1982; Tuckman, Kleiner, & Lavell, 1959) indicated the following: suicidal ideation varies with age; inwardly directed aggression is more prevalent in younger adults; younger adults are more harsh, self-critical, and self-depreciating; and older adults exhibit a greater wish to die.

A problem with the present-day age studies is that various researchers have divided their age samples differently, resulting in some difficulties in direct comparison among studies. Age divisions have often been determined by the sample itself; for example, Lester and Hummel (1980), Lester and Reeve (1982), and Leenaars and Balance (1984c) defined "young" as less than the sample mean of 42 (although from a theoretical perspective this mean is within the mid-life age range). Other definitions of young, old, etc., are present in the literature. Such a problem is largely reflective of the difficulty in obtaining adequate samples of notes themselves. Given our current archive of over 400 suicide notes, an a priori classification of our age sample was possible. We propose the following schema as our sample groups which is not only based on extensive research on adult development (Colarusso & Nemiroff, 1981; Kalish, 1975; Kimmel, 1974; Troll, 1975) but also Erikson's theoretical model on the stages of such development (Erikson, 1963, 1968) with the understanding that overlap between these groups as well as even more refined classifications within these groups is possible. The three groups which are proposed are the following:

	Classification	*Erikson's Stage*	*Chronological Age*
Group 1	Young Adulthood	Intimacy vs Isolation	18–25
Group 2	Middle Adulthood	Generativity vs. Stagnation	25–55
Group 3	Mature Adulthood	Integrity vs. Despair	55 and up

It is the purpose of this study to investigate the suicide notes of Young Adults, Middle Adults, and Mature Adults.

Method: Two independent individuals who have graduate degrees in psychology and are currently in clinical practice served as judges. These individuals were different from the judges in the previous studies reported in this volume. They were asked to verify whether the classification (presented in Table 14-1 and Table 14-2) described by the individual protocol sentence did, in fact, occur in 60 suicide notes, 20 notes representing each age group. No demographic or other information about the individual was provided.

The three groups, based on our sample of notes, are the following:

	Classification	*Age Range*	*Mean Age*	*Male/Female*
Group 1	Young Adulthood (18–25)	18–25	22.25	M = 13 F = 7
Group 2	Middle Adulthood (25–55)	26–52	37.25	M = 14 F = 6
Group 3	Mature Adulthood (55 and up)	55–77	65.15	M = 9 F = 11

The overall mean age is 41.59; the age range is 18–77; and the sample includes 24 female notes and 36 male notes. The notes were written between 1966 and 1983.

Findings: A coefficient of concordance of .76 between the two judges indicated substantial inter-judge reliability ($p < .05$). Chi-square tests for two independent samples (Siegel, 1956) were performed to assess the significance of differences in verification instances for each protocol statement. The protocol sentences (presented in Table 14-1 and Table 14-2) that were verified significantly more frequently within the Young Adult group as compared with the Middle Adult group were as follows: (Table 14-1, 2) The person considering himself too weak to overcome difficulties, rejects everything except death (X^2 (1,N=40) = 7.29, p. < .01); (Table 14-1, 10; Table 14-2, 8) the suicide appears to be motivated by more than what the person manifestly communicates (X^2 (1,N=40) = 5.74, p. < .05); (Table 14-1, 11) the suicide is functional for the person for it abolishes pain and intollerable suffering (X^2 (1,N=40) = 7.93, p. < .01); and (Table 14-2, 7) the person, who wishes to die, exhibits a weakness in constructive tendencies (X^2 (1,N=40) = 6.41, p. < .05).

The protocol sentences that were verified more frequently within the Young Adult group as compared to the Mature Adult group were the following: (Table 14-1, 2) The person considering himself too weak to overcome difficulties rejects everything except death (X^2 (1,N=40) = 5.38, p. < .05); (Table 14-1, 4) the person's aggression appears to be turned inward (X^2 (1,N=40) = 10.67, p. < .01); (Table 14-1, 12) the suicide appears to be related to unsatisfied needs (X^2 (1,N=40) = 8.18, p. < .01); (Table 14-1, 14) there is evidence for egression and desertion (X^2 (1,N=40) = 5.39, p. < .05); and (Table 14-1, 18) the suicide appears to be determined by the individual's history and the present interpersonal relations (X^2 (1,N=40) = 5.83, p. < .05); (Table 14-2, 6) suicide is seen as fulfillment of self-punishment (X^2 (1,N=40) = 5.16, p. < .05); and (Table 14-2, 7) the person, who wishes to die, exhibits a weakness in constructive tendencies (X^2 (1,N = 40) = 8.18, p. < .01).

Only one sentence was verified more frequently within the Middle Adult group as compared to the Mature Adult group; namely, (Table 14-1, 19; Table 14-2, 11) the reported feeling, attitudes, and/or thrusts of ambivalence (X^2 (1,N=40) = 4.82, p. < .05). No other significant differences were noted between the three age groups.

Despite considerable similarities across age, the comparison between the three age groups suggested that individuals describe their behavior as significantly different in some critical respects, depending on age. These results support the findings of the previous age studies and suggest that a life span developmental perspective is essential in understanding suicidal phenomena.

It is our age group from 18 to 25 that is most different from other adults, consistent with recent research (Leenaars, 1986b, 1987). Differentiations for these Young Adults were found from the other age groups in their suicide on several essential characteristics. Young Adults (as compared to Middle Adults) report to be experiencing more frequently a situation that is unbearable. They perceive their suicide more frequently to have adjustive value and to relieve pain. The Young Adults (as compared to Mature Adults) more frequently see their action as an egression. They more frequently want to leave, to exit, to escape, and to desert a situation. Interpersonally, Young Adults (as compared to Mature Adults) describe more frequently a disturbed—an unbearable—interpersonal situation as well as a history to their disturbed relations and their suicide.

The latter observation is important in understanding suicide because one's history—childhood and adolescent stress or, more accurately, trauma—is a major factor in the adult suicide. One will rarely find a Young Adult in his note discussing childhood and adolescent stress, and the Middle and Mature Adult even less so. Yet, the individual when he enters adulthood from adolescence is not a static "finished product." Development in adulthood continues to be an ongoing, dynamic process (Colarusso & Nemiroff, 1981). Adult trauma (such as rejection by a spouse, or illness) are very important in understanding the individual's suicide. Our observations show that the suicidal person in his suicide note often describes such stress as the primary reason for his death; in fact, he is often singularly preoccupied with a situation and his unbearable painful reactions to that situation. External sources, e.g., spouse, friends, etc., have also been noted to isolate the same situation as the cause for the suicide (Tuckman, Kleiner, & Lavell, 1960).

However, it is only a full understanding of the interrelationship between the childhood and adolescent antecedents and the current adult reaction patterns that provide us with a meaningful insight into the suicide. Adult development is not only dynamic and ongoing, but also *serial.* The suicide does respond anew to a new trauma in his adult life, but his reactions (e.g., relational, affective states, and cognitive states) are essentially *consistent* with that individual's previous reactions to loss, threat, impotence, etc. The adult not only shows change in his reactions, but enormous consistency. There is a steadiness over time, regardless of whether one is in Young, Middle, or Mature Adulthood. Development is both discontinuous and continuous (Piaget, 1968). Furthermore, it is the steadiness, rather than the current precipitating event, that will allow us to be more accurate in our predictions of the suicide.

The emotional state in the suicidal person appears to be generally ubiquitous across the adult life span except that Young Adults (as compared to Mature Adults) more frequently exhibit inwardly directed aggression. One more frequently reads in their notes themes of humility, subordination, submission, flagellation, and masochism. Likewise, the cognitive state appears to be similar across the age span, with two exceptions. First, Young Adults (as compared to Middle Adults) more frequently communicate *one thing* in their notes as causing their suicide, although *other* motives are clearly evident to a reader of the same notes. Second—the only non-Young Adult difference—Middle Adults (as compared to Mature Adults) exhibit more frequently an ambivalent attitude in relation to their situation, relations, and death.

Additionally, differences were noted among the age groups on a number of protocol sentences that were theoretically classified under Ego. Young Adults are apparently significantly more often psychologically perturbed, which possibly contributes to their high rate of suicide. Young Adults (compared to Middle and Mature Adults) were more frequently judged to exhibit a relative weakness in their capacity to develop constructive tendencies and to overcome their personal difficulties. They more often in their suicide notes communicate that they reject everything to escape their perceived unbearable and unmanageable pain. Young Adults (as compared to Mature Adults) also more often see their suicide as an act committed because of thwarted or unsatisfied needs and perceive the act as a necessary fulfillment of self-punishment.

The current observations can be easily nested (with a few exceptions) within the previous literature. The observations support the position that when constructing a model to interpret suicide, age is a significant variable to be accounted for in that model. However, despite these differences, even more important similarities exist across the age span. We believe that we can cautiously transpose our findings, presented in Chapter 14, across the adult life span—the differences are an issue of *more* or *less*, not presence or absence.

SEX

Leenaars and Balance (1984a) have noted that in previous research on suicide notes, sex has been a relatively neglected demographic variable. Although not the primary focus of the research, two studies (Cohen & Fiedler, 1974; Lester & Reeve, 1982) have reported the following sex differences: Females appear to be less direct and less negative in their communications about the forthcoming suicide; females exhibit greater concern for others whom they know interpersonally; females express greater negative emotions, specifically, despondency, grief, and disappointment; and females appear to be more disorganized in their writings. Other studies have not focused on sex although a few did investigate this variable, but reported no differences.

It is the purpose of this study to investigate the suicide notes of males and females.

Method: The suicide notes that were classified by the two independent judges in the age study were reanalyzed. The notes were matched according to sex and were controlled for age. A set of 20 pairs was analyzed; 7 pairs from Group 1 (Young Adults); 6 pairs from Group 2 (Middle Adults); and 7 pairs from Group 3 (Mature Adults). The male-female pairs ranged in age within 3 years from each other (with 2 possible pairs being eliminated from Group 3 because this criterion could not be met). Thus, the male-female notes represent the three age groups almost in an equal fashion, virtually eliminating age as a confounding variable in our sex study.

Findings: No sex differences were found; i.e., we found no significant differences on any of the protocol sentences, a finding supported in recent research (Leenaars, 1986b; 1987). Thus, one can cautiously transpose the previous findings in Chapter 14 (based on male notes) to females, possibly suggesting the generalizability regarding situation, relations, emotional state, cognitive state, and ego in suicide for *both* males and females. There may be *phenotypic* differences (e.g., method) but not *genotypic* ones. Yet, these observations raise the following question: Why should males commit suicide three times more often? It may well be that these differences are related to sociological (see Durkheim, 1897/1951), biological (see Maris, 1986, especially the chapter by Motto), neuropsychological (see Luria, 1973), or some other factor(s).

These negative observations, however, do raise a question about Cohen and Fiedler's finding (1974) that females express greater negative emotions and Lester and Reeve's finding (1982) that males in their notes are less disorganized than females, since both males and females to a notable degree exhibited heightened emotions, constriction, and other fallacious logic in our sample. Whether females are less direct about their communication and exhibit greater concern for others cannot be evaluated, since we have not addressed these areas. The differences between Cohen and Fiedler's content analysis and Lester and Reeve's content (rating) analysis and the current protocol analysis may be one possible source for the noted discrepancies. Alternatively, sampling differences may account for the discrepancies. Future studies need to further address these discrepancies as well as to further investigate whether sex is, indeed, a discriminating variable in the genotypic study of suicide notes. We need to know whether gender makes a difference on such issues as "I love you," "I am in unbearable pain," "I am hopeless and helpless," and "This is the only way out for me."

SUMMARY

The observations, in keeping with previous research, suggest that age is an important variable when analyzing suicide notes, and, by implication, suicide itself, as well as when constructing theories or making discriminations within a theory. It became evident in this series of observations, that females and males whether in Young, Middle, or Mature Adulthood, often describe their behavior as highly similar. Despite the fact that the dynamics and reaction patterns of suicide appear to differ with age in some respects, the dynamics and reaction patterns are also similar in other critical respects. The observations in our study of sex reflect only similarities. We believe that suicide is generally ubiquitous across sex and age although some "differences" exist, depending not on sex but on age.

Chapter 17

FINAL COMMENTS

Our attempt has been to define suicide through a study of suicide notes. We now see that suicide can be best understood, predictively and discriminitively, as a multidimensional malaise. It is constituted, at least, by a painful situation, a disturbing relation, an overpowering emotional state, a constricted cognitive state and the person's own ego. Suicide has adjustive value for the individual, not adaptive (survival) value. It is perceived, consciously and unconsciously, as the best solution to a problem or injustices. Suicide, as our findings indicated, is a complicated human act.

To recapitulate our findings: Our studies of suicide notes from 1945–1954 and 1983–1984 indicated that suicide has been generally the same across this short time span. We can raise the question whether notes from very much earlier times would be the same or different; for example, Thomas (1980) presented an idiographic study of an ancient Egyptian suicide note, written about 4,000 years ago. Thomas suggested that the note communicated (among other factors) the following: a situation that may have been more fantasy than reality; a perception that all, even his own soul, had forsaken him; a deeply depressed emotional state; and a cognitive state that was constricted, if not delusional (e.g., "no one loved him," "the world is only full of sin"). Suicide was seen as "sweetness" and "joy" for this Egyptian. It was a welcome escape. Thomas, indeed, reflected on the stability of the man's personality. The suicide wrote, for example:

> Death is before me today. As a man longs to see his house.
> When he has spent years in captivity.

There are a number of other "historical" suicide notes worthy of an archival dig. Here, we decided to begin this effort by an analysis of Werther's—actually Goethe's simulated—suicide note, written in the eighteenth century, reproduced in Chapter 1. Independent judges, while scoring the 1983–1984 sample of notes, were also provided blindly with this note. The reliable results within the context of Werther's life as described by Goethe—which will also serve as a review of the 10 suicidologists' formulations for the reader—are as follows.

Young Werther was, according to his own communication, in what he perceived to be a traumatic situation, the unrequited love of Lote. He was experiencing unendurable psychological pain, being stressed and frustrated by his need for affiliation. He was unwilling to accept this unsatisfied wish or need and thus wanted to egress. Suicide had an adjustive value. His only ideal or solution was beyond life, "the ecstasy of death."

Werther's suicide, as is so frequently the case, was a dyadic event. His relation to Lote was disturbing (to him, Lote, her husband, and her family). His attachment (identification) to Lote was painfully intimate and, given Lote's own affection for him and a deep ambivalence, was simultaneously stimulating and inhibited. However, Werther's wish for closeness was frustrated. The relation had been doomed to failure from the beginning since she had been betrothed to another before they met. In the end, Werther was singly preoccupied with the loss and rejection; he believed that possession of Lote was the only possible way of going on living.

Werther's emotional state was overpowering; his own word was "intoxication." He was overly perturbed, experiencing feelings of pitiful forlornness, deprivation, distress, grief, and aggression turned inward. In his suicide note, he communicated that he was hemmed in, feeling hopeless and helpless.

Werther's suicide note was about one thing, his love for Lote. His thoughts were constricted on his loss. He provided only permutations and combinations of this grief-provoking content in his note. Lote was "heaven" and "the purest joy of life." However, as our judges verified, Werther's suicide was not only caused by this grief, for other motives and needs were evident in his note.

Werther was described in the book as a narcissistic person. His capacity for developing constructive tendencies, not only with Lote, was poor; he continually experienced defeat in employment, relations, travel, etc. At the end, he needed to adapt but he was paralyzed. His life was colorless, and all had became wholly unattractive. The only happiness was to die for Lote, to sacrifice (punish) himself for Lote to "restore the peace and happiness of your life." Death was the only solution. Yet, much more than the written words described Werther's life; unconscious psychodynamic implications were verified by the judges to be evident in his last letter.

The historical study of Werther can be related to our present day findings. The actual protocol sentences that were reliably verified in Werther's note are as follows: in Table 14-1, sentences 4, 5, 10, 11, 12, 13, 14, 15, 16, 20, 22, and 23; and in Table 14-2, sentences 1, 3, 6, 7, 8, 9, 10, 12, 13, 14, 15, 16, 17, and 18.

A *genuine* suicide note of 1689 written by twenty-five-year-old John Temple, son of Sir William (the famous English statesman), highlights further how classical the psychological characteristics in suicide may be. He wrote:

> 'Tis not out of any dissatisfaction with my friends, from whom I have received infinitely more kindness and friendship than I deserve, I say it is not from any such reason that I do myself this violence, but having been long tired with the burden of life, 'tis now become insupportable. From my father and mother I have especially of late all the marks of tenderness in the world. (Quoted in D. Nokes, 1985, *Johnathan Swift,* p. 17.)

John had been Minister of War (his father obtained him the post) and advised the king to free the Irish general Hamilton, thinking he would get the rebels to surrender; but instead, Hamilton joined them. John then drowned himself in the Thames. (See Nokes, 1985; Sir William Swift was the patron of Jonathan Swift).

As a final summing up, we thought that we would attempt to simulate a suicide note of our own. It is a fictional prototypical note from the work done (although it is likely that no genuine note will contain *all* these elements). It is meant to reflect the essential hallmarks of a genuine note.

> Dear Mary,
>
> I was really in love with you. Remember the Rockies. I guess it was all my fault. I'm no good. I caused all the trouble. I'm sorry for losing my job.
>
> I can't go on without you. I feel so alone. It would have been easier if you had listened to me. I thought we were happy for all those years.
>
> I walked outside last night. No one talked to me. You can have the house back. And the girls they will get the insurance money. There is $500,000. Call Mr. Taylor at 000-0000. And my brother always wanted the car.
>
> I don't want the girls to worry. You said that I always hurt them. They'll be better without me. Tell them that I love them and died in an accident. You don't have to tell my family. It is not important.
>
> All I have is bad dreams. I don't sleep. I'm so mixed up honey. I can't handle it. Forgive me for I know what I do. This is the only way as long as you feel as you do. Now you can be free. It is just too hard to live.
>
> Please no service. I'm not worth it.
>
> Your husband forever,
> Bill

We believe that personal documents have an important place in psychology and are indispensable in the study of human lives. Suicide notes especially have an important place in the study of the suicidal person.

People in general have considerable difficulty appreciating significant characteristics of suicidal individuals, evident by the fact that genuine notes are different in critical respects from simulated ones, although there are similar (common) characteristics in both. This finding is consistent with Goffman's idea (1974) that "as-if frames" are similar but also different than real "frames." The simulated notes (like Goethe's and our own) are "fabrications," like our own formulations (hypothesis, models, theories), and these are in some way outside of the genuine "frame." A person who simulates a note or constructs a theory to interpret suicide has some important ideas about it; in fact, some of these formulations can be logically and empirically verified. But, like a person who simulates a note, theorists and clinicians fail to know some of the significant characteristics of the genuine "frame." This is understandable because the simulator, theorist, and clinician have only been drawn to imagine suicide, but the person who kills himself is experiencing this final egression. We cannot construe all of the genuine "frame" of the suicide. We cannot completely define suicide. It is impossible to appreciate and understand objectively and completely the suicide; we only have our formulations. We can assume, however, that our investigations have allowed us to be somewhat closer to it. It is also our hope that researchers will continue to develop models to interpret suicide that can be logically and empirically tested and, most importantly, can be made useful and life-saving.

APPENDICES

APPENDIX A

An Annotated Bibliography of Suicide Notes: 1856–1987

A bibliography of suicide notes, arranged chronologically, from 1856 to 1987, together with a brief abstract of each paper is presented.

1. Boismont, B. de (1856). *Du suicide et de la folie suicide* (On suicide and the suicide of insanity). Paris: Germer Bailliere.

Presented an analysis of 1,328 suicide notes expounding a moralistic viewpoint.

2. Wolff, H. (1931). Suicide notes. *American Mercury, 24,* 264–272.

Provided a presentation of 14 suicide notes (6 male; 8 female) with descriptive comment.

3. Michael, C. (1944). *Abshied. Briefe und Auszeichnungen vib Epikur bis in Unsere Tage.* (Farewell: Letters and notes from Epicurus to Our Time). Zurich: Verlag Oprecht.

Presented a collection of 166 suicide notes written by historical figures from Epicurus to the 1940s, emphasizing the ubiquitous human elements and focusing on the changes in attitudes towards life and death.

4. Morgenthaler, W. (1945). *Letzte Aufzerchnungen von Selbstmorten* (Last notes of suicide). Bun: Varlag Hans Huber.

Presented verbatim 47 notes from Berne, Switzerland from 1928–1935.

5. Shneidman, E., & Farberow, N. (Eds.) (1957). *Clues to Suicide.* New York: McGraw-Hill.

Presented an edited book on suicide with several chapters reporting studies on suicide notes. Thirty-three genuine and 33 matched simulated notes are also presented, which have been the primary data in many subsequent studies. The genuine notes were randomly obtained (with the cooperation of the Los Angeles County Coroner's Office) from a sample of 721 notes. Shneidman and Farberow had subsequently obtained the simulated notes from independent, nonsuicidal individuals who were matched by sex, age, and occupation. The notes had been written by white, Protestant, married, native-born males.

6. Shneidman, E., & Farberow, N. (1957). The logic of suicide. In E. Shneidman and N. Farberow (Eds.), *Clues to Suicide,* pp. 31–40. New York: McGraw-Hill.

Examined 700 notes and concluded that the person who is about to kill himself is prone to fallacies in the logical process that leads him to the suicide. The suicidal person shows problems in identification; the person exhibits fallacious identification between the self as experienced by oneself and the self as experienced by others.

7. Farberow, N., & Shneidman, E. (1957). Suicide and age. In E. Shneidman and N. Farberow (Eds.), *Clues to Suicide,* pp. 41–49. New York: McGraw-Hill.

Utilizing a theoretical analysis, based on Menninger's theory of suicide, examined 619 notes (489 males; 130 females) that were grouped according to age. The results indicated that the wish to kill and the wish to be killed decreased with age and the wish to die increased with age.

8. Shneidman, E., & Farberow, N. (1957). Some comparisons between genuine and simulated suicide notes in terms of Mowrer's concepts of discomfort and relief. *The Journal of General Psychology, 56,* 251–256.

Utilizing a comparison of 33 genuine and 33 simulated notes, concluded that the suicidal person departs with hate and self-blame and attempts to leave definite instructions and restrictions for the survivors.

9. Hayakawa, S. (1957). Suicide as a communicative act. *ETC, 15,* 46–50.

Presented a discussion of suicide notes as an act of communication.

10. Osgood, C., & Walker, E. (1959). Motivation and language behavior: A content analysis of suicide notes. *Journal of Abnormal and Social Psychology, 59,* 58–67.

Utilizing a content analysis of 69 genuine notes (40 male and 29 female) and 72 matched "ordinary" letters, found that suicide notes (as compared to the letters) display greater stereotypy than would be expected under high degrees of motivation; greater disorganization; greater conflict in motives; greater directiveness; and a greater demanding, commanding, and pleading style. A second, more stringent analysis of Shneidman and Farberow's 33 matched notes resulted in a few significant differences being noted; genuine notes reflected greater ambivalence and greater demands, as well as exhibiting several differences in grammar and sentence structure.

11. Tuckman, J., Kleiner, R., & Lavell, M. (1959). Emotional content of suicide notes. *American Journal of Psychiatry, 116,* 59–63.

Provided an analysis of the emotional content in 165 notes (107 male; 58 female); the results indicated that over half of the notes showed positive affect (e.g., gratitude, affection, concern), about one-quarter showed hostile or negative feelings (which appeared to be more pronounced in persons who were separated or divorced than those single, married, or widowed), and one-quarter were neutral in affect. Results also suggested that older (45 and above) persons showed less affect than younger persons in the notes.

12. Shneidman, E., & Farberow, N. (1960). A sociopsychological investigation of suicide. In H. David and J. Brengel-

mann (Eds.), *Perspectives in Personality Research.* New York: Springer.

Examined 948 genuine suicide notes and other sociopsychological data and found that socioeconomic factors play important roles in the suicide. Not only are different methods used but people commit suicide for different stated reasons (e.g., lower status people spoke more of everyday stress, whereas higher status people spoke more of "being tired of living"). The age of the suicide was also found to be an important variable.

13. Gottschalk, L., & Gleser, G. (1960). An analysis of the verbal content of suicide notes. *British Journal of Medical Psychology, 33,* 195–204.

Examined the verbal content in Shneidman and Farberow's 33 genuine and 33 simulated notes plus 37 additional genuine notes (27 male; 10 female). The results indicated that certain categories of words distinguished the genuine notes from the simulated: a high percentage of references to other people and things (although the reference may be vague or tenuous) and a low percentage of references to cognitive operations.

14. Wagner, F. (1960). Suicide notes. *Danish Medical Journal, 7,* 62–64.

Provided a descriptive analysis of 60 notes of 57 attempters and 3 completers, suggesting that the suicidal person is in mental agony and psychic tension, which has grown to a point where the suicide is more of a threat than a plea directed towards others. The suicide is seen as a desperate way out of an unbearable situation.

15. Capstick, A. (1960). Recognition of emotional disturbance and the prevention of suicide. *British Medical Journal, 1,* 1179–1182.

Examined 136 suicide notes (83 males; 53 females), concluding that depression occurred or had occurred frequently in the suicides. Conclusions, however, indicated that the age of the suicide was an important factor: the older suicide exhibited the greatest depression and communicated complaints of physical illness, references to the hereafter, and a concern of others, whereas the younger suicide exhibited less depression and communicated notable harmful and malicious motives.

16. Tuckman, J., Kleiner, R., & Lavell, M. (1960). Credibility of suicide notes. *American Journal of Psychiatry, 116,* 1104–1106.

Studied the reason for the suicide in 63 suicide notes and the reason stated by informants. Results indicated a very high (90%) agreement or compatibility between these sources, suggesting that some credibility could be given to suicide notes.

17. Spiegel, D., & Neuringer, C. (1963). Role of dread in suicidal behavior. *Journal of Abnormal and Social Psychology, 66,* 507–511.

Examined Shneidman and Farberow's 33 genuine and 33 simulated notes to evaluate whether a process inhibits the experience of dread in the suicide. Results indicated that the genuine notes were less explicit in expressing suicidal intention, contained less suicide synonyms, had more instructions to the reader and were more disorganized.

18. Tuckman, J., & Ziegler, R. (1966). Language usage and social maturity as related to suicide notes. *The Journal of Social Psychology, 68,* 139–142.

Examined Shneidman and Farberow's 33 genuine and 33 simulated notes and found no difference in social immaturity.

19. Bjerg, K. (1967). The suicidal life space: Attempts at a reconstruction from suicide notes. In E. Shneidman (Ed.), *Essays in Self-Destruction,* pp. 475–493. New York: Science House, Inc.

Provided a theoretical analysis of 568 notes from a Lewinian model. The results indicated that suicides show unfulfillable desires, high perturbation, intolerable inner tension, unrealistic expectations of others, personal devaluation, and feelings of worthlessness.

20. Tuckman, J., & Ziegler, R. (1968). A comparison of single and multiple note writers among suicides. *Journal of Clinical Psychology, 24,* 179–180.

Compared single and multiple note writers in a sample of 158 notes. Results indicated that multiple note writers communicate through their notes with more than one person; however, this appeared to be related to the overrepresentation of separated and divorced persons in the multiple note group, whose notes also contained a greater combination of hostility and positive feeling tone.

21. Frederick, C. (1968). An investigation of handwriting of suicide persons through suicide notes. *Journal of Abnormal Psychology, 23*, 263–267.

Examined 45 notes plus three control handwritten copies for each note and found that the handwriting of a suicidal person was distinguishable by highly trained and professional people.

22. Darbonne, A. (1969). Suicide and age: A suicide note analysis. *Journal of Consulting and Clinical Psychology, 33*, 46–50.

Tested the hypothesis that suicidal ideation varies with age in 259 notes. Results indicated that young adults (20–39) were overwhelmed by rejection and especially problems concerning heterosexual love objects and competition for them. Individuals from ages 40 to 49 left a communication of the vanquished (i.e., they were unequal to the demands of life and were tired or bored and wanted a way out). The 50–59 group often used the notes to leave instructions and to convey information and unemotional messages. The 60 and over group cited illness, pain, and physical disability and often described loneliness and isolation.

23. Oglivie, D., Stone, P., & Shneidman, E. (1969). Some characteristics of genuine versus simulated suicide notes. *Bulletin of Suicidology,* March, 17–26.

Examined Shneidman and Farberow's 33 genuine and 33 simulated notes using *The General Inquirer* (a dictionary of tag words). Discriminations were noted in the following: genuine notes had a higher reference to concrete things, persons and places; genuine notes had higher use of the word "love"; genuine notes had a fewer number of references to the process of thought and decision.

24. Frederick, C. (1969). Suicide notes: A survey and evaluation. *Bulletin of Suicidology,* March, 27–32.

Presented a review of the literature with evaluation and recommendations for future research.

25. Darbonne, A. (1969). Study of psychological content in the communications of suicidal individuals. *Journal of Consulting and Clinical Psychology, 33*, 590–596.

Presented a theoretical analysis of 40 suicide notes and 71 simulated notes (40 individuals and 31 therapy patients who were threatening suicide) from Adler's formulations of suicide. The suicides reflected heightened dependency needs, problems in maintaining interpersonal relationships, a high degree of activity and a veiled aggression which included hurting the self in order to hurt and manipulate others. Suicide threateners were found to be in some ways like suicides and in others like normals.

26. Hood, R. (1970). Effects of foreknowledge of manner of death in the assessment from genuine and simulated suicide notes of intent to die. *The Journal of General Psychology, 82,* 215–221.

Examined Shneidman and Farberow's genuine and simulated notes and found that retrospective distortion may occur in studies of suicide notes when the judges have foreknowledge that the note writer committed suicide.

27. Hood, R. (1971). Effect of foreknowledge of sex and manner of death in the assessment from suicide notes of intent to die. *Journal of Social Psychology, 84,* 73–79.

Examined Shneidman and Farberow's genuine notes and found that foreknowledge of sex and manner (natural causes/suicide) effects people's judgment of the note; a clear sex difference was noted; i.e., notes by females known to have died later from natural causes were judged as indicating more intent to die than equivalent notes written by males, whereas males and females known to have died later from suicide were judged as identical on intent to die.

28. Lester, D. (1971). Need for affiliation in suicide notes. *Perceptual and Motor Skills, 33,* 550.

Examined Shneidman and Farberow's 33 genuine and 33 simulated notes for need for affiliation; no differences were found.

29. Jacobs, J. (1971). A phenomenological study of suicide notes. In A. Geddens (Ed.), *The Sociology of Suicide,* pp. 332–348. London: Frank Cass and Co., Ltd.

Presented a descriptive study of 112 suicide notes of adults and adolescents, finding in the notes references to begging for forgiveness, describing illnesses, making accusations towards others, taking precautions to exclude problems from themselves, leaving instructions, and using the note to leave a will.

30. Lester, D. (1971). Choice of method for suicide and personality: A study of suicide notes. *Omega, 2,* 76–80.

Examined 47 suicide notes (43 completed suicides; 4 attempted suicides) of 23 individuals who used a passive method and 24 individuals who used an active method; no differences were found between the passive and the active group.

31. Arbeit, S., & Blatt, S. (1973). Differentiation of simulated and genuine suicide notes. *Psychological Reports, 33,* 283–297.

Evaluated whether 93 judges could discriminate Shneidman and Farberow's 33 genuine and 33 simulated notes based solely on the clues in the notes; only 13 judges were able to distinguish the genuine notes from simulated notes above chance levels. Conclusions indicated that the accuracy of a judge was based on the clinical skills of that judge rather than the characteristics of the notes themselves.

32. Edland, J., & Duncan, C. (1973). Suicide notes in Monroe County: A 23-year look (1950–1972). *Journal of Forensic Sciences, 18,* 364–369.

Provided a summary of the suicide statistics in Monroe County, N.Y., particularly in relationship to the role of suicide notes. Twenty-three percent of suicides left a note. A classification is provided to categorize suicides for coroners.

33. Lester, D. (1973). Temporal perspective and completed suicide. *Perceptual and Motor Skills, 36,* 760.

Examined Shneidman and Farberow's 33 genuine and 33 simulated notes and found no difference in temporal perspective. Genuine notes did contain more imperatives (i.e., instructions to others) and greater involvement with fantasy.

34. Shaffer, D. (1974). Suicide in childhood and early adolescence. *Journal of Child Psychology and Psychiatry, 15,* 275–291.

Examined 31 suicides, ages 14 and under, and reported that 14 left a note; no differences in age, IQ, personality description, and method used were noted between children who left a note and those who did not. Results indicated that hostility was frequently expressed in the notes.

35. Beck, R., Morris, J., & Lester, D. (1974). Suicide notes and risk of future suicide. *Journal of American Medical Association, 228,* 495–496.

Examined 33 notes of attempted suicides and 43 notes of completed suicides in a study of 231 attempted and 194 completed suicides, utilizing a suicide intent scale. Results indicated greater suicide intent among note writers than non-note writers.

36. Cohen, S., & Fiedler, J. (1974). Content analysis of multiple messages in suicide notes. *Suicide and Life-Threatening Behavior, 4,* 75–95.

Compared 195 suicides who left a note and 813 non-note writers and found differences in such variables as sex, marital status, and the method used to kill oneself. The results raised questions as to whether or not, note writers can be accepted as representative of all suicides. Content analysis suggested several sex differences (females expressed greater despondency; grief and disappointment; greater concern for others; and greater evidence of humor, irony, and sarcasm), as well as a few age and marital status differences, although the study suggested greater *similarity* in demographic variables than differences.

37. Duncan, C., & Edland, J. (1974). Suicide notes. *Legal Medical Annual,* 113–120.

Noted that the suicide note is of interest and importance to certifying death as suicide because, when valid, it is prima facie evidence of the manner of death. It is argued that the note must be retained as relevant documentary evidence in such cases.

38. Tripodes, P. (1976). Reasoning patterns in suicide notes. In E. Shneidman (Ed.), *Suicidology: Contemporary Developments,* pp. 203–228. New York: Grune & Stratton.

Examined Shneidman and Farberow's 33 genuine and 33 simulated notes from multiple aspects of reasoning. The persistent finding was that the suicide is unable to distinguish the subjective from the objective. In his estimation one is being objective in one's views, whereas others are unrealistic. Results also indicated that the suicide is disorganized; is unable to implement impressions and convictions; tends to oversimplify and thinks that everything is obvious; tends to be focused, rigid, fatalistic and dogmatic; projects his views on the world; and is unable to see any difference between his feelings and the outside world.

39. Neuringer, C. (1976). Current developments in the study of suicidal thinking. In E. Shneidman (Ed.), *Suicidology: Contemporary Developments,* pp. 229–252. New York: Grune & Stratton.

Provided a review of the research literature on suicidal thinking, including previous cited references on the topic.

40. Shneidman, E. (1976). Suicide notes reconsidered. In E. Shneidman (Ed.), *Suicidology: Contemporary Developments,* pp. 253–278. New York: Grune & Stratton.

Indicated that suicide notes are best understood when examined within the context of the life in which they occur.

41. Henken, V. (1976). Banality reinvestigated: A computer-based content analysis of suicidal and forced death documents. *Suicide and Life-Threatening Behavior, 6,* 36–43.

Examined 22 suicide notes, 18 simulated notes, (both from Shneidman and Farberow's collection) and 8 forced-death documents. Results indicated that the writings of the suicides were more "deviant" (e.g., alienation, preoccupation especially with others of the opposite sex), as well as more concrete and constricted in focus, whereas the forced-death group were more in contact with life, such as an illness, and were more aware of their responsibility. Writings of the simulated group were different from both the other writings although some (stereotypical) similarities were evident with the genuine suicide notes.

42. Chynoweth, R. (1977). The significance of suicide notes. *Australian and New Zealand Journal of Psychiatry, 11,* 197–200.

Examined the content of 25 suicide notes from a descriptive point of view, noting that suicide notes may be important in understanding suicides; the examination suggested that depression and hostility occurred frequently.

43. Lester, D., & Hummel, H. (1980). Motives for suicide in elderly people. *Psychological Reports, 47,* 870.

Examined 52 (35 male; 17 female) suicide notes (mean age was 42 years; standard deviation was 17 years; range was 18 to 74 years) and found that older (above the mean) suicides were less likely to indicate a desire to be killed. No sex differences were noted.

44. Thomas, C. (1980). First suicide note? *British Medical Journal, 281,* 284–285.

Presented a study of an early ancient Egyptian document that may be the earliest suicide note in existence.

45. Shneidman, E. (1980). *Voices of Death.* New York: Harper & Row.

Composed a book of personal documents written or recorded by people threatened by death, including verbatim transcripts of suicide notes and an analysis of these notes. The analysis of the notes indicated that common themes in suicide were the following: the simultaneous presence of love and hate (i.e., ambivalence); a sense of shame, "loss of face," disgrace or a sense of dereliction of duty; a reflection of fear; a sense of total rejection in a personality that already depreciates itself; a creed; and other themes. A conclusion is presented that suicide notes are somewhat barren in telling us everything we want to know about suicide because of the special state of mind of the suicide; i.e., a state of relatively fixed purposes, ambivalence, and mental constriction. However, suicide notes are seen as providing a great deal of meaning when put in the context of the life history of the individual who wrote the note.

46. Shneidman, E. (1981). Logical content analysis. In E. Shneidman, *Suicide Thoughts and Reflections, 1960–1980.* New York: Human Sciences Press.

Presented an analysis of reasoning and cognitive maneuvers that explicate the idiosyncrasies of concludifying (choosing death) that an individual might manifest in his flow of thought, utilizing suicide notes to illustrate these processes. A four-part scheme is presented: Idio-logic—which explicates the details of a man's logical styles; Contra-logic—which attempts to explain why his reasoning seems reasonable to him; Psycho-logic—which surmises the traits found with the logical styles and underlying epistomology; and Pedago-logic—which extrapolates from the other three how to respond to the individual's reasoning and cognitive maneuvers.

47. Leenaars, A., & Balance, W. (1981). A predictive approach to the study of suicide notes. *Journal of Clinical Psychology, 37,* 50–52.

Presented a protocol analysis of Shneidman and Farberow's 33 genuine and 33 simulated notes from the theoretical perspectives of Binswanger, Freud, and Kelly. Results indicated that only specific protocols from Freud's formulations discriminated in favor of the genuine notes; statements of loss, rejection, preoccupation with a significant other, and identification with the lost person were noted more frequently in the genuine notes.

48. Lester, D., & Reeve, C. (1982). The suicide notes of young and old people. *Psychological Reports, 50,* 334.

Examined 52 (35 male; 17 female) suicide notes (mean age was 42 years; standard deviation was 17 years; range was 18 to 74 years) and found that older (above the mean) suicides were more concerned with feelings rather than action and less explicit about the suicide. Notes of male suicides (as compared to female suicide) contained more negative thought units and were rated as less disorganized.

49. Schwibbe, M., & Räder, K. (1982). Kontentanalytische untersuchungen zur emotionalität in suizidbriefen und anderen todesnah verfassten texten (Content analytic studies of emotionality in suicide letters and other texts written near death), *Zietschrift für Klinische Psychologie. Forschung und Praxis, 11,* 280–291.

Content-analyzed 34 private letters, 29 suicide notes, and 28 letters composed by the writer before execution for emotionality. Results indicated that suicide notes were impaired in their positive evaluations, whereas forced-death documents were enhanced in positive evaluation, potency and emotionality.

50. Schwibbe, M., & Rader, (1982). K. Kontent—analytische untersuchung zur konkretheit von suizid—briefen. *Crisis, 3,* 16–31.

Investigated the concreteness of suicide notes, finding both a high concreteness and high abstract form. The abstractness was assumed to be related to the verbal concentration and summary of life events in the notes.

51. Edelman, A., & Renshaw, S. (1982). Genuine versus simulated suicide notes: An issue revisited through discourse analysis. *Suicide and Life-Threatening Behavior, 12,* 103–113.

Presented a discourse analysis (i.e., a tool for analyzing the underlying structure of verbal messages) of Shneidman and Farberow's 33 genuine and 33 simulated notes. Results indicated the following: Suicides are more cognizant of objects and these appear to be concrete and negative; specific people, places, things, and the concept "you" are negated, while generalized others are seen as more "positive"; relations are reviewed with a specific notion of time (e.g., as decrease in the use of future references and the conditionality of relations).

52. Peck, D. (1983). The last moments of life: Learning to cope. *Deviant Behavior, 4,* 313–332.

Examined 132 suicides notes written by individuals below 35 years of age, for a *fatalistic attitude* (defined as failure to achieve goals while engaging in normative activities). The results indicated that 43 notes contained elements of fatalism, suggesting suicide to be one plausible response to stress in young people.

53. Fishbain, D., D'Achille, L., Barsky, S., & Aldrich, T. (1984). A controlled study of suicide pacts. *Journal of Clinical Psychiatry, 45* (4), 154–157.

Reviewed suicide-pact victims and single suicides, finding that the former differ on a number of factors, including leaving significantly more notes.

54. Leenaars, A., & Balance, W. (1984). A logical empirical approach to the study of suicide notes. *Canadian Journal of Behavioural Science, 16,* 249–256.

Described a logical empirical method which calls for suicide notes to be treated as an archival source and to be subjected to a protocol analysis. Investigation of various theoretical formulations and a reliability study are presented to explicate the method.

55. Leenaars, A., & Balance, W. (1984). A predictive approach to Freud's formulations regarding suicide. *Suicide and Life-Threatening Behavior, 14,* 275–283.

Presented a protocol analysis of Shneidman and Farberow's 33 genuine and 33 simulated notes from Freud's formulations regarding suicide. Results indicated that the following occurred more frequently in the genuine notes: loss and/or rejection; preoccupation, ambivalence, and identification with a lost person; communicating feelings of anger towards oneself but appearing to be angry towards someone else; turning back upon oneself murderous wishes or impulses; and seeing the act as a fulfillment of self-punishment.

56. Leenaars, A., & Balance, W. (1984). A predictive approach to suicide notes of young and old people from Freud's formulations regarding suicide. *Journal of Clinical Psychology, 40,* 1362–1364.

Described a protocol analysis of 52 (35 males and 17 females) suicide notes (mean age was 42; standard deviation was 17 years; range was 18 to 74 years) from Freud's formulations of suicide. Results indicated that younger (less than the mean) people were more self-critical, were more harsh towards themselves, perceived themselves as having less worth, and treated themselves more as an object.

57. Sherman, S., Presson, C., & Chassin, L. (1984). Mechanisms underlying the false consensus effect: The special role of threats to self. *Personality and Social Psychology Bulletin, 10,* 127–138.

Noted that motivational factor may affect judges' construal of suicide notes.

58. Stephens, B. (1984). Vocabularies of motive and suicide. *Suicide and Life-Threatening Behavior, 14,* 243–253.

Summarized previous research on suicidal motivation, concluding that one can view suicide motives as social constructions learned in interaction which permit the individual and others to assign meaning and acceptability to the suicidal act.

59. Leenaars, A., Balance, W., Wenckstern, S., & Rudzinski, D. (1985). An empirical investigation of Shneidman's formula-

tions regarding suicide. *Suicide and Life-Threatening Behavior, 15,* 184–195.

Presented a protocol analysis of Shneidman and Farberow's 33 genuine and 33 simulated notes from Shneidman's formulations regarding suicide. Results indicated that the following occurred more frequently in the genuine notes: the experience of adult trauma; rejection and withdrawal of a significant other; expressions of ambivalence; feelings of love and hate; helplessness; overpowering emotions and constricted perception; and psychodynamic implications. The importance of frequency counts in genuine notes was made.

60. Allen, N. (1985). An annotated bibliography to suicide and life-threatening behavior. *Suicide and Life-Threatening Behavior, 15,* 364–366.

Presented an annotated bibliography of investigations on suicide notes that have been published in the journal of the American Association of Suicidology.

61. Leenaars, A. (1986). A brief note on latent content in suicide notes. *Psychological Reports, 59,* 640–642.

Presented a beginning study of the unconscious psychodynamic forces in a sample of 93 suicide notes. Results suggested that these forces may be most associated with the dyadic nature of suicide.

62. Leenaars, A. (1987). Protocol analysis studies of suicide notes. In J. Morgan (Ed.) *Suicide: Helping Those at Risk.* London: King's College.

Presented a series of studies (genuine vs. simulated, age, and sex) of suicide notes to investigate Shneidman's formulations regarding suicide. Results indicated a number of differentiating elements between genuine and simulated notes, and a large number of commonalities across the life span of both males and females although differences exist across age but not sex.

63. Rudestam, K., & Angelli, P. (1987). The effects of the content of suicide notes on grief reactions. *Journal of Clinical Psychology, 43,* 211–218.

Presented an analog study of 48 individuals' response to four types of simulated notes (other-blaming, incongruent, self-blaming, and neutral) to investigate grief reactions. Results indicated that survivors may well respond differently to a suicide note (and, by implication, suicide), depending on the content of the note; the self-blaming note elicited the greatest amount of distress (especially blame and guilt), followed equally by the incongruent and the other blaming notes, and the neutral note, the least.

64. Lester, D., & Leenaars, A. (1987). Differentiation of genuine suicide notes. *Psychological Reports, 61,* 70.

Examined Shneidman and Farberow's 33 genuine and 33 simulated notes to identify differences between genuine notes in their obviousness as genuine suicide notes to people in general. The results indicated that individuals (N = 24) construed some notes consistently as "genuine" (17 were correctly judged above 50% of the time) and others as not (16 were correctly judged 50% or below of the time); it was suggested that further research was needed to isolate what characteristics of notes are salient for people and allow perception of a suicide note as genuine.

65. Leenaars, A. (1987). An empirical investigation of Shneidman's formulations regarding suicide: age & sex. *Suicide and Life-Threatening Behavior, 17,* 233–250.

Presented a protocol analysis of 60 suicide notes, 20 written by individuals—females and males—in Young, Middle, and Late Adulthood. Results indicated that age (notably in regard to Young Adults) but not sex was a significant variable on a number of specific classifications and clusters of these classifications (perturbation, relations, self-cognitions, and long-term instability), although an even greater number of similarities exist.

66. Leenaars, A. (1988). Are women's suicides really different from men's? *Women and Health,* 14, 17–33.

Reviewed the literature on sex differences in suicide and examined 20 suicide notes written by males and females on a variety of psychological variables. No differences were found on such issues as "I love you," "I am in unbearable pain," "I am hopeless and helpless," and "This is the only way out for me."

APPENDIX B

Suicide Notes: 1983–1984

This archive contains, verbatim, except identification changes, with grammar, spellings, and punctuation preserved, suicide notes from females and males who committed suicide in Los Angeles County, California between June 1983 and July 1984. It contains the first 33 suicide notes (of over 100) that matched the age range (25–59) and sex (i.e., male) to the 33 genuine notes reported in Shneidman and Farberow's *Clues to Suicide* for 1945–1954. This archive also contains 20 suicide notes written by females—all the 1983–1984 female notes in the 25–59 age range. We would like to thank Dr. E. Shneidman for making this collection available.

Male Notes

(1)
Mary
I have signed all of the pink slips for the cars so it will be easier for you dispose of them I don't want to be here when all the Buzzards pick through of my stuff But if I were you I would

Move Back Here And Keep an eye on things for I am sure there will be a lot of looting [rest not clearly reproduced]

MARY-

CALL ME AND LET ME KNOW IF THIS GOT TO YOU

The best advice I have for you is talk to John I think he is honest, maybe you could make some kind of deal to restore them for you say you could get the most money—don't [rest not clearly reproduced]

Please notify my wife Mary Smith

Phone (#)

c/o (?)

BE CAREFUL
CYANIDE GAS IS
IN THIS BATHROOM

(2)

Mary, Jane, Joe, John cant take it
lecturing will get worst now
forgive if you can

Dad

(3)

Dear Mary

After last night I know you do love me. You tried so hard to say you don't but your not speaking from your heart. Listen to it Baby remember in sickness and in health, richer or poorer till Death remember its going to Be our wedding date so very soon. I love you you stupid head. SMO I hope you Shno so Deeply. I've been wrong but I'm still you loveing husband forever. I'am not sick to do what I have to. Your not like Jane she was a pig your so very different and so special of a person I love you and miss you so very much. Dont drink Don't let another man touch you honey. Put your ring back in the right place. I cant see how to live with you rebelling from me this is me honey Bill. SMO come to me Baby let me take care of you. I long to hold you in my arms make love to you forever *remember!* Please I'm your husband Baby.

I set up outside to look like home. My home is with you NO MATTER WERE. Lets go home honey let me love you. Dont rebell any more. Your realy the only one who knows me Bill. Not any one else. *I know you* also. the cats are gone everything but I know you love me.

Stop it right now. Its me honey Bill stop this nightmare come to me your husband Its not wrong to love me not matter who said it is. I'am here honey I'll be out back I have a change of clothes for you. You can take porsch Butt to the park again just our family. I know you love me honey I know I'm in your heart. I'll be waiting for you no matter where I go. I love you mush pleace rember all the love I have shown you. rember please for God sake rember.

Love
Bill

(4)

Mary,

Please take care of my affairs, this was all my fault of selling house and everything I brought on myself. I can't go on living like this. I hope God will forgive me for taking my own life. I know the church was true if only we could of lived it better. Take care of yourself. I can't live without you:
Love Bill

(5)

I William Smith Do not want to Live anmore I am sick Mary I want to feel Better

William Smith
P.S. I want to DIE

(6)

Mary

First of all I'd like to say I really don't know how this is going to come out on paper. This is a first. These past few days I've had more than enough time on my hands to think. (only of us/ you.) I want only one thing right now that is for us to pull this together God I don't know why in the hell it has taken me all these years to be able to tell you I love you. You needed this all this time. My heart is puring out for you now. I can only hope its not to late.

I want your love the way it was when you gave me your all. I now its probably impossible. I'd give anything

What I want to ask is there is chance that we can rebuild a healthy relationship. I want you to be able to say thats my old man. Be proud + supportive of me I want to be able to stand behind you with the same type of actions and feelings I need some time to open up the way you expect + deserve. I know now I need this counseling to open my mind and soul to make me a person worth giving your all to + myself being able to throw this damn sheild Ive been carrying around for so long. I gave everything I had to a relationship that wasnt worth the fucking powder to blow it to hell. I guess since that time Ive always been afraid to be vulnerable. I sat in solitary confinement for weeks crying my heart out. I swore to myself at that time there would never be another time. I've blown it to hell with you. I can only ask for your understanding and this guidence Im reaching out for now. I can state truthfully I should have looked for help earlier. I know I'll be able to express love to you if you will find it in your heart to let me. I want you and need you. I know you feel I've let you down. I readily admit its be a one way street.

I'm sitting just waiting for this phone to ring + pick it up with your voice on the other end. Everytime a car pulls up I pray that its you. Maybe it will be before the end of tonight Im reaching out please tell me its not to late. I love you. I'll tell you as often as you want to hear it if you'll let me in. love you

Bill

We have got to pull together

(7)

I sit alone. Now, at last, freedom from the mental and physical torment I have been experiencing. I'm damned if I do and damned if I don't. What a choice.

This should come as no surprise. My eyes have spoken for a long, long time of the distress I feel. The self-imposed isolation, the rejection, the failures and frustrations overwhelm me. The laughs are all gone and irrationality has control. There is no way to pull myself out of the hell where I've placed myself.

Please, please respect the dignity of respecting my wishes regarding no services, etc. It is all spelled out in the personal file of papers. If the XYZ program does not work out, use the alternate plan.

I truly wish this could all have ended in a different way, but that was just not to be.

Goodbye, love, forgive me. May you all find happiness.

Bill

1 The personal file is up to date. All important documents (stocks, etc.) are in the safe-deposit at (bank). The deposit box key is on the car key chain. The box at (bank) just holds some copies of items which are not vital.

2 Don't forget there will be an extra $2000 in the (credit union) as life insurance.

3 My IRA and account funds are available to you as cash as beneficiary. Both at (bank).

4 The Travel file is on the file cabinet in the bedroom. Contact Joe for an appointment and perhaps he can offer some new way to collect for the estate. At least he can review what has occurred and tell you what property of John's is attached.

5 A good attorney can probably effect some kind settlement on the medical situation and explain the legal obligations for whatever is unpaid.

(8)

honey I don't know how to say this When you read this Don't feel Bad or Sad about *me*—Im my own way I am trying to straiten things out I got us in such a mess it's my own fault—you should have some pension and Insurance from the local—change the lot on (street) to your name *only* spend the money will take of yourself Just help the Boys if you can

Bury or Burn me as cheap as possible I don't care where. You should find a lot and let the Boys build you a little house and get the rest of the Insurance money. You only need one car now sell the truck it will help get things squared away Tell Bill I have no hard feelings to him I think he knows that. You don't have to call my whole family I don't think its that Important. I wish I could turn Back time But I cannot do that

I know I had a job But the way my mind is I don't think I could handle it—like you said honey I give to everybody But you and I feel like I am a leech You have worked hard for years and you deserve something Better than *me* I hope you forget me real soon.

Love Bill

PS Boys I Love You

I called Joe I wanted to here his voice one more time I told him that the fight was not your fault.

(9)

I have taken my life because I tried shock treatment at the (hospital) and I became unbearably worse! I have no further desire to live. I am very bitter about what the shock treatments did to me. They made me worse than I've ever been in my whole life.

(10)

I tried to get this car to San Francisco where I was happy to die. The carburetor wont co-operate

I can't live in VA Hosp. And I wont live without you.

I'm sorry I hurt you and scared you Christmas. It scared me to death but nobody cared

If I don't kill myself I'll kill her and I love her to much

I love you

They wont even admit it was there because what I did

Let the VA bury me

I dont care what happens to this body

To whom it MAY CONCERN UPON MY DEATH I RE-LISE ALL INTEREST IN THIS VEHICLE.

1980 BMW

Lic. ____

AND WILL IT TO ____ FOR DEBTS OWED TO HER

Dear Mary

I'm sorry swearhart I know everything thats happened to us was my fault.

I wish I could have been your white knight I just couldn't take pressure.

You gave me the only happiness I've ever known

I gave you all the love and will to live that I had left

Please remember the good times

I wish you could have had our kid. I would have been good to them

I always loved you there was never anyone else

(11)

I cannot continue any longer. The pain has become too unbearable. Jane is not responsible. My problems are insoluble. I should have done it thirty five years ago

Bill

(12)

Lay in bed detsying all day

Life?? is so boreing. Back into the same old rut. No lights in Chev. Joe has got car. Truck wont start, stereo quit, caint sleep. Women left me. I feel like shit.

(13)

Mary

Youve always told me not to play phone games.

I passed you on the street today we seen each other but you kept going like you didn't even know who I was.

I called your house but you unplugged your phone

You would never answer my calls at your work.

You could at least call me

I think you are seeing someone else if you are I think you should tell me. We are both grown up enough to understand

I love you very much and I know you loved me at onetime but like you said I will drive you to someone else. Well I see that what happened.

You must like him because your never home and when you are you won't even call me. You unplug the phone

I know I fucked up your life, like they say misery loves company well I guess thats me misery. I hope we can work it out,

But if you feel happier with someone else there is nothing I can do But regret every bad thing Ive did + said to you.

MOM PLEASE SELL THE BIKE AND PAY JANE $2000 I OWER HER MORE BUT THAT ALL I GOT

Bill

(14)

Evaluation + Options present situation

Received Last Check	220.00
Cash on hand approx.	50.00

Rent O'due 13 days
225.00
Food for 1 wk. (Less milk)

Options

1 Effort for job by 19th (and pit off rent?) until 30th + 7th Oct
This option with owner of Bldg. (If not, go to option *5*)
2 Same as above Less Rent, move 1st Where?
3 Wait for evaluation, live on street, etc.?
4 Beg from friends?
5 Buy a Steak, Dope, Booze and go out with a BANG!
(And see a couple of ladies first!!!)
Discussion closed!———

(15)

Do you rememeber a Halloween Party 24 years ago? You were so warm that night and now are filled with ice and frigid dislike of me. How appropriate. Halloween, the start and end of our lives. And at the start, the vows that were made; for richer or poorer, in sickness and in health, for better or worse. And now death do us part.

In a month, Thanksgiving. I was away just after our first one. Bet you can't remember what I gave you on our first Christmas? Oh, what's the use of reminiscing? I'm gone and you have cold and hard thoughts of me. I just know I can't live in rented room after all these years. The final failure.

(16)
Joe

Everything I can think of is in the best possible order. I am truly sorry to leave without notice. I did my best to leave everything set up. I have expressed my personal feelings in the past and they still stand. I always tried to do my best for you and you reciprocated.

Me sincere thanks for all the help and education, as well as the personal assistance.

There could be a lot more said but I don't think it is necessary.

The only things I removed from my office were personal.

In my car is my briefcase with company info etc. including various company keys.

If you can help Mary + she wants it, please try.

My most personal best
to You + Yours,
Bill

Mary

You know so many ways to say "I love you" . . . with a kiss, a touch, just everything you do . . . But I don't know any way to really thank you, except to say how much I love you, too.

Happy Anniversary

We almost made the 15 years honey.

Thanks for all the good times and happiness.

Love,
Bill

(17)

I can't handle the responsibility of life.

I have tried to cope with the pressures but find that I just can't do it.

I'm sorry to leave behind those people I love—Mary, Jane, Joe, John, my mother, sisters, niece and nephews—I hope they find peace and happiness in this difficult life.

I've tried to make it and failed—just can't get it together anymore!

This terrible depression keeps coming over me and I can't bear feeling so bad. Thanks to the people who tried to help me but I became beyond help!

Bill Smith

(18)

Please call my children first

Can't Take much more Love you all to much
gone to See Mary

I can't live without Mary this pain + misery is to much
Love all you kids forgive me ain't going to Die in Hosp. Like Mom

Love Dad

(19)

Well he couldn't Hack It, (OH Well)

If your interested you are welcome to what ever you want in the garage. Ask Joe for the key I've let him know that you may ask for it. Anything you don't want that is valuable I would appreciate it broken, burned or buried. Perhaps you may take some things to Miss Jane. OH Yeah She has a fine place. The key to the chest on the small Round table against the Southe wall of garage next to chest. If you don't want the skulls please crush them. There is an excellent supply of incense some very choice vintage.

You may also have the musical instruments that I once had. Do with them as you wish.

Yes, Yes, any books you want you may have.

See Ya Around
Bill

(20)

(top of note missing)

. . . with Jesus + that I have prayed for him to lookafter you and Jane. I have prayed that you arent destroyed by this because that would be something I could never be forgiven for. My love for you has always been the deepest and hopefully I'll see you again. You are my miracle. I have accepted the lord Jesus as my saviour but I kow that he wouldn't condone this. I accept the just dues. and pray that maybe you wont hurt anymore. Make our kid something! for your strength and love does work miracles. You and Jesus I pray can forgive me for copping out. Its me who accepts the responsbility of my actions. I apolagize to all of you + beg Jesus forgiveness. I love all of our friends + loved ones. Pray for me for I know if there is a heaven, I'll hopefully meet you there someday. You have been and will always be the brightest ray of sunshine that eve entered my life and no one can take that away. If I see mom I'll see that Joe is taken care of + will try to be with him too! I Love thos kids and am asking yours + Jesus forgiveness for the trauma I have caused them. Eternity is the best way of saying how long I (?) love you. Dad I hope will find strength in (?)

May the lord bless + keep you + forgive me for something I have no earthly rights to do.

Your loving husband
Your loving father
Your loving Son
Bill

(21)
Joe You to are a good kid. If you had given me more of a chance I would have done anything for you. But I love you just the same. Your mother and I had our difference but I still love her very much so please take good care of her for me please.

P.S. Joe The bike is still yours. But please be carefull with it. Drive it with the utmost safty *please*

Good bye Joe remember I love you

Your Father
Bill

To: My wife Mary

Mary all I can say is Im sorry for the why things turned out. I guess you where right we could not make it with our marriage.

I do wish I could undo the thing I had done but I can't. But do know I could have made it up to you in other ways. So this is it I just cant cope anymore say good bye to your mother and Jane + John and give all my love to Joe he was my pride + joy. I love him very much so give him a special good bye from

Pap-pa. Mary Im sorry and I love you please nver forget that I love you.

Good bye your husband
Bill

(22)
But, if there's a force & I'm given to control any of it, it shall be with you—

Just don't know why Joe didn't call me for so damn long-always punishing me for something. You literally own her oil have for over two yrs. R & E Me? Bye all becoming very hard to cogi-type-tate-should've planned ahead more—

John, thanks for tol'rat'n the abuses

Xev-Needn't tell you. . . . You were? There was sorry too for things said but I was just trying to see you the baddest way tickets I could

All love to & warm heart to

(23)
Mary

Everything we have should go for the kids I left another $230.00 on the bottom of the steps Just have the state bury me. Its cheaper After all we are not legally married. They can not make you pay for anything.

Good Bye
I Love You
Bill

The grass is greener on the outher side

(24)
Mary

I Love You.

I know you can't cope with Me. Please don't think I did this because of you. I'm fucked. But I do love you very *much.* I just can't cope. Please try to be good + remember all the good times.

Good Times

I was happy
Bill

The car is Mary's

Bill Smith

Please sent vamp. to (name, ph. #)
I gave Jane my stereo.
Don't let Sue have anything.
Put me to sea *please*
I love you Mary
See you later!!!

(25)
I just checked out may God have mercy on my soul

(26)
Dear Joe—

I'm sorry it seems the only way.

Love—
Bill

(27)

Jane give all of my possessions to Mary and dont want Sue to attend my funeral.

Bill ______

Mary Please take this check and withdraw all the money from my account

Thank you
Bill

Please Pay Joe at (business) $1400.00 (tel. #)

Bill ______

The BMW License/ ______ should be retrieved from (auto shop) across the street and given to Jean when she turns 21 and is not to be sold

My share of the houses should go to Jean and she is to retain full possession until such time that she remarries and at such time the share of this house that belongs to me should go to alchoholics Anonamous

(28)
Dear Mom and Dad,

I love you both and I want to thank you for everything that you did from bringing me up to helping me with this current problem. As you know I have been a saver all my life and have spent almost nothing on myself all these years. I have been a prisoner of this discipline all my life; you taught me well. I can not face the future for what these people might want to do to me. So I am putting an end to my life.

I will everything I have to both of you. I have accounts with Bank of ____ in ____, ____ Bank in ____, ____Bank in ____ and ____ Savings and Loan of ____ whose office is in ____. As well as ________AAA account: I hve a $50,000, CD with B of A and a $35,000 with ____ Bank. My safety deposit box is with B of A. The note that is in the Box from Mr. ____ has not been paid back to me yet and he will owe you the money now according to the terms of the note. He still works at ____ and his home phone is ____. His work number is ____.

I do not fit in this current society and I hope that whatever happens to my spirit, if there is such a thing, it will be happier there.

I hope you understand why I have done this—I just don't fit in to this world.

Please use the money to have fun, we both know there is no need to invest it.

I want Mary to share in this also. She has been wonderful to me and I feel that I should help her financially. You be the judge as to how to do this distribution.

My radio equipment should be given to my wonderful friends Jane and Joe. They are both friends indead.

I hope that I can find happiness out there somewhere.

With all the love in me.

Bill

(29)
I am tired of failing

If I can do this I will succeed

(Phone #) Police
(ext. #) Sgt. ____

?Bear

my love

I can't help myself + I can't do any more damage than I already have.

1. *First call Mary*
2. Don't forget that you can call on friends like Mary for support + to take care of Maitai
3. Sign my unemployment check + deposit it—(mail box toy is right here).
4. Car needs gas
5. You *will* live a happy healthy life.
6. I am sorry
7. Forever + a day is red

Love
Bill

XXXXXXXX

When you read this I will be dead (_____) take care of *you* get my other letters from the file

(30)
Post man—call Sherrif
Shooting in back yard.
no news papers

(31)
Mom!

Please forgive me. I'm too ill.
Please take care of Mary and the children.
Mary was really good to me—*a great wife.*

Love—
Bill

Dearest Mary, I beg you forgiveness for what I have done to myself, to you, the children and all the family. I am sick—too sick to continue on this painful path.

After all the pain and suffering subsides, write to the insurance companies and the Veterans Administration, so that you can obtain the insurance benefits to live on for a time.

What else can I say in this painful letter. Please remember

all the beautiful times that we shared together. I thank you for all of it.

You have two beautiful children as a rememberance of these good times and our good marriage.

I am truly sorry, the end came like this. I hope you can carry on, alone for a time.

May God help you—

Bill

I see no way that I can recover from the illness that I have. It is now worse then ever.

Thank you for all the good times. You are a *great* wife

Love—
Bill

(32)
Forgive me For today I die I just can't live without Mary. I might as well be dead may be their will be piece. I have this empty feeling inside me that is killing me everyday I just can't take it any more When Mary left me I died inside I cry to God to help me but he dosn't listen.

whom it may concern:
Please notify the following people what has happened to me
My son + daughter: (names, address)
My father—(name, address)
My mother—(name, address)
My sister—
I will everythin I own to my son John and my daughter Jane—divided 50-50.

I have *$4000* in my money market account no. ____ at the (bank) at the (city) office # ____

I have *$747.92* in my checking account no. ____ at the (bank) at the (city) office # ____

There is $649 i my wallet—in cash.

My car is the blue Ford in the parking lot out back. License No ____.

I also leave them the two endorse checks—one for 20.00 + the other for $65.30.

Sincerely
Bill Smith

(33)
Suicide (?) Note.

I hope this works

There is an envelope at my feet for Dr. X in the Psychology Dept. Please see to it that he gets it.

Also, class rosters for Trade-Tech are in my brown bag.

Farewell, farewell, what a ridiculous way to pretent to go.

Maybe this will go off by mistake.

I hope! (Am terrified)

What a rotten sham to pull. It's too bad I don't have enough personality to be ashamed of myself.

I should shoot my cat first.

Fleas everywhere.

You just can't continue leaning on everyone like this. This is a petty criminal mentality. It's sick! & you don't want to get better, you want to get worse. Those who have befriended you (or loaned you money) get it the worst.

Female Notes

(1)

I wish I could explain it so someone could understand it. I'm afraid it's something I can't put into words.

There's just this heavy, overwhelming despair—dreading everything. Dreading life. Empty inside, to the point of numbness. It's like there's something already dead inside. My whole being has been pulling back into that void for months.

Everyone has been so good to me—has tried so hard. I truly wish that I could be different, for the sake of my family. Hurting my family is the worst of it, and that guilt has been wrestling with the part of me that wanted only to disappear.

But there's some core-level spark of life that just isn't there. Despite what's been said about my having "gotten better" lately—the voice in my head tha'ts driving me crazy is louder than ever. It's way beyond being reached by anyone or anything, it seems. I can't bear it any more. I think there's something psychologically twisted-reversed that has taken over, that I can't fight any more. I wish that I could disappear without hurting anyone. I'm sorry.

(2)

Dear God

I love you so much I can not express the way I feel about you you have been so good to me + my Daughter in so many way.

God I thank you for all the thing you have bless me with my life + home clothes everything I love you so much, God you know, but what even it is Iran putting it in you hard I can not deal with need more

1 Let your will be.

2 bless me with a job.

(3)

Dear Dad & Mom

I Love you Very Much. I am Sorry for any problems that may have resulted from the way I treated my family. I wanted to know you But *I just wasn't there.* I wanted to be Strong for you & I went the *wrong way. Father* thank you for being *my friend* It would have been much easier to have just been a father but you wanted to be my friend & I have just wasn't their (*Thank you for that* & everything youv'e done for me)

Mother; *I Love you so much you were always their* when I needed you. you are very strong please forget aboutme I know it hurts but I was wrong. *I Love you both so very much.*

Your Son Bill

(4)

Mom,

Thanks for waiting up for me. Thanks for not inviting me. Please do not give [dog] to anyone. you can have my furniture but nothing absolutely nothing is to Bill.

Thanks for the Memories

Mary

(5)

Dear Jane,

I found a relative (a nice one) up North to stay with. I've left the keys, etc. where you can find them. I'll be back for the rest of my stuff as soon as I can.

Take Care of Yourself

Mary

MOVING TO SAN FRANCISCO BECAUSE OF

X Mary

PLACE TO LIVE

MARY'S PEOPLE

Find 2 Jobs in San Francisco

JOB

EMOTIONS

Deal With Them

Learn From Mistakes

Commit Suicide

Hospital

PROBLEMS

EMOTIONS

BETTING OVER LOSING Betty

Mary

DON'T

COME

IN

CALL

THE

POLICE

I HAVE COMMITED

SUICIDE

(6)

Hello Jane

I just wanted to tell you i still love you very much Babe I'll always love you very much.

My God i don't know how all this happen but it did. I wish it never did happen. All i know it hurts real bad just thinking of it makes me cry and say why. I never thought you would do this to me.

Byi my Lady I love you forever,

Mary

P.S. talk

Byi

You're always be part of me and thought

Jane I just want you to know I love you very much You know I still love you sweetie, I don't understand how all this happened, but you know what, I wish this would never have happened. Jane It hurts me very much. Just thinking of what happened makes me wonder why. I never thought you would do this to me! BABE I miss you.

respectfully
Mary

P.S. I love you BABY

(7)
I commit suicide because I want to be with my father forever—Don't rescue me otherwise I will die by harder way and harm others.

Mary

(8)
Mother—

I know the words that I am about to write will never answer why or ease any sorrow you may feel.

These last 13 months of my life have been the most painful of my 30 years. I've been thru so much that along the way I lost myself. This is the way I want it; if that will help.

Unfortunately I must once more be faced with what to do about loose ends.

Most importantly Mom I want you to understand I must be cremated, not buried, and I do not want any kind of service! Death should be just that. No mourning or sadness. If you like, on my 1 year of being gone have a mass for my soul to be found.

Disability will be sending me a white slip to mail on the 30th.

Do that and use the money on whatever you can. You know I have no money to leave anyone.

I don't want those assholes Jane & Joe to get my car. You'll have to tell them I had severe breakdown and can only afford to pay $50.00, as I have been, because I'm away in a hospital.

Enclosed are my keys. The smallest one is for my storage. Mom I want you to contact John for me. I am leaving everything of mine to him because he loved me and was my very truest friend!

He is to take over payments of $50.00 on my car (without Jane & Joe knowing) when its paid off he gets the pink slip. Everything personal & otherwise in my storage is his to do with what he likes.

Tender words only make matters difficult. I would like to say I love you and thank you for your love.

Mary

(9)

Honey, I know you will be upset so call Jane or Sue or Jean across street for children

over

call police + cover me up
Don't let the kids in the bedroom. I'm dead

Mary

(10)

So many people—

have loved me + tried to help—Thank you—but I couldn't pull that together to let it be enough

—I have too much anger to face—I can't do it

Will

All my possessions go to my mother—
+ my sister—

Selling my car should pay off outstanding debts to
(X) Counseling Service
Master Charge—(X) Bank
Student Loan

All other possessions are paid for

Mary Smith
SS # ____

(11)

When you receive this I will be dead.

Please feed my pets—cats as soon as possible.

Put them to sleep at the *Vets* not the pet shelter. The *vets* will charge about $10 each.

You will find enough money in the house to pay for it.

You may also have my 2 rings + my earrings.

The $5000 trust you + Bill can deceide about

Me
At peace at last
Mary

I did not move—my body will be at the ____ address

I AM
NOT MOVING
SORRY

(12)

Mary
(tel #)
Jane
(tel #)

If I havent the Love I want so bad there is nothing left

(13)

8:30 A.M.

My Last Will and Testament

I leave any money or possessions left, if any, after debts are paid, to Joe, my brother, and Jane, my therapist, split 50-50.

I'm sorry that I couldn't put the important papers in order. I can't organize anything any more. Tax receipts are in blue accordion folder on bookcase. John of (bank) has my savings (ph. #)

I just can't go on like this anymore. The depression and lonliness are too much for me. Being off of work will just make things worse. I tried to make it and failed.

Cremate me.

Love to all,
except Sue & Tony
Mary Smith
SS # ____

Thurs. A.M.
This is a Tx for competence + clear thinking.

P.M.

I talked to Jane this A.M. + she was very understanding, saying my work was good as anyone else's + just not to push myself so hard + not to panic when I can't remember something.

I went to the Depression clinic They have one study that would take me off drugs for one week on a placebo + then be on one of two drugs. She believes I'm getting worse on (drug) + that I need to get off of it + onto (drug) ASAP. I do

P.M.

I had another day of fear and trepidation. Praying not to be caught up in emergencies which I can't handle. By day's end, I felt that there is no way out.

Then, had my session with Jane. All she can do is nitpick about how I need to feel small + helpless—yes I do feel that way, but it doesn't help me to get back on my feet quickly. Damn her! She could be fixing me up better somehow, I'm sure. She doesn't know how it is—though I've tried my best to show her. I'm f . . . . . g mad at her—All right. Maybe my expression of that anger is good for me. Maybe it'll help me—It has already helped—I'm sure of it. I feel angry + that's better than feeling empty. I'm "some better" as she says.

The Art of Listening

The Art of Listening
Be Patient—listen to the whole question
Don't start thing @ your response
Listen to Nature/God
Listen

Behold I stand at the door and knock

The Art of Listening

Shut out the useless
The more we know of our being the better instruments
Bill
Separated from Supply
Recognize God
Reunify (?)
Realization
Thank
How Religious Science Works

How Religious Science Works
Go *slowly.* Listen carefully

Peace Corps
(ph. #)

I slept 'til 10 + finally got up at @ 10:30. I don't know what I'm going to do. The only two avenues open, if I continue so depressed, are *1* Kill myself *2* Quit the job + retreat to New York. Both seem hopelessly awful. I rode bicycle for 1 mile
Monday
I feel just awful. What am I going to do? Called Dr. —— San Francisco left message ? roade bike a little. Flailed on floor + worked up sweat.

The Situation is Hopeless but not Serious

Dr. ——
(ph. #)

(14)

I am so tired of feeling sick
I cant go on anymore. This was the only way out for me.
Please all forgive me, but
its best for me.
Mary

(15)
Jane, Sue, Joe, John
Personal
My Darlings,

Please forgive me. I hope I don't shame you too much. I have loved you all so much. The happiest times of my life was when we love *together.* We had so much fun—but it seems a hundred years ago.

I swear to you all—I have never done a bad thing all these years. Jane, I'm sorry you've never believed that—but it is true, so help me God.

I needed desperately someone to talk to. *Everything* I do turns out wrong. I've been so stupid. I don't deserve to live—I am worthless. I am so unhappy—please pray for me.

I'm sorry. I hope all three of you children get married and *be happy*—money can't buy it. Peace + tranquility is a blessing. Life is so short. Don't wast time arguing.

Choose who you want—if you're lucky, you'll find someone like your Father. Loyal. Honest. The only thing he wasn't was understanding. But he couldn't help that. So I managed to mess up when I tried to help you kids. I'm so stupid. The failing is mine. Remember always—he has always been here—love him—he deserves it. But I don't. I'm not worth anything.

I adore you.
Mom

Here is your money for car payment—please use it. I love you. I didn't do anything.

Mom
suicide

DO NOT ENTER
Call Paramedics (#)

(16)
Bill

I love you so much.
Forgive me for doing this.

(17)
Please leave $5000 for Jane and $5000 for Sue

And all my devoted love to my dearest family and friends always.

Mary Smith

(18)
Dearest Jane Wed.

I went to the little park (with all the eats) because I wanted to be by myself. If I'm not home when you get home would you please come + get me.

My brown purse is in top drawer!

Love Mary

Dearest Jane

I'm doing this against Bill, not you!

He said (over the phone in Holland) that he loved me, but I havn't seen him more than 10n times since I've returned.

The keys to *all* my metal boxes are in the pocket of Mama's blue coat hanging in the closet nearest the bathroom (in the long beige plastic bag). The keys to all my trunks + suitcases are in the large metal box (with unbroken handle) on the floor of the closet. The jewelry is all real + I want only *you* to use it—*no one* else.

The negatives of all the pictures I took in Germany and Holland (for 10 years) are in the large metal box on the shelf; the prints themselves are in one of the soft sided bags on the shelf in closet.

Anything you might need is in the brown purse in the top drawer of the chest: hospital forms (Blue Cross) (I have Medicare stamps with me). If you have any questions about the Blue Cross, call Equity in New York tel. (#). My social security number is (#).

Ask Bill if it would help his tax situation, if he sent a letter to New York to get my W2 from for the year I worked there (I think it was X-X) Only address I can remember
(address)

I want to be buried near mama + daddy, not one of the burials at sea, nor cremation.

Bill's tel # at "home" is (#)
His work number is Tel (#)

Love,
Mary

Call Dr. _____, and be sure + return check + medicare when they arrive.

P.S. Every document you will need, is in "smallish" brown purse in upper drawer. I'm out target practising.

P.S. I bought the gun because I was very scared when I went to New York; also I can't find the copy of my birth certificate.

(19)
To wait 1 month for Death certificate is too much. I don't think I can make it. (CROSSED OUT)
Dr. _____ is a very kind person
I went to apply for welfare—they put me on some kind of work house arrangement. and I have to run around all over the area for 10 Jobs. why am I being punished. it is a cruel and inhuman punishment. I'm too old for this. I don't have the stamina anymore. for a younger person it would be O.K. So I won't qualify.

I'm to old to live on the street. I'm a nonperson I've never been a compitant person
things like going to an office and filling our forms never work for me they always want something I dont have like Death certificate, marriage license etc. "What is your address" I dont have one. I cant even get mail Why is everything so hard for me. I give up. (CROSSED OUT)

My Husband was a manic Depressive in July he became very high in a manic state and uncontrollable I managed to get him Hospitalize many times but he wouldn't stay in Hospt. We live on my small VA (#) Disability pension. Comes on 1st of month. I've got into our August check and by the 3rd or 4th all our money was gone. I've no idea what he did with it. So I decided to go to his father and try to borrow some money to see us through the month of August. I was unsuccessful. I learned that Bill was finally in Hosp a few days after I'd left.

While I was up north at Bills parents and Bill was in the hosp. the owner of our apt Bld. Broke into our apt. and cleaned it out of all our possessions our rent was pay up until the end of August. I wrote and told him that I wasn't coming Back right away + if at the end of the month Bill was still in the Hospital to call the good will and give our things to them. I stressed in this letter that our rent was paid up until the end of August.— But he didnt wait like I expected him to the very day he got my letter he instigated the removal of our possessions. Leaving nothing we were totally wiped out, no Belongings, no place for Bill to go when or if he was released from the Hosp.

When He Broke into our Apt it was ____ or ____ of August, the middle of the month. I later learned that he didn't want a person with mental problems living in his Building so befor I could return, he had the apt painted and rented I beleave by the ____ th

When my apt was being emptied a neighbor called me and told me what was taking place. I was horrified. I was 300 miles away, my Husbands in the Hospt. and I'm helpless. I called another neighbor and asked her to collect my Husbands clothes and T.V. which she did. everything else is gone my clothes, furniture Now my husband is dead. I have no place to live and zero income. [the following crossed out]

My Husband was released from the Hosptal knowing he had no home go to to (He was 57 years old and not well) If that might not have been a contributing factor to his Heart Failure. I feel a great wrong has been committed. I am very Hurt, very alone and very Angry.

Tuesday August ____

Bill called me from Hosp. and told me they were finally going to release him Wed. Aug ____ and to catch a bus Friday night which would arrive Sat morning Sept ____. He would meet me at the Bus Station and since we had no place to live he had made arrangements with a friend who has trailor.

We would stay there over the labor day week end and come tuesday we would find us a place to stay.

I arrived as planned Sat morning but Bill wasnt there. I waited 2 hours, then started to phone I finally called Main General and was told he was in intensive care due to heart failure. 2 weeks later he died.—I lived at the Hospital by day and slept on a friends sofa at night in the same Apt Bld. where my Husband and I use to live. and I'm still there now.

Mary Smith

Bill entered the psych. ward in the 2nd week of August. was released 3 weeks later on Wed. August ____.

Sometime thursday nite 9/____ Bill had trouble breathing and was taken to Western Hospital and left there. How he got to Main General or when heart failure occured is not clear. I arrived Saturday Sept. ____. Finally found him in intensive care at Main. He was on respiration but concious and aware I was there. Monday Sept ____ he was taken off respirator was Breathing well on his own He suddenly stopped Breathing and his heart stopped they Cartiovented him 2nd time and brought him back but not until he died Sept ____ MON

I signed paper signifying no more cardioventing. To let him go, for his mind was allready gone. I also signed a paper permitting an autopsy to find out why he stopped Breathing ehn he shouldn't have.

until recently he had managed to control it.

We've lived in apt. 13 yrs

(20)

Dear Jane!

Write to my parents and explain and write *gentle* and *nice,* mail the upper part to them! Thank you! Love Mary

Please, go to Joe's wedding!

My Darling Bill

I *love* you very much, all my *life,* and you have been the *best* Husband that I have ever know. But I can't take it any more, please, forgive me!

You know where the keys are to the Safty Deposit Boxes. One is in the Fridgedaire bottom, the other one is in the green box in a brown leather case, you will find them. The leather case from my Opa's.

Take care of yourself, and please stay *healthy* and live a *happy life!*

Please, forgive me again!

over!

We had a *very good* Marriage!

Safty Deposit Box at (bank)

Dear Jane, Sue, John, Tony.

Thank you for being so *nice* and *good* to me, I appriciate it very much. You have done *soo* much for me thanks. I *love* you all! Love, Mary

Please, go to my Joe's *Wedding* and make him *happy! Please* go!

And *please* take care of my *darling* Bill, he *needs* your *help* now! I hate to do this, but I can't go on any more. May God forgive me!

Love, Mary

Show Bill how to run the Washer and Dryer, and please *help* him out as much as you can! Stay with him!

My *Parents* I *love* very much too!

I *love* my Bill and my Joe *sooo* much!

My Darling Son Joe

I love you very much, but I can't take it any more. Please forgive me! That I can't make it to your Wedding!

Have a very *happy Marriage* with Sue and be happy for *ever,* and all your *life.*

Have a happy Marriage, and don't let this upset you!
Please, be happy!
you have been
a good Son.

Love you always
Mom

REFERENCES

Aaron, D. (Ed.). (1985). *The Inman diary*. Cambridge, Mass.: Harvard University Press.

Adams-Webber, J. (1985). Self-other contrast and the development of personal constructs. *Canadian Journal of Behavioural Science, 17,* 303–314.

Adler, A. (1951). *The practice and theory of individual psychology* (P. Radin, Trans.). New York. The Humanities Press, Inc.

Adler, A. (1956). *The individual psychology of Alfred Adler* (H. Ansbacher & R. Ansbacher, Eds.). New York: Harper & Row.

Adler, A. (1964). *Superiority and social interest* (H. Ansbacher & R. Ansbacher, Eds.). Evanston, Ill: Northwestern University Press.

Adler, A. (1967). Contribution to discussions of the Vienna Psychoanalytic Society—1910. In P. Friedman (Ed.), *On suicide.* New York: International Universities Press, Inc. (Original published in 1910).

Allport, G. (1942). *The use of personal documents in psychological science.* New York: Social Science Research Council.

Allport, G. (1962). The general and the unique in psychological science. *Journal of Personality, 30,* 405–422.

Anderson, B. (1971). *The psychology experiment* (2nd ed.). Belmont, Calif.: Brooks/Cole Publishing Co.

Ansel, E. & McGee, R. (1971). Attitudes toward suicide attempts. *Bulletin of Suicidology, 8,* 22–28.

Aristotle (1941). Nicomachean ethics. In R. McKeon (Ed.), *The basic works of Aristotle.* New York: Random House.

Balance, W. (1975). Frustrations and joys of archival research. *Journal of the History of Behavioral Sciences, 11,* 37–40.

Battin, M., & Maris, R. (Eds.). (1983). Suicide and ethics. *Suicide and Life-Threatening Behavior, 13,* 223–345.

Beauchamp, T. (1978). What is suicide? In T. Beauchamp & S. Perlin (Eds.), *Ethical issues in death and dying.* Englewood Cliffs, NJ: Prentice-Hall.

Berlyne, D. (1971). *Aesthetics and psychobiology.* New York: Appleton-Century-Crofts.

Binswager, L. (1958). The case of Ellen West (W. Mendel & J. Lyons, Trans.) In R. May, E. Angel, & H. Ellenberger (Eds.), *Existence.* New York: Basic Books, Inc. (Original published in 1944)

Binswager, L. (1963). *Being-in-the-world* (J. Needleman, Trans.). New York: Harper & Row.

Bjerg, K. (1967). The suicidal life space: Attempts at a reconstruction from suicide notes. In E. Shneidman (Ed.), *Essays in self-destruction.* New York: Science House, Inc.

Bringmann, W. (1975). Design questions in archival research. *Journal of the History of Behavioral Sciences, 11,* 23–26.

Camus, A. (1955). *The myth of sysyphus* (J. O'Brien, Trans.). New York: Vintage Books.

Capstick, A. (1960). Recognition of emotional disturbance and the prevention of suicide. *British Medical Journal, 1,* 1179–1182.

Carnap, R. (1959). Psychology in physical language. In A. Ayer (Ed.), *Logical positivism.* New York: Free Press. (Original published in 1931).

Carnap, P. (1959). The elimination of metaphysics through logical analysis of language (A. Pap, Trans.). In A. Ayer (Ed.), *Logical positivism.* New York: Free Press. (Original published in 1932).

Chynoweth, R. (1977). The significance of suicide notes. *Australian and New Zealand Journal of Psychiatry, 11,* 197–200.

Cohen, S. & Fiedler, J. (1974). Content analysis of multiple messages in suicide notes. *Suicide and Life-Threatening Behavior, 4,* 75–95.

Colarusso, C. & Nemiroff, R. (1981). *Adult development.* New York: Plenum Books.

Darbonne, A. (1969a). Study of psychological content in the communications of suicidal individuals. *Journal of Consulting and Clinical Psychology, 33,* 590–596.

Darbonne, A. (1969b). Suicide and age: A suicide note analysis. *Journal of Consulting and Clinical Psychology, 33,* 46–50.

Domino, G., Moore, D., Westlake, L., & Gibson, L. (1982). Attitudes toward suicide: A factor analytic approach. *Journal of Clinical Psychology, 38,* 257–262.

Douglas, J. (1967). *The social meanings of suicide.* Princeton, NJ: Princeton University Press.

Durkheim, E. (1951). *Suicide* (J. Spaulding & G. Simpson, Trans.). Glencoe, Ill.: The Free Press. (Original published in 1897).

Edelman, A. & Renshaw, S. (1982). Genuine versus simulated suicide notes: An issue revisited through discourse analysis. *Suicide and Life-Threatening Behavior, 12,* 103–113.

Erikson, E. (1963). *Childhood and society* (2nd ed.). New York: W. W. Norton.

Erikson, E. (1968). *Identity: Youth and crisis.* New York: W. W. Norton.

Exner, J. (1978). *The Rorschach: A comprehensive system (Vol. 2).* New York: John Wiley & Sons.

Farberow, N. (1961). Summary. In N. Farberow & E. Shneidman (Eds.), *The cry for help.* New York: Harper & Row.

Farberow, N. (1972). Cultural history of suicide. In J. Waldenstorm, T. Larsson, & N. Ljeingstedt (Eds.), *Suicide and attempted suicide.* Stockholm: Nordiska, Bokhandelns, Forlag.

Farberow, N. (Ed.). (1980). *The many faces of suicide.* New York: McGraw-Hill.

Farberow, N. & Shneidman, E. (1957). Suicide and age. In E. Shneidman & N. Farberow (Eds.), *Clues to suicide.* New York: McGraw-Hill.

Freud, S. (1974). Psychopathology of everyday life. In J. Strachey (Ed. & Trans.), *The standard edition of the complete psychological works of Sigmund Freud, Vol. VI.* London: Hogarth Press. (Original published in 1901).

Freud, S. (1974). Fragments of an analysis of a case of hysteria. Ibid. (Original published in 1905).

Freud, S. (1974). A case of obsessional neurosis. Ibid, *Vol. X.* (Original published in 1909).

Freud, S. (1974). Mourning and melancholia. Ibid, *Vol. XIV.* (Original published in 1917).

Freud, S. (1974). General theory of neurosis. Ibid, *Vol. XVI*. (Original published in 1917).

Freud, S. (1974). A case of homosexuality in a woman. Ibid, *Vol. XVIII*. (Original published in 1920).

Freud, S. (1974). Group psychology and the analysis of the ego. Ibid, *Vol. XVIII*. (Original published in 1921).

Freud, S. (1974). The ego and the id. Ibid, *Vol. XIX*. (Original published in 1923).

Freud, S. (1974). New introductory lectures. Ibid, *Vol. XXII*. (Original published in 1933).

Freud, S. (1974). An outline of psycho-analysis. Ibid, *Vol. XXIII*. (Original published in 1940).

Frey, R. (1980). Did Socrates commit suicide? In M. Battin & D. Mayo (Eds.), *Suicide, the philosophical issues*. New York: St. Martin's Press.

Gergen, K. (1977). Stability, change and chance in understanding human development. In N. Daton & H. Reese (Eds.), *Life-span developmental psychology: Dialectical perspectives on experimental research*. New York: Academic Press.

Ginsburg, G. (1971). Public conceptions and attitudes about suicide. *Journal of Health and Social Behavior, 12*, 200–207.

Goethe, J. (1951). *Die Leiden Des Jungen Werther. Goethes Werke, Vol. 6*. Hamburg: Christian Wegner Verlag. (Original published in 1774).

Goffman, E. (1974). *Frame analysis*. New York: Harper & Row.

Gottschalk, L., & Gleser, G. (1960). An analysis of the verbal content of suicide notes. *British Journal of Medical Psychology, 33*, 195–204.

Graber, G. (1981). The rationality of suicide. In S. Wallace & A. Eser (Eds.), *Suicide & euthanasia: The rights of personhood*. Knoxville, TN: University of Tennessee Press.

Hayakawa, S. (1957). Suicide as a communicative act. *ETC, 15*, 46–50.

Heidegger, M. (1962). *Being & time* (J. Macquarrie & E. Robinson, Trans.). New York: Harper & Row. (Original published in 1926).

Henken, V. (1976). Banality reinvestigated: A computer-based content analysis of suicidal and forced death documents. *Suicide and Life-Threatening Behavior, 6*, 36–43.

Husserl, E. (1973). *The idea of phenomenology* (W. Alston & G. Nakhnikian, Trans.). The Hague: Martinus Nijhoff. (Original published in 1907).

Jacobs, J. (1971). A phenomenological study of suicide notes. In A. Geddens (Ed.), *The sociology of suicide*. London: Frank Cass & Co., Ltd.

Jung, C. G. (1974). A medical opinion on a case of simulated insanity (R. Hull, Trans.). In H. Read, M. Fordam, & G. Adler (Eds.), *The collected works of C. G. Jung, Vol. I.* London: Routledge and Kegan Paul. (Original published in 1904).

Jung, C. G. (1974). The psychological diagnosis of evidence. Ibid., *Vol. II.* (Original published in 1906).

Jung, C. G. (1974). Psychological types. Ibid., *Vol. VI.* (Original published in 1921).

Jung, C. G. (1974). The relations between the ego and the unconscious. Ibid., *Vol. VII.* (Original published in 1928).

Jung, C. G. (1974). On the nature of dreams. Ibid., *Vol. VIII.* (Original published in 1945/1948).

Jung, C. G. (1974). Basic postulates of analytic psychology. Ibid., *Vol. VIII.* (Original published in 1931).

Jung, C. G. (1974). Mind and earth. Ibid., *Vol. X.* (Original published in 1927/31).

Jung, C. G. (1974). Problems of modern psychotherapy. Ibid., *Vol. XVI.* (Original published in 1929).

Jung, C. G. (1974). Child development and education. Ibid., *Vol. XVII.* (Original published in 1928).

Jung, C. G. (1974). The development of personality. Ibid., *Vol. XVII.* (Original published in 1934).

Jung, C. G. (1977). Symbols and the interpretation of dreams. Ibid., *Vol. XVIII.* (Original published in 1961).

Kalish, R. (1975). *Late adulthood: Perspectives on human development.* Monterey, Calif.: Brooks/Cole Pub. Co.

Kalish, R., Reynolds, D., & Farberow, N. (1974). Community attitudes toward suicide. *Community Mental Health Journal, 10,* 301–308.

Kelly, G. (1955). *The Psychology of Personal Constructs, Vol. 1 & 2.* New York: Norton.

Kelly, G. (1961). Suicide: The personal construct point of view. In N. Farberow & E. Shneidman (Eds.), *The cry for help.* New York: McGraw-Hill.

Kelly, G. (1969). A mathematical approach to psychology. In B. Maher (Ed.), *Clinical psychology and personality.* New York: Wiley.

Kelly, G. (1977). Confusion and the clock. In F. Fransella (Ed.), *Personal Construct Psychology.* London: Academic Press.

Kerlinger, F. (1964). *Foundations of behavioral research.* New York: Holt, Rinehart & Winston, Inc.

Kimmel, D. (1974). *Adulthood and aging.* New York: John Wiley & Sons, Inc.

Leenaars, A. (1979). *A study of the manifest content of suicide notes from three different theoretical perspectives: L. Binswanger, S. Freud, and G. Kelly.* Unpublished Ph.D. Dissertation. University of Windsor, Windsor, Canada.

Leenaars, A. (1985, Aug.) Freud's and Shneidman's formulations of suicide investigated through suicide notes. In E. Shneidman (Chair), *Suicide notes and other personal documents in psychological science.* Symposium conducted at the meeting of the American Psychological Association, Los Angeles, Calif.

Leenaars, A. (1986a). Brief note on the latent content in suicide notes. *Psychological Reports, 59,* 640–642.

Leenaars, A. (1986b). Protocol analysis studies of Shneidman's formulations regarding suicide. In J. Morgan (Ed.), *Suicide: Helping those at risk.* London: King's College.

Leenaars, A. (1987). An empirical investigation of Shneidman's formulations regarding suicide: Age & sex. *Suicide and Life-Threatening Behavior, 17,* 233–250.

Leenaars, A., & Balance, W. (1981). A predictive approach to the study of manifest content in suicide notes. *Journal of Clinical Psychology, 37,* 50–52.

Leenaars, A., & Balance, W. (1984a). A logical empirical approach to the study of suicide notes. *Canadian Journal of Behavioural Science, 16,* 248–256.

Leenaars, A., & Balance, W. (1984b). A predictive approach to Freud's formulations regarding suicide. *Suicide and Life-Threatening Behavior, 14,* 275–283.

Leenaars, A., & Balance, W. (1984c). A predictive approach to suicide notes of young and old people from Freud's formulations regarding suicide. *Journal of Clinical Psychology, 40,* 1362–1364.

Leenaars, A., Balance, W., Wenckstern, S., & Rudzinski, D. (1985). An empirical investigation of Shneidman's formulations regarding suicide. *Suicide and Life-Threatening Behavior, 15,* 184–195.

Leenaars, A., Balance, W., Pellarin, S., Aversano, G., Magli, A., & Wenckstern, S. (1988). Facts and myths of suicide in Canada. *Death Studies.* In press.

Lester, D., & Hummel, H. (1980). Motives for suicide in elderly people. *Psychological Reports, 47,* 870.

Lester, D., & Reeve, C. (1982). The suicide notes of young and old people. *Psychological Reports, 50,* 334.

Luria, A. (1973). *The working brain* (B. Haigh, Trans.). New York: Basic Books, Inc.

Malinowski, B. (1926). *Crime and custom in savage society.* New York: Harcourt Brace & Co. (Cited in Zilboorg, 1936a).

Mallon, T. (1984). *A book of one's own: People and their diaries.* New York: Ticknor & Fields.

Maris, R. (1981). *Pathways to suicide.* Baltimore, MD: The Johns Hopkins University Press.

Maris, R. (Ed.). (1986). *Biology of suicide.* New York: Guilford Press.

Maslow, A. (1966). *The psychology of science.* New York: Harper & Row.

McIntosh, J., Hubbard, R., & Santos, J. (1983, April). Suicide facts and myths: A compilation and study of prevalance. Paper presented at the American Association of Suicidology Conference: Dallas, Texas.

Menninger, K. (1933). Psychoanalytic aspects of suicide. *The International Journal of Psycho-analysis, 14,* 376–390.

Menninger, K. (1938). *Man against himself.* New York: Harcourt, Brace & Co.

Menninger, K. (1945). *The human mind.* New York: Alfred A. Knopf.

Menninger, K. (1963). *The vital balance.* New York: The Viking Press.

Menninger, K. (1969). Expressions and punishment. In E. Shneidman (Ed.), *On the nature of suicide.* San Francisco: Jossey-Bass.

Motto, J. (1986). Clinical considerations of biological correlates of suicide. In R. Maris (Ed.), *Biology of suicide.* New York: Guilford.

Murray, H. (1938). *Explorations in personality.* New York: Oxford University Press.

Murray, H. (1967). Death to the world: The passions of Herman Melville. In E. Shneidman (Ed.), *Essays in self-destruction.* New York: Science House, Inc.

Murray, H. (1981). *Endeavors in psychology: Selections from the personology of Henry A. Murray* (E. Shneidman, Ed.). New York: Harper & Row.

Neuringer, C. (1976). Current developments in the study of suicidal thinking. In E. Shneidman (Ed.), *Suicidology: Contemporary developments.* New York: Grune & Stratton.

Nokes, D. (1985). *Jonathan Swift.* New York: Oxford University Press.

Oglivie, D., Stone, P., & Shneidman, E. (1969). Some characteristics of genuine versus simulated suicide notes. *Bulletin of Suicidology,* March, 17–26.

Osgood, C., & Walker, E. (1959). Motivation and language behavior: a content analysis of suicide notes. *Journal of Abnormal and Social Psychology, 59,* 58–67.

Peck, D. (1983). The last moments of life: Learning to cope. *Deviant Behavior, 4,* 313–332.

Piaget, J. (1970). *Structuralism* (C. Maschler, Trans.). New York: Harper & Row.

Plato. (1963). Phaedo. In E. Hamilton & H. Cairns (Eds.), *The collected dialogues of Plato.* Princeton, N.J.: Princeton University Press.

Ramsay, R., & Bagley, C. (1985). The prevalence of suicidal behaviors, attitudes and associated social experiences in an urban population. *Suicide and Life-Threatening Behavior, 15,* 151–167.

Rosenblatt, P. (1983). *Bitter, bitter tears.* Minneapolis: University of Minnesota Press.

Rosenblatt, P. (1985, August). Diaries of loss and theories of grief. In E. Shneidman (Chair), *Suicide Notes and Other Personal Documents in Psychological Science.* Symposium conducted at the meeting of American Psychological Association, Los Angeles, Calif.

Runyan, W. (1982a). In defense of the case study method. *American Journal of Orthopsychiatry, 52,* 440–446.

Runyan, W. (1982b). *Life histories and psychobiography.* New York: Oxford University Press.

Runyan, W. (1983). Idiographic goals and methods in the study of lives. *Journal of Personality, 51,* 413–432.

Seligman, C. (1929). Temperament, conflict and psychosis in a Stone-Age population. *British Journal of Medical Psychology, 9,* 187. (Cited in Zilboorg, 1936a).

Sherman, S., Pressow, C., & Chassin, L. (1984). Mechanisms underlying the false concensus effect: The special role of threats to self. *Personality and Social Psychology Bulletin, 10,* 127–138.

Shneidman, E. (1963). Orientations towards death. In R. White (Ed.), *The study of lives.* New York: Atherton.

Shneidman, E. (1967). Sleep and self-destruction: a phenomenological approach. In E. Shneidman (Ed.), *Essays in self-destruction.* New York: Science House.

Shneidman, E. (1973). Suicide. *Encyclopedia Britannica.* Chicago: William Benton.

Shneidman, E. (1976). Suicide notes reconsidered. In E. Shneidman (Ed.), *Suicidology: Contemporary developments.* New York: Grune & Stratton.

Shneidman, E. (1980). *Voices of death.* New York: Harper & Row.

Shneidman, E. (1981). Logical content analysis. In E. Shneidman, *Suicide thoughts and reflections 1960–1980.* New York: Human Sciences Press, Inc.

Shneidman, E. (1981). *Suicide thoughts and reflections: 1960–1980.* New York: Human Sciences Press, Inc.

Shneidman, E. (1982). The suicidal logic of Cesare Pavese. *Journal of the American Academy of Psychoanalysis, 10,* 547–563.

Shneidman, E. (1983). *Deaths of man.* New York: Jason Aronson, Inc. (Original published in 1973).

Shneidman, E. (1985). *Definition of suicide.* New York: John Wiley & Sons.

Shneidman, E. (1987). A psychological approach to suicide: In G. Vanden Bos & B. Bryant (Eds.), *Cataclysms, crisis, and catastrophes: Psychology in action.* Washington, D.C.: American Psychological Association.

Shneidman, E., & Farberow, N. (1957a). *Clues to suicide.* New York: McGraw-Hill.

Shneidman, E., & Farberow, N. (1957b). The logic of suicide. In E. Shneidman & N. Farberow (Eds.), *Clues to suicide.* New York: McGraw-Hill.

Shneidman, S., & Farberow, N. (1957c). Some comparisons between genuine and simulated suicide notes in terms of Mowrer's concepts of discomfort and relief. *The Journal of General Psychology, 56,* 251–256.

Shneidman, S., & Farberow, N. (1960). A socio-psychological investigation of suicide. In H. David & J. Brengelmann (Eds.), *Perspectives in personality research.* New York: Springer.

Shneidman, E., & Mandelkorn, P. (1970). How to prevent suicide. In E. Shneidman, N. Farberow, & R. Litman, (Eds.), *The psychology of suicide.* New York: Science House.

Smith, K. Conroy, R., & Ehler, R. (1984). Lethality of suicide attempt rating scale. *Suicide and Life Threatening Behavior, 14,* 215–242.

Spiegel, D., & Neuringer, C. (1963). Role of dread in suicidal behavior. *Journal of Abnormal and Social Psychology, 66,* 507–511.

Siegel, S. (1956). *Nonparametric statistics.* New York: McGraw-Hill.

Stengel, E. (1964). *Suicide and attempted suicide.* Baltimore: Penguin Books.

Sullivan, H. S. (1940). Conceptions of modern psychiatry. In H. Perry & M. Gawell (Eds.), *The collected works of Harry Stack Sullivan, Vol. I.* New York: W. W. Norton.

Sullivan, H. S. (1956). Clinical studies in psychiatry. In H. Perry, M. Gawell, & M. Gibben (Eds.), *The collected works of Harry Stack Sullivan, Vol. II*. New York: W. W. Norton.

Sullivan, H. S. (1962). Schizophrenia as a human process. Ibid, *Vol. II*.

Sullivan, H. S. (1964). The fusion of psychiatry and social science. Ibid., *Vol. II*.

Thomas, C. (1980). First suicide note? *British Medical Journal, 281*, 284–285.

Tripodes, P. (1976). Reasoning patterns in suicide notes. In E. Shneidman (Ed.), *Suicidology: Contemporary developments*. New York: Grune & Stratton.

Troll, L. (1975). *Early and middle adulthood.* Monterey, Calif.: Brooks/Cole Pub. Co.

Tuckman, J., Kleiner, R., & Lavell, M. (1959). Emotional content of suicide notes. *American Journal of Psychiatry, 116,* 59–63.

Tuckman, J., Kleiner, R., & Lavell, M. (1960). Credibility of suicide notes. *American Journal of Psychiatry, 116,* 1104–1106.

Tuckman, J., & Ziegler, R. (1968). A comparison of single and multiple note writers among suicides. *Journal of Clinical Psychology, 24,* 179–180.

Volant, E. (1986, April). The religious content in suicide notes. Paper presented at the American Association of Suicidiology Conference, Atlanta, Georgia.

Wagner, F. (1960). Suicide notes. *Danish Medical Journal, 7,* 62–64.

Windelband, W. (1904). *Geschichte und Naturwissenchaft* (3rd ed.). Strassburg: Heitz.

Windt, P. (1980). The concept of suicide. In M. Battin & D. Mayo (Eds.), *Suicide, The philosophical issues.* New York: St. Martin Press.

Zilboorg, G. (1936a). Differential diagnostic types of suicide. *Archives of Neurology and Psychiatry, 35,* 270–291.

Zilboorg, G. (1936b). Suicide among civilized and primitive races. *American Journal of Psychiatry, 92,* 1347–1369.

Zilboorg, G. (1937). Considerations on suicide, with particular reference to that of the young. *American Journal of Orthopsychiatry, 7,* 15–31.

Zilboorg, G. (1943). *Mind, medicine and man.* New York: Harcourt, Brace & Company.

ABOUT THE AUTHOR

Dr. Antoon A. Leenaars is a clinical psychologist in private practice in Windsor, Canada. He is on the Board of Directors of the Canadian Association for Suicide Prevention and a member of the American Association of Suicidology. Dr. Leenaars has received the American Association of Suicidology's 1988 Edwin Shneidman Award for distinguished research in suicide. A Consulting Editor to the journal *Suicide and Life-Threatening Behavior,* Dr. Leenaars has written numerous papers and chapters and has lectured internationally on the subject of suicide. His specialty within suicidology is suicide notes. He has written and presented over 20 papers on this topic. Currently, he is actively involved in the following: research on suicide notes regarding women's studies, life-span psychology, youth suicide, terminal illness, and unconscious processes; development of Thematic Test for Suicide Prediction; and work on the clinical applications of the current volume.

NAME INDEX

SUBJECT INDEX